Management Challenges in IS: Successful Strategies and Appropriate Action

Wiley Series in Information Systems

Management Challenges in IS:
Successful Strategies and Appropriate Action

JAMES D. McKEEN
HEATHER A. SMITH
Queen's University
Kingston, Ontario, Canada

JOHN WILEY & SONS
Chichester – New York – Brisbane – Toronto – Singapore

Other Wiley Editorial Offices

John Wiley & Sons, Inc., 605 Third Avenue,
New York, NY 10158-0012, USA

Jacaranda Wiley Ltd, 33 Park Road, Milton,
Queensland 4064, Australia

John Wiley & Sons (Canada) Ltd, 22 Worcester Road,
Rexdale, Ontario M9W 1L1, Canada

John Wiley & Sons (Asia) Pte Ltd, 2 Clementi Loop #02-01,
Jin Xing Distripark, Singapore 129809

British Library Cataloguing in Publication Data

A catalogue record for this book is available from the British Library

ISBN 0-471-96516-2

Produced from camera-ready copy supplied by the author.
Printed and bound in Great Britain by Bookcraft (Bath) Ltd, Midsomer Norton, Somerset.
This book is printed on acid-free paper responsibly manufactured from sustainable forestati
for which at least two trees are planted for each one used for paper production.

Contents

Series Preface

The information systems community has grown considerably since 1984, when we first started the Wiley Series in Information Systems. We are pleased to be part of the growth of the field, and believe that the series books have played an important role in the intellectual development of the discipline. The primary objective of the series is to publish scholarly works which reflect the best of research in the information systems community.

As the information systems field matures, there is an increased need to carry the results of its growing body of research into practice. The series desires to publish research results that speak to important needs in the development and management of information systems and our editorial mission recognizes explicitly the need for research to inform the practise and management of information systems. The present volume provides another good example of the series' intent. *Management Challenges in IS: Successful Strategies and Appropriate Action*, by Jim McKeen and Heather Smith, directly applies theory to practice. Based on the need of IS managers to assimilate and then translate technical and managerial information into effective strategies, the authors report on the results of their 'IT Management Forum.' The Forum was designed to allow IS executives the opportunity to express concerns, share experiences, and explore key topics in the broad area of the management of IT. The results of these executives' discussions were written up in the form of papers. This volume represents a compilation of these interesting and topical papers. They should prove valuable and insightful to anyone interested in the challenges facing the IS manager.

PREVIOUS VOLUMES IN THE SERIES

Boland & Hirschheim: *Critical Issues in Information Systems Research*

Schäfer: *Functional Analysis of Office Requirements—A Multiperspective Approach*

Mumford & MacDonald: *XSEL's Progress—The Continuing Journey of an Expert System*

Swanson & Beath: *Maintaining Information Systems in Organizations*

Friedman: *Computer Systems Development—History Organization and Implementation*

Huws, Korte & Robinson: *Telework—Towards the Elusive Office*

Lincoln: *Managing Information Systems for Profit*

Ward: *Strategic Planning for Information Systems*

Silver: *Systems that Support Decision Makers—Description and Analysis*

Irving & Higgins: *Office Information Systems—Management Issues and Methods*

Cotterman & Senn: *Challenges and Strategies for Research in Systems Development*

Walsham: *Interpreting Information Systems in Organizations*

Watkins & Eliot: *Expert Systems in Business and Finance— Issues and Applications*

Lacity & Hirschheim: *Information Systems Outsourcing— Myths, Metaphors and Realities*

Österle, Brenner & Hilbers: *Total Information Systems Management—A European Approach*

Ciborra & Jelassi: *Strategic Information Systems*

Knights: *Managers Divided*

Krcmar: *EDI in Europe*

Ward & Griffiths: *Strategic Planning for Information Systems*

RUDY HIRSCHHEIM
University of Houston,
Houston, Texas

DICK BOLAND
Case Western Reserve University,
Cleveland, Ohio

Preface

We never planned to write a book. When we started the Queen's IT Management Forum, our interests were purely academic. We wanted to find out what was happening on the front-line of the information technology 'wars' in organizations. Through focusing on current IT management concerns in a variety of businesses, we hoped to be better able to focus our own research on the impact of IT on organizations.

However, it was not long before we realized that, not only was there a need in academia to learn more about IT in organizations, there was also an enormous need in organizations to learn more about the 'big picture' trends in using and managing IT. IT managers have both the fortune *and* the misfortune of being able to peer into the future long before the rest of us. It is they who make the decisions that will affect how IT is used in organizations. They therefore have a direct influence on the impact of IT on businesses and ultimately, through their employees and customers, on a large portion of society as a whole.

This book is therefore the outcome of a new form of scholarship. It bridges the gaps between the practical, everyday knowledge of the IT manager and the measured, thoughtful knowledge of the academic researcher. The first type is characterized by 'flying by the seat of your pants'—it is anecdotal and incomplete at best. The second type is methodologically sound and thorough, but often of little help to the practitioner by the time it is completed. As a result, two bodies of knowledge about IT management exist—each with their own dynamics and timeframes. Intersections between the two are haphazard.

Through the IT Management Forums and the resulting papers, we have sought to connect these two bodies of knowledge by creating a third body which has significant intersections with both current experience and trends, and academic knowledge. These, in turn, have become the start of a number of industry-academic collaborations to explore effective IT management:

- In 1991, we began an annual **CIO Forum** to provide Chief Information Officers with an opportunity to share knowledge with each other and to learn about current academic research.

- In 1994, we implemented an **Associate Membership** in IT Management Forum which has enabled a larger number of organizations to participate in our work.

- In 1995, we started a quarterly **CIO Brief** to facilitate the sharing and documentation of the experiences of leading edge IT organizations so that others could benefit from them.

Each of these efforts has the potential to affect how IT is used in organizations and to provide academics with useful insights for future research.

We see this type of work as the way of the future in IT. While the 'after the fact' type of analysis practised by academics will always be worthwhile, it will not be useful to practitioners unless it is made available in a more accessible form. No IT manager of our acquaintance has the time to read through dozens of academic articles to find the gems hidden therein. Yet, it is becoming increasingly dangerous and expensive for organizations to undertake massive technical and organizational change without thorough planning and research. Every IT manager we know has a 'war story' about significant and costly initiatives being championed by executives on the basis of a two-page article in an airline magazine.

This book is therefore designed for both the thoughtful practitioner and the practical academic. It does not set out to be the final word on any topic or to provide any 'silver bullets.' Instead, it is designed to fill the void left between the fast-paced world of technical and organizational change and the more moderately-paced world of trying to make sense of it all. In the process, we hope to have provided not only useful information to the reader, but also a new way to approach understanding change.

Acknowledgements

Writing a book is one of those tasks that rarely comes to fruition without the help of many individuals. This book is no exception. Indeed, because of the collaborative nature of the activities which provided its genesis, this book would not have even been possible without them. To those individuals we are truly indebted. They have, to a person, willingly offered their insights, experience and perceptions to aid our understanding of the varied and complex issues of managing information systems effectively. We have developed strong ties over the years—indeed, close friendships—surpassing normal business relationships. John Bailey, Prem Agrawal, Gary Davenport, Gary Plomske, George Oliver, Jan Schwartz, Hugh Forbes, and Dave Burkett were founding members and many are still associated with our Forum today. Harvey Baumgarten, Doug Croth, Dan Howard, Jim Breen, Dorothy Pang, Bob Parsons, Robin Hewson, Clive Howard, Nancy Morrow, Rick Haier, Rick Boddy, Wendy Merkley, Steve Duncan, Fred Taggart and Henry Lynn have each made significant contributions to these chapters as well.

We would also like to thank Mrs. Linda Freeman who took a collection of unorganized word processing files and produced a camera-ready version of the book you are now reading. Linda's expertise, ingenuity, creativeness and foresight solved problems before they developed and helped us meet a challenging publication deadline.

Finally, we would like to acknowledge the role of Queen's University's School of Business in this book. The School has encouraged and supported our work in a number of ways and made it possible to explore and develop this collaborative approach to the study of IT management.

School of Business   James D. McKeen
Queen's University   Heather A. Smith
Kingston, Ontario
April, 1996

1
The Importance of Effective Information Systems Management

INTRODUCTION

Today's Information Systems (IS) manager must face a great deal of uncertainty in his or her work: decisions have to be made using only partial information; risks taken with new technologies; and new and untried strategies implemented. IS managers who are charged with the responsibility of maximizing the benefit of information technology (IT) within their organizations often find themselves forced to make critical decisions regarding IT with little guidance. While there is a great deal of information (some would say too much information) available to IS managers from vendors, consultants, trade shows, industry associations, and the popular press, very little of it deals with the *management* issues surrounding IT and its implementation. Worse, much of this information is biased in favour of the products or services provided by the information source. As a result, the majority of IS managers have very little information about how to *combine* technical and managerial information into effective and workable strategies that could be used in their day-to-day job.

The IT Management Forum was developed in response to this need—a need for information focused on the unique set of problems faced by IS managers. The Forum, founded by the authors in 1990, is an opportunity for IS executives to share their experiences, learn from their peers, and to work out solutions to the critical issues surrounding information technology management. Forum membership is limited to ten companies and is selected from leading-edge organizations in a variety of industries. Representatives from these organizations meet quarterly to discuss the topics they feel are of critical concern to them and their organizations. We act as facilitators to guide and structure the meetings to ensure they reach practical and effective conclusions that are of *immediate* use in organizations.

After each session, a paper is written for the members that addresses practitioner concerns and summarizes the group's conclusions. It also tries to incorporate the 'bigger picture' to help the IS manager put an issue into perspective. All too often, IS organizations are subject to industry fads, media pressures, and vendor 'hype.' The papers are designed to present strategies that IS managers could use *immediately* in their organizations. As one manager remarked to us, 'Everyone agrees where we'll be in fifteen year's time; we just don't know how best to get there from here.' To ensure that Forum sessions are relevant to the needs of IS managers, each follows the same format:

- members jointly select a topic of interest to them;
- they research each topic within their own organizations following an outline prepared by the facilitators;
- each member makes a presentation about how his or her organization is managing the issue;
- members have an opportunity to critique and discuss each presentation and to agree on best practices;
- draft copies of each paper are reviewed by members as well as selected IS and user managers in the member's organizations;
- responses are incorporated into the final papers.

The reaction to these papers has been extremely positive. Manager after manager has told us that they address a need for a balanced, thoughtful discussion of important IS management issues. However, until now, readership has been limited to

Forum members only. This book represents a compilation of Forum papers and is the first time they have been available to non-Forum members. We hope that they will be helpful to anyone who has an interest in the challenges and dilemmas faced by today's IS managers. The stories below describe some of these.

THE CASE OF THE RELUCTANT PARTNER

John Anderson, the CIO of Acme Financial, is ready to implement a 'new paradigm' for IS. He has attended seminars about how to be a true partner with the business rather than simply a service provider. He has read all the articles about it in Datamation *and* CIO Magazine. *He has even restructured his organization to be more proactive with business to help them find the optimal strategies they need to run their business more effectively. John knows IS can be a much bigger contributor to the company than it has been in the past and that this is the way of the future for businesses.*

The problem is, while John is ready for this new vision of IS, his senior management is not. 'Just give us the systems we ask for' they keep telling him when he tries to suggest that IS could contribute to the company's strategic plans. Sure, IS and the users have not always seen eye-to-eye on everything. There was that time a few months back that the customer data base crashed because of a programming error and company business was shut down for four hours. Even the president was pretty steamed about that one. IS is not the best at delivering systems on time without cutting out function, but IS is working hard to be courteous and responsive to its users.

John feels that the company is missing a major opportunity to work together with IS to develop more effective systems. But management simply does not want to listen to him. 'They're locked into an '80s timewarp' he thinks and wonders HOW he can get them to see that IS has much more to offer them now than it did in the past.

John has a classic IS dilemma. There are many conflicting and confusing ideas about the role of IS in business today. Some visions suggest that IS should aim to be a mere service provider, delivering systems as requested, on time, and on budget. Other visions, recognizing the role systems have played in corporate strategy, suggest IS needs to be more proactive, participating as equals at the highest levels of organizational planning.

Management's acceptance of new roles for IS is frequently coloured by how effectively IS has worked in the past. If IS has a poor image in the organization, it is unlikely that senior management will want to share decision-making with it. There are many possible reasons for John's problem. Unfortunately, all too often, IS still has a reputation for being 'tekkies' who do not know their way around the business and do not understand how it really operates. In some organizations, there has been significant user-IS conflict. In others, IS has delivered ineffective or inappropriate systems which provide little benefit to the business. Sometimes, IS simply has not marketed its services well internally. Regardless of the reason, John must recognize that management of IS' role and responsibilities within Acme is an important element of his job. IS cannot be effective without a clear agreement with management about these. And senior management will not let IS take on new roles unless it is convinced that they will be beneficial for the company.

The chapters in Part 1 of this book, **Managing IS in the Organization**, each address some aspect of managing the role of IS in the contemporary organization. For example, IS must be marketed and promoted internally, but not in the ways that many IS managers think. Marketing IS involves more than simply telling the business it needs more information technology. IS has an important role to play in a company's re-engineering efforts, but the company needs to understand where IS involvement is necessary and appropriate and where it is not. It is John's job to clarify this with his senior management. Finally, IS' relations with users are a significant source of conflict in organizations and this conflict can often retard IS' acceptance by business managers. Management of this relationship is therefore critical to gaining credibility within the company.

THE CASE OF THE RETICENT RE-ENGINEER

Barbara Simpson knows that IS organizations need to change. As CIO of Greenshields Insurance she has seen the company go through a major re-engineering process as a result of the economy and the changing business climate. She knows that to contribute effectively to the organization she needs to streamline her own organization and to adapt to meet the new demands the users will be placing on it. The problem is, she is not sure where IS is heading. Should IS change to become more business-oriented? or does it need to become more technical? A few years ago, many IS organizations decentralized their development staff to the user departments to become more responsive to user needs. Now, centralization seems to be 'in' to avoid functional solutions to organizational problems.

Senior management is also pressuring Barbara to re-engineer IS itself. Every other department in the company except IS has had to take serious budget cuts. IS has reorganized itself several times in recent years, but somehow its staff and budget numbers never seem to go down. There are so many essential IS services—data management, security, quality control, end user services. It seems next to impossible to do everything IS is supposed to and cut down at the same time.

'What I need is a game plan,' she thought. 'If I knew where IS is heading over the next five years, I could design a strategy to get there. At present, all we do is move from crisis to crisis. For once, I'd like to do more than simply react to problems.'

Managing an IS organization today is a major challenge. CIOs like Barbara are struggling to adapt both the role and structure of IS in light of a rapidly changing technology and rapidly changing business needs. All too often, restructuring IS is seen as a cure for many of IS' management problems. As a result, it is not uncommon for IS to be reorganized every two or three years as its management tries to keep up with evolving organizational needs, technical trends, and the latest IS fashions.

But 'poor structure' should not be used as an excuse for poor performance. When restructuring IS is used as a substitute for clarifying IS' role and responsibilities in the organization, bureaucracy and infrastructure tend to increase, not decrease. Effective structure is, in fact, the logical outcome of a clear articulation of IS' goals and objectives. If Barbara takes the time to think through what IS will be doing and how it will be working in the organization in the short and medium term, she will be much more likely to develop a workable structure for her IS department than if she simply responds to the latest crisis or fad.

Part 2 of this book, **Managing the IS Organization**, looks at the issues associated with managing IS from a tactical perspective (i.e., the next two to five years). It examines the key changes that IS will have to make in the next few years and presents an overall strategy for getting there. It then explores more specific trends in how IS does its work and links these both to larger trends in organizations and the industry, outlining practical plans for achieving change. Contrary to the prevailing wisdom, this book concludes that there is no single 'best' structure or strategy for managing IS but rather a variety of appropriate structures and objectives which will work for a particular company. It is management's job to assess these and to select a strategy and structure in keeping with the changes it wishes to make. In short, this section presents a managerial game plan for IS change in the medium term.

THE CASE OF THE PRODUCTIVITY PREDICAMENT

Kevin Wang of Superior Gas is under the gun. Users and senior management are pressuring him to develop more systems faster. Although his function point productivity has improved dramatically over the past five years, the users do not care about that. 'Who knows what a function point is?' the CFO snapped at him recently. 'What we want is a faster turnaround time for systems and we're not getting it! I've had two companies in here this month who claim they can do the work faster and cheaper. Why can't you?'

Kevin has already implemented many new tools and strategies such as, CASE, RAD, JAD, and new methodologies, not to mention an expensive project control package. It seems that every day there is another consultant at his door trying to sell him more 'silver bullets.' But the software and methodologies he has right now were supposed to solve all his problems, and did not. Right now, everyone is talking about OO. All the industry 'hype' suggests that it improves productivity threefold! But he has heard that story before. He has been around long enough to realize that there are almost always tradeoffs when new tools and technology are involved.

'I've got to find a way to get more done faster, but how? We've got all the technology in place but somehow it's not working the way it should,' he muses. 'Is there something I'm missing?'

Kevin is not the only CIO in a productivity crunch. While business has always pressured IS to do more, faster, with the increasingly competitive environment it finds itself in, these pressures are taking on a new imperative. In the past, IS has looked to technology to improve its productivity. Although more and better tools are certainly an important component of productivity, all too often IS managers see them as the *only* avenue of improvement.

There is much more to effective performance management. While IS staff have always intuitively recognized the value of a good manager in getting things done, a recent study by Boston University (Guinan, 1994) has concluded that the *only* significant factor in project performance was the effectiveness of the project leader. Measurement too can be a contributor to improving performance, but only if it focuses the team's attention on what is truly important. An organization can easily spend a lot of time calculating function points, collecting project control information, and creating project status reports to the detriment of the project's overall productivity. Finally, organizations need to take a new look at how their work itself is organized to ensure that time and effort are not wasted. System testing is a prime example of one kind of IS work that has not changed substantially over time in spite of the fact that it frequently takes up 30–40% of the development effort.

The chapters in Part 3, **Managing IS Performance**, address IS performance from two complementary perspectives:

* the role of tools and techniques in improving productivity
* the role of other factors, such as measurement, good management, and work design.

Improved performance results from an effective combination of both. IS management cannot simply rely on tools and techniques to speed up system development. This section points to the critical role management at all levels can have in improving IS performance and outlines some practical suggestions for ensuring that optimal performance is reached.

THE CASE OF THE OVER-CHALLENGED CIO

Lynn D'Angelo is working 12 hours a day and still not getting everything done! Although she has been at the job for five years, she just cannot seem to get things under control. There are so many tasks that need her attention and with tight staffing restrictions in her company, National Hospital Management, more and more responsibilities seem to be falling in her lap. At present, she is trying to work out a strategy to cope with the millennium change. Many of the company's core systems were written in the 1970's and no one ever dreamed they would last this long. As a result, many of the company's systems are not going to make it past 1 January, 2000. A thorough assessment of every single system is necessary, and changing them will entail many person-years of work. Somehow, this has to be worked into an already challenging development timetable!

Now on top of everything, the President has just come back from a business trip where he read an article in Business Week *about corporate information warehouses. He thinks it is a perfect idea for the company; Lynn is not so sure. The consultants she has talked to seem to have rather vague answers to her questions. She suspects its because there are no real answers. In spite of this, Lynn has three weeks to prepare her recommendations to senior management.*

Lynn feels overwhelmed. She looks back wistfully to the days when the company had a single mainframe and used COBOL for all its systems and change was more manageable. If only there was a way to get all this complexity under control!

There is no question that the job of managing IS is growing increasingly complex. This results not only from the increasing amount of new technology that IS must cope with, but also from the growing number of legacy systems that need to be maintained. It is no wonder that Lynn is feeling she cannot keep up. Traditionally, it has been assumed that the lifetime of a system is five to seven years. After that, it should be replaced. The approaching millennium has made many managers realize that many of their core 'workhorse' systems are up to 20 or more years old! The effort of coping with systems and technology that span 30 years, as well as the challenging job of moving a company's information resources and technology forward, leaves many CIOs with little time to spare.

Managing the information resources of a company—the systems and the data IS produces—is a growing aspect of a CIO's responsibilities. Managers need to find new ways of coping with them as they eat up increasing amounts of IS resources. IS organizations can no longer afford to maintain multiple system platforms for example. Legacy systems cannot be allowed to become a drain on the organization's development capabilities. At the same time, companies cannot buy into every new technical fad that comes along. There must be a clear business case to be made before new technology is added to the ever-burgeoning array of hardware and software. In short, CIOs must be more proactive in this area than they have been traditionally. Without definite strategies for managing their information resources, many more CIOs will end up like Lynn—overworked and overwhelmed.

The chapters in Part 4 of this book, **Managing the Information Resource**, deal with strategies for managing a company's systems and data, i.e., its information resource. The chapter on 'Managing Complexity' addresses a question faced by all IS managers—how to deal with the growing number of issues they are facing on a regular basis from both the

technology and the business. Other chapters look at dealing
with the complexity generated by older, legacy systems and
how to design information and systems for the future. Together,
they are designed to focus the IS manager's attention on the
specific issues and concerns surrounding managing a company's
information resource and to distinguish this aspect of IS
management from other parts of a CIO's job.

A GUIDE TO THIS BOOK

This book is designed to be read by anyone who wants a
practitioner's view of IS management issues. Each chapter is
based on a topic selected by a group of practising senior IS
managers as being critical to their work today. These managers
came from a wide range of businesses. The resulting chapters
incorporate the issues, ideas, and strategies presented by them
to the group as a whole and subjected to the scrutiny of other
practising managers.

   While they can be read as self-contained units, chapters have
been grouped into four major themes which reflect the
challenges facing IS managers in the 1990s. At the end of each
unit, a CIO responds to the ideas presented in one of the
chapters and discusses his strategies for managing IS in his
own organization. An overview of each section is presented
below.

Part 1: Managing IS in the Organization

This section presents issues that reflect on IS' relationship with
the larger business of which it is part. It points out that
contrary to popular opinion, there is no single appropriate role
for IS to play in an organization. In some companies, IS is a
trusted and valued partner and no decisions are made without
its input. In others, IS is viewed as a service and business
managers want to call the shots. In either case, IS has an
important role to play within the organization and needs to
manage it appropriately.

Re-engineering the Corporation: Where does IS Fit In? discusses the topic of organizational re-engineering from the standpoint of IS. It examines three different types of reengineering—process re-engineering, business re-engineering, and corporate re-engineering. It then focuses on the critical role IS plays in business re-engineering because of the importance of information technology to this work. Four primary prerequisites for the successful implementation of a re-engineering effort are then discussed and the role of IS in achieving success is explored.

Managing IS-User Conflict explores four key underlying sources of conflict between IS and user groups: differences in goals and timeframes; lack of measurable benefit; and disagreement over roles and responsibilities. It then explores those emerging trends that influence the IS-business relationship; the routinization and standardization of managerial work; changes to work content and skill requirements; and the erosion of managerial control and decision-making. Guidance for managers involved in conflict relationships is then provided.

Marketing the IS Function examines why the IS function needs to market itself to the rest of the organization and to do it effectively. Since marketing is a process of identifying and satisfying needs, IS managers cannot promote particular IT strategies and plans without reference to how well they are meeting the organization's needs at present. The chapter presents a three-tiered marketing needs hierarchy and suggests strategies for IS management to follow in order to address the organization's needs at each level of this hierarchy. When marketing is approached in this step-by-step fashion, the IS function and business gradually build a relationship of respect and trust, which form the basis for a committed partnership between the two. This in turn enables the organization to achieve its maximum potential.

Part 2: Managing the IS Organization

This section deals with the issues involved in managing the IS organization itself. IS departments are highly complex 'mini-enterprises' that frequently have a great deal of autonomy within the organization because of their special needs. IS managers must oversee a wide variety of technical and professional staff, manage large operating budgets, keep up with rapidly-changing technical trends, and be able to deliver IS services effectively in a cost-appropriate fashion. They need to be able to discern trends in what is needed and design their organizations to deliver information and information services well.

To do this, managers first must understand how IS' role is evolving within the organization, and then take a hard look at their internal operations. Often, IS' internal structure and procedures can use significant restructuring. It is not uncommon to find that certain IS activities follow cumbersome and time-consuming processes that would not be acceptable elsewhere in the business. This can be the result of IS managers being unable to be as objective about their own organizations as they can be about others; or it can result from the business being unwilling to fund appropriate IS infrastructure. In either case, IS managers need to be more proactive about ensuring their own internal operations are functioning effectively.

Human resource management in IS also requires special attention in order to ensure that staff is well-prepared to meet future technical demands in addition to coping with existing requirements. There is a very real danger that many IS organizations will not be able to make the transition from older to newer technologies unless a substantial effort is made to train and upgrade today's IS professionals. This section highlights the issues associated with managing the IS enterprise and suggests ways to ensure that it is well-positioned to meet current and future company needs.

Retooling Information Systems: A New Vision for IS describes how to build an IS function to handle the formidable challenge of change and upheaval being faced by many IS organizations. Like the process of retooling an outdated factory to produce products faster and more efficiently, the IS function must undergo a change that is no less comprehensive if it is to fulfil its organizational mandate. This chapter sets out to identify and articulate a blueprint for a future direction for IS.

Re-engineering IS discusses how organizational re-engineering can be specifically tailored for IS to achieve the dramatic improvements in performance, product quality, and customer service promised by re-engineering experts. While information technology plays an important role in enabling the re-engineering process, many senior managers are wondering whether IS itself is designed to deliver IT to the organization most effectively. This chapter focuses on how IS managers might re-engineer their own function to achieve similar re-engineering goals as other business units.

Managing the IS Infrastructure addresses the large number of specialties which have been created within IS to support both the business and the IS function in the past few years. Recently, many organizations have begun to question the value of this IS infrastructure. It was developed for a number of reasons: to improve productivity, upgrade skill levels, and ensure standards. But has this infrastructure been responsible for the high degree of bureaucracy and long lead times that are all too often characteristic of IS organizations? This chapter examines the composition, function, and contribution of the IS infrastructure and discusses a variety of ways that IS goals can be met without creating additional overheads.

Human Resource Management for IS looks at the growing discrepancy between the skills available in most IS organizations and those that will be needed over the next decade. Employment projections predict a growing number of IT workers whose skills are irrelevant over the next decade. This chapter looks first at the current human resources practices of IS managers and then outlines strategies for making human resources management a more proactive and effective process.

Part 3: Managing IS Performance

Improving IS performance is a major IS management concern. As pressures on business have increased in the current decade, pressures on IS to help them cope have increased correspondingly. IS managers have begun an all-out assault on IS productivity, but in spite of expensive tools, and massive attention to the subject, it is unclear what has been achieved in system development. This section addresses how IS organizations are attempting to improve their performance and looks at the most effective strategies for doing so.

Benchmarking IS looks at how IS performance is measured. IS is one area of the company that is extremely difficult to measure and evaluate. While IS management is placing new emphasis on measurement to demonstrate its contribution to overall corporate performance both through improved quality and cost-effectiveness, achieving useful evaluations of IS is easier said than done. This chapter explores how IS organizations are evaluating and comparing themselves and makes suggestions about how the measurement and evaluation of IS both internally and externally could be improved.

Improving System Development Productivity examines IS' management of the development process. While previously, IS has focused on creating using bureaucracy and multi-step methodologies to meet its own needs, now all facets of the development process must be designed to further the business' overall goal—to make money. This chapter looks at ten assumptions about the systems development process which, if challenged, can lead to new and more productive methods of developing systems.

System Development Tools: Do They Make a Difference? discusses the wide variety of tools that have been introduced into organization in the past 20 years. Each has promised to vastly improve the system development and maintenance processes. Yet managers are still continually barraged with pitches for more tools and techniques that promise more and greater flexibility, maintainability, effectiveness, or productivity. This chapter looks at the bottom-line on system development tools to determine the impact they have had on the systems IS develops. From this assessment, a clearer understanding of the role of tools in the development process is gained and managers will learn how to select effective tools for their organizations.

Object-Oriented Technology: Getting Beyond the Hype explores the hyperbole about object-oriented technology that is putting IS managers under pressure to get on the OO bandwagon. Many IS practitioners are speaking about OO as a 'revolution' that will dramatically change how IS does its work and which has the potential to eliminate or significantly reduce IS staff. Other managers, however, know from bitter experience the problems and costs of introducing a new technology. This chapter looks critically at the current state of OO technology and identifies the issues IS managers must face in making decisions about using it in their own organizations.

Improving Testing looks at the process of testing systems. Very little about testing has changed since the earliest days of system development, yet testing has become increasingly complex as different technologies have proliferated in recent years. As a result, testing has begun to take up more and more development time. There are enormous benefits to be gained from improving the process of testing and major business risks associated with it being done poorly. This chapter examines other complex design processes to determine what can be learned from them that can be applied to improving testing and present strategies for changing and upgrading the testing process in IS.

Part 4: Managing the Information Resource

Most businesses have come to realize that information is a significant resource for their organizations. However, how this resource is to be used and managed presents IS with a host of difficulties. Systems produced 20 or 30 years ago, written by programmers who have long since disappeared, with minimal documentation, share computer space with contemporary modular or object-based programs. Data fields designed for one piece of information, have been modified to hold totally different information, as the needs of the company have changed. Systems produced for a single function of the company have evolved over time to serve totally different needs than were ever anticipated. Data are produced at different levels of abstraction, from all parts of the company, and cannot be compared easily. Managing this mess into some sort of order will be one of the biggest jobs facing IS managers in the immediate future. This section addresses some of the most important steps that need to be taken in this area.

Managing Complexity explores sources of complexity in IS and methods for managing it effectively. There is little doubt that the transition to an information society has increased the level of complexity in people's lives to an unprecedented level. IS has assumed a front-line position in coping with this accelerated complexity within the organization. It falls to IS to decide what technology will be introduced, how fast it will be introduced and how it will be integrated into the organization. IS' ability to manage the complexity associated with this work will have a major impact on the well-being of organizations.

Mining for Corporate Information. Almost all large organizations today produce mountains of data. Some organizations have recently been successful in 'mining' operational data to discover important nuggets of information that have been used to improve their business' effectiveness. This has prompted many senior managers to pay attention to the importance of the information resource in their organizations. However, most IS managers, while recognizing the value of this information, know that extracting it is not a trivial task. This chapter discusses strategies for delivering information to the corporation, determining the benefits derived and the costs involved, and examines the significant technical, organizational and people issues associated with effective information management.

Managing Legacy Systems. Most organizations have hundreds or even thousands of programs and data files that need revitalization. These systems not only take up a significant amount of developer time (up to 50% in some organizations), they also severely restrict IS' flexibility and responsiveness to the business. This chapter looks at strategies for managing these systems, the organizational and people issues surrounding them, ways of upgrading them to current standards without bankrupting the organization, and how to prevent creating legacy systems in the future.

Preparing for the Millennium Change looks at a humble problem that is causing IS considerable worry: the date field. Date fields are ubiquitous; virtually every transaction is 'date-stamped' and the comparison of dates is endemic to business functioning. Because many systems do not identify the century, almost every organization today faces potential chaos. Companies that are unprepared for the century change will face disruptions in computer processing ranging from a few hours of relatively inconsequential inconvenience to a few days with realized losses in activities like billings, orders, or shipments to losses that will be unrecoverable and which jeopardize the organization's health. This chapter examines the nature of the millennium problem from a number of perspectives and presents proven strategies for managing this situation, including a framework for approaching the problem in a logical fashion.

Although these chapters are designed to be read on their own and are thus useful for those who wish to consult this book about a particular IS management issue, taken as a whole, these chapters present a perspective on IS that is often undervalued. They emphasize the important role a manager can play in ensuring that information technology is delivered effectively and cost–efficiently. All too often IS managers have been guilty of looking for a 'silver bullet' from technology—the one magic answer that will solve all of their problems. If this book has one message, it is this: there are no silver bullets; there are only good managers.

The world of IS presents many challenges to managers. They operate in environments that are continually changing; they face situations that no one has ever faced before; they have to combine effective organizational and technical management techniques; and, they have significant responsibilities to the organization. But IS is not as special as many managers think it is. In fact, there is much to be learned from other disciplines and more experienced business managers. It is only by looking at the *management* aspects of IS, as opposed to the *technical* aspects, that these become clear. Inasmuch as this book does this, it will present new ways of approaching and dealing with the common problems faced by today's IS manager.

PART 1

Managing IS in the Organization

2

Re-engineering the Corporation: Where Does IS Fit In?

INTRODUCTION

Re-engineering is a 'hot topic.' The appearance of articles describing organizations achieving quantum leaps in productivity, substantially reduced costs, and improved customer service through re-engineering provides evidence of this. But the problem confronting executives is how to sift fact from fiction amid all the hoopla. They need to know: What exactly is re-engineering? and, How does one do it?

A recent review of the literature reveals that there is very little consensus concerning re-engineering. Some authors believe that the central focus of re-engineering should be process redesign (Davenport and Short, 1990) while others suggest it should be integration (Boudette, 1991; Carlyle, 1990). Because information technology plays an important, if not, central role, some writers suggest that the information systems function must be the driving force behind these changes (Senn, 1991). Others believe that IS should be involved in only a limited way (Krass, 1991). In some cases, it is suggested that re-engineering needs to be accomplished by an improved development methodology (Emery, 1991); in others, the key approach is changed management thinking and organization structure (Hammer, 1990; Carlyle, 1990); still others believe it can only be accomplished by information technology but *not* by IS (Donovan, 1993). Some wonder what makes re-engineering substantially different from good, old-fashioned business/ systems analysis? And what role should IS assume in the re- engineering process?

This chapter looks at the issue of re-engineering and how it works in organizations. It outlines the types of re-engineering taking place and examines the role IS is playing in the process. Recommendations for managers currently involved in re- engineering activities are then presented and a method of implementing re-engineering effectively is then described.

WHAT IS RE-ENGINEERING?

Much of the confusion surrounding re-engineering stems from the lack of an accepted definition. Adding to this, cited re- engineering examples vary from organizational restructuring to arming a salesforce with laptop computers. At a basic level, re-engineering means radically redesigning the way an organization performs its business to achieve dramatic improvements in performance. On closer examination, however, it can be seen that re-engineering actually involves three quite distinct activities—each requiring a different approach and attempting to re-engineer in quite a different manner.

Process Re-engineering concentrates on making processes more efficient. These could be manufacturing processes or business processes. Here, the emphasis is on process simplification, streamlining activities to make them run smoother, reduce paperwork, improve quality, and improve response time. Process re-engineering generally takes place within existing organizational boundaries and encompasses much of what is usually called business or system analysis. Because of this, it is typically driven by IS. Examples include: improvements in existing processes with few or minor system changes, rationalization of processes and systems to achieve productivity improvements and expense savings, simplification or standardization of procedures and forms, using new hardware and/or software to simplify processes or reduce costs (e.g., substitution of PC-based technology for a mainframe system). In each of these examples, IS worked together with business units to achieve significant improvements in existing processes saving time and money. Analysts challenged the methods whereby existing processes were implemented but current organization structures and fundamental business assumptions remained unaffected.

Business Re-engineering broadens the scope of the re-engineering effort so substantially that it becomes a distinctly different activity. Business re-engineering attempts to re-establish the natural business entity, such as a customer or a product, and to link all of the processes and activities relating to that entity together. The emphasis here is on reintegrating activities and processes that have become fragmented over time due to the size of the organization. As one Forum member stated, 'We try to ask how a "Mom and Pop" business would handle an issue and redesign with this goal in mind.' While business re-engineering's goal is integrative in nature, it must accomplish more than simply 'putting the pieces back together.' Integration of systems merely automates more effectively. It does not challenge the rules about how a business is organized and conducted. As Michael Hammer (1990) states:

'At the heart of re-engineering is the notion of **discontinuous thinking**—of recognizing and breaking away from the outdated rules and fundamental assumptions that underlie operations. Unless we change these rules, we are merely rearranging the deck chairs on the Titanic.'

An example of true business re-engineering is the restructuring of the organization to focus on customers. In at least two companies we know, customer representatives were given the information and the authority to handle all customer-related activities. Whereas previously, customers would have to go to different individuals for service, new products, and billing inquiries, now one customer representative is able to handle any customer problem and has access to all the information and systems required. While this concept is simple, it has meant a significant consciousness-shift for the organizations involved. They needed to recognize that old organizational divisions such as customer service, repairs and maintenance, accounts receivable, and sales are unnecessary (and indeed, undesirable) from a customer perspective. In this situation, IT is the **enabler**. Once the basic decision has been made to re-engineer, IT can provide the most effective means of implementing it. However, a substantial number of organization issues that are not IT related, such a structure, personnel, and politics, need to be addressed by senior management as well.

Corporate Re-engineering is the third type of re-engineering. It involves changing the entire organization by splitting it into separate businesses or 'spinning off' pieces that are not directly related to the core functions of the company. An example of corporate re-engineering is the 'Saturn project' where General Motors approached the design and marketing of a new car by creating a different company not hamstrung by old methods of work, old ways of thinking, and old management and labour practices. In another case, the IS function of a major organization was spun off into its own company that now competes for business. A third example of corporate re-engineering is the creation of Stentor Ltd, a new communications corporation that is composed of the engineering and marketing functions of the ten major telephone companies in Canada. While these companies will continue to exist, and from a customer perspective will not change, they will be very different internally. Stentor will enable Canadian telephone companies to compete internationally as a single entity, while maintaining their local character in each province. In these cases, the role of IT is supportive. Corporate re-engineering is and should be the responsibility of CEOs and boards of directors. This form of re-engineering calls the very existence of the organization itself and what it does into question.

WHAT IS NEW ABOUT RE-ENGINEERING?

Today's competitive environment means that increasingly, management is willing to question current practices at all levels to achieve competitive advantages, improve productivity, reduce costs, and improve services. While each form of re-engineering is taking on more prominence in organizations as managers struggle with the challenges of the modern business environment, what is really new about them? Process re-engineering has been around since Frederick Taylor first suggested productivity would be improved by task decomposition (Davenport, 1990). It has been substantially enhanced in recent years by the introduction of IT, but process re-engineering is still essentially the same activity industrial engineers and systems analysts have been doing for many years.

Corporate re-engineering has also been around in a variety of guises for a long time. EDS was successfully spun off from GM over 15 years ago. Simpsons-Sears was created in the 1950s by two separate companies—Robert Simpsons and Sears Roebuck—to take advantage of new market opportunities. More recently, banks have been merging with investment houses to take on a wider range of functions. While the stakes may be higher, and more companies may be doing it, there is nothing intrinsically new or different about this form of corporate restructuring.

Business re-engineering is truly innovative. This is because it is being stimulated and enabled by new forms of information technology. In the past, *Datamation* notes, 'business priorities and organizational form were limited by technology not enhanced . . . The essence of technologies in the 1990s is their inclusiveness and their ability to allow a multitude of things to happen simultaneously rather than serially' (Carlyle, 1990). Thus, it is the potential of IT to enable new ways of looking at the organization that makes business re-engineering different from what has happened in the past. The remainder of this paper addresses the issue of business re-engineering and IS' role in the process.

FOUR ESSENTIALS OF BUSINESS RE-ENGINEERING

The possibilities and potentials of business re-engineering are many and complex and are limited only by organizational restraints and the constraints of the technology. This makes the **management** of business re-engineering crucial. We suggest that there are four components of business re-engineering considered to be essential in the successful management of this activity:

• A New Vision.
• Top Management Leadership.
• Attention to Non-technical Issues.
• Participation by the IS Function.

1. *A New Vision*

The importance of a top management 'vision' of where the organization should go cannot be underestimated. Successful examples of re-engineering are the result of thinking big, thinking boldly, and thinking differently. Michael Hammer (1990) notes 'if managers have the vision, re-engineering will find the way.' Vision is not something that can be approached in a stepwise fashion. It occurs when a manager refuses to be limited by traditional organizational constraints and begins to question what things are truly valuable about the work being done. Some executives have found the vision by working temporarily in front-line positions. Others have brought outsiders into the organization to get a fresh point of view. Still others have found this vision by considering new business partnerships with suppliers, customers, or competitors.

A vision is a mental picture of the ideal organization given no structural or bureaucratic limitations. The old-style organization dismembered natural entities (e.g., customers or shipments) into functional pieces (e.g., order taking, customer service, billing, delivery, or credit) with each handled by a separate part of the organization with its attendant bureaucracies and systems. This approach was usually mandated by the limitation of existing technologies. Because of recent developments in IT, however, the re-engineered organization can now reassemble the pieces to recreate these natural entities in order to serve them more effectively. Vision is required because business re-engineering is not an evolutionary process but a clarion call to change in many areas of the organization.

Business re-engineering is a difficult, confusing and disruptive task. What prompts and inspires this new organizational vision? An obvious response is cost reduction. Eliminating hand-offs, overheads, excess management, and redundant departments are attractive goals in difficult financial times. However, Davenport and Short (1990) caution that a proper vision for the organization must have goals beyond cost reduction. 'Excessive attention to cost reduction results in tradeoffs that are usually unacceptable to . . . stakeholders. While optimizing on other objectives seems to bring costs into line, optimizing on cost rarely brings about other objectives.' Similarly time, quality and service objectives are important but must be secondary to management's overall vision of an organization that is structured to deal with natural entities and handle natural processes.

The law of entropy states that all conditions tend to deteriorate over time. When applied to organizational change, this means that changes made will tend to revert to their original condition, unless extra efforts are made to maintain the goal or vision of the change in the minds of the individuals involved. The vision as conceived by management must be continually refreshed, rejuvenated, and reinforced throughout the organization.

2. *Top Management Leadership*

Along with vision, the involvement of top management is critical to the outcome of re-engineering. There are several reasons why senior managers **must** be the drivers of this process:

• Re-engineering goals must be aggressive and challenging ones. These kinds of goals stimulate the creative thinking necessary to challenge existing mindsets. Senior managers have the scope of control to establish such objectives. Examples of such objectives include: substantial cost reductions, time reductions, improved output quality, or improved quality of work life and empowerment.

- Only senior managers can force the people and departments involved to work together. The 'functional chimney' structure of many modern organizations can prevent the cross-functional integration of processes that is essential to effective business re-engineering. Breaking down or through these chimneys requires management that can see across these organizational barriers and which has the organizational clout to deal with the concerns and objections that are bound to arise when the *status quo* is threatened.
- It is unfortunate, but true, that it often takes a crisis to stimulate the kind of thinking and cooperation that leads to significant organizational change. Forum participants unanimously agreed that it is unlikely that effective re-engineering could take place without one. Top management therefore has the responsibility of creating or communicating a sense of crisis that will incite managers to action.
- Re-engineering is not without risks. It requires a motivated team that really wants to solve a problem. Top management can create an environment where taking risks is not only acceptable, but desirable. As one manager put it: 'You need to feel you can try.' Top management must shield the re-engineering effort from company cynics eager to gloat over a failed initiative.
- As noted above, business re-engineering is revolutionary, not evolutionary. When changes have been identified, they need to be implemented quickly. Top management has the ability to act with the speed and the force that are necessary to drive such an implementation.
- Finally, top management must demonstrate 'commitment, consistency and maybe a touch of fanaticism' (Hammer, 1990) to outlast those who believe business re-engineering is simply another 'get-rich-quick, band-aid approach to resolving business' many and complex ills' (*Information Week*, 1991). If top managers exhibit persistence and fortitude, combined with vision, re-engineering can be an effective long-term strategy for companies to preserve competitive advantage. If they do not, 'it will deteriorate to nothing more than a repackaging of old theories and will be a waste of time and resources.' (*Information Week*, 1991).

3. *Attention to Non-Technical Issues*

Although IT is the stimulus behind current business re-engineering activities and the means by which businesses carry out these activities, the non-technical issues that arise during re-engineering are just as critical to the success of the endeavour. Too often, re-engineering efforts focus on improving processes and underestimate the complexity of the other issues involved. These issues fall generally into two categories: human relations and organizational.

Human relations issues include cultural factors such as feelings, politics, values, and resistance as well as more formal personnel functions such as training and compensation. The key to addressing the former is to focus on building a motivated team. In addition to ensuring that top management's vision and objectives are clearly articulated throughout the organization, individuals at all levels need to feel involved in the process of change. The changes should clearly empower workers and give them ownership of their work. This can be threatening to more traditional managers who like to maintain a high degree of control in their areas, but as Davenport and Short (1990) warn, 'managers who ignore this dimension risk failure . . . for organizational and motivational factors.'

More formal personnel factors need to be addressed as well. The process of re-engineering may lead to layoffs or restructuring that can be painful for people. Delayering the organization leaves the critical issue of compensation up in the air. These issues cannot be left until all of the re-engineering decisions have been made but need to be addressed and integrated into a complete re-engineering programme. One manager involved in a major re-engineering effort that will result in substantial savings for her company (and a large reduction in jobs) estimated that personnel issues represent about one-third of the work involved in re-engineering. In this case, advance planning has resulted in some innovative programmes to retrain and upgrade employees at all levels.

Organizational issues also need to be addressed in association with the re-engineering process. As processes are re-designed to focus on natural entities, organizations will tend to be more process-structured and less functionally-structured. When functional chimneys in organizations break down and layers of management flatten, companies will find it necessary to develop structures that maximize activities within and across the entire organization. These will cut across a variety of existing structural dimensions including functions, products, or geography. Hammer has suggested the following guidelines for restructuring organizations:

- Organize around outcomes, not tasks.
- Treat geographically dispersed resources as though they were centralized.
- Link parallel activities while they are occurring instead of integrating their results.

Re-engineered organizations may not eliminate traditional structures altogether but they will recognize that responsibilities will tend to cut across these structures and that they must be able to respond to new challenges with more flexible, team-oriented, coordinating work capability.

4. *IS Participation*

As noted above, re-engineering is possible only because IT is enabling business to take a fresh look at itself. Whereas IT has traditionally been used to speed up and simplify work processes, today it can also facilitate organizational transformation, if management has the vision, the skills, and the motivation to do it. This is because IT has the ability to overcome many traditional organizational constraints. For example, IT can transfer information quickly and easily across large distances, making many processes independent of geography. It can link together all information about a single entity, e.g., a customer or a product, or enable multiple tasks to be accomplished simultaneously.

Because of the centrality of IT to re-engineering solutions, the IS function has an important role to play in the re-engineering process. Few re-engineering solutions will be effective without the support of the IS function. However, many people believe that there is a larger role for IS staff in re-engineering. Often, IS professionals have the organizational perspective and a knowledge of technical potentialities that place them in the position of being catalysts for the re-engineering effort. In fact, some writers feel the IS professionals should be the prime candidates for leading the re-engineering process because they have the cross-boundary vision and multi-dimensional way of thinking that will enable them to rise above old-style organization constraints (Hammer, 1990).

Whether as supporter, catalyst, or leader of the activity, the IS function and IS staff are essential contributors to the re-engineering process. The scope of this role will depend on two factors. First, IS staff must be able to rise above their traditional procedural and analytic thinking. Re-engineering is not simply another systems project, neither is it an automation effort. Rather, the IS function must take on the role of enabler and facilitator of the process and attempt to encourage cross-functional communication and collaboration as well as integration of the technical and the non-technical tasks involved. Second, IS professionals must be able to take a more integrative approach to their own work. Highly skilled specialists are of limited value to the re-engineering process. Instead, IS staff involved in re-engineering must be multi-disciplinary generalists who are able to tackle all parts of the task, from its inception until its roll-out into the organization.

AN APPROACH TO RE-ENGINEERING

Even with vision, top management involvement, IS participation, and a recognition of the people and organizational issues involved, the re-engineering process can still flounder because it is not clear how to do it. While some organizations have developed methodologies and written process manuals on how to re-engineer, it is fair to say that re-engineering remains a new-enough process that there is very little agreement on how to do it. In fact, some would suggest that a 're-engineering methodology' is a typically rigid old-style

IS approach to the issue and that attempts to rationalize re-engineering will end up torpedoing it.

While our knowledge of business re-engineering is not complete, there are some approaches that we **know** work. These should be considered and included in any strategy to re-engineer at a business level, in addition to the other essentials we have identified above:

- **Start with Discontinuous Thinking:** the importance of being able to keep a fresh perspective throughout the re-engineering process has been mentioned above, but cannot be over-estimated. The questions Why ? and What if ? should be constantly asked if the re-engineering team truly wishes to break away from current organizational constraints.

- **Identify the Natural Entities:** these might be processes, like shipping, or physical objects, like a customer, around which re-engineering efforts will focus. A natural entity is like a picture that has been broken into many pieces like a jigsaw puzzle. The job of re-engineering is to put as many pieces of the puzzle together again as possible.

- **Identify High Impact Areas:** rather than undergoing an exhaustive analysis of all entities in the company, identify a few that are the most critical to your organization's success or the few that are most in need of repair. Companies using this approach have found it as effective as the exhaustive approach and considerably less time-consuming (Davenport and Short, 1990).

- **Establish a Cross-functional Team:** establish a team that represents all the areas affected by the re-engineering process and that has a good understanding of what is being accomplished in these areas. In other words, team members should be high enough up in the organization to be able to take a cross-functional perspective, but should be close enough to the work in an area to be able to answer questions about it.

- **Broaden the Scope:** too narrow a perspective will ensure the activity deteriorates into a process redesign project that will not achieve the organization's objectives. Ensure that all parts of a process or functions that deal with an entity are included in the scope of the re-engineering effort.

- **Look for the Best Demonstrated Practices:** look around at what your competition is doing; or look at how similar objectives are achieved in other companies; review business journals for case studies on how other organizations are approaching their problems. The best approach may not be a unique solution but a modification of an approach that has worked well in other companies. This is what Ford did when it looked at how Mazda handled its accounting procedures.

- **Consider Baseline Measurements:** if not too expensive, measuring the performance of the organization's existing practices can identify problems and serve as a baseline from which improvements can be demonstrated. Simple graphs of the costs and time involved in each step can be useful. However, the experts caution that this step can be overemphasized, and can limit the team's approach to a problem or simply take too much time (Davenport and Short, 1990).

- **Identify IT Capabilities:** while technology should not be driving it, what IT can do will seriously influence the re-engineering process. This approach is significantly different from traditional systems analysis methods in which IT is not considered until after a process has been redesigned. However, in business re-engineering, Davenport and Short (1990) note that 'IT can actually create new process design options, rather than simply supporting them.'

- **Build an Organizational Prototype:** developing a low-risk, small-scale prototype of both the systems and the organizational processes that surround them can be the most effective way to design and implement your ideas (*Information Week*, 1991; Davenport and Short, 1990). While system prototypes have been in use for some time, the use of organizational prototypes as well will ensure that the non-technical issues discussed above get the attention necessary to ensure implementation goes smoothly. Prototypes enable the team to see how the new methods work and to modify them simply and inexpensively. An iterative prototyping process is both an effective design tool and an excellent first step in implementation.

• **Do Not Forget Roll-out:** attention to the roll-out of new systems and procedures is often forgotten in the euphoria of a successful prototype implementation. Forum participants cautioned that many anticipated benefits can be lost with inadequate attention to this vital step. Michael Hammer (1990) notes: 'No-one in an organization wants re-engineering. It is confusing and disruptive and affects everything people have grown accustomed to. . . . The strain of implementing a re-engineering plan can hardly be overestimated.' To avoid entropy, a careful roll-out of both systems and organizational procedures must be planned, carried out, and followed up.

CONCLUSION

Re-engineering business is clearly THE challenge for management at present but nowhere is it more challenging than for IS. With re-engineering, IS has the opportunity to demonstrate conclusively its value to the organization and to be invited to participate in business decisions at the highest organizational levels. However, not everyone agrees that IS will be able to rise to the occasion. It is no longer enough for IS professionals to see themselves as service providers and supporters of the *status quo*. Their new function must be as facilitators who can support, collaborate in, or mobilize business re-engineering as necessary. To do this, they will need improved consulting and communications abilities and to become visionaries with an appreciation for enterprise-wide business operations and the transformational nature of IT.

3
Managing IS-User Conflict[1]

INTRODUCTION

The executive of the national retailer was frustrated. His entire Point of Sale (POS) system was down and there was nothing he could do but wait. The situation was serious. Irate store managers were phoning to know when the problem would be fixed. Clerks were having to write up sales by hand. A call to the information systems department revealed that all five members of the POS team were at a conference. The problem would have to wait.

This true story illustrates three points regarding the role of IS in organizations. First, it shows how dependent organizations have become on IS. Second, it demonstrates the increasing involvement of senior user management with IS issues as IS departments gain more visibility and seniority within organizations. No longer can upper management afford to delegate their responsibilities *vis-à-vis* information systems—the associated costs and organizational implications are too great.

---

[1] Adapted from *Information and Management* Vol 22 (1992) by H.A. Smith and J.D. McKeen in *Computerization and Management: A Study of Conflict and Change* (1992) pp. 53-64, with kind permission from Elsevier Science–NL, Sara Burgerhartstraat 25, 1055 KV, Amsterdam, The Netherlands.

Third, the story highlights the rift between IS and business management—one that often results in conflict between the two groups. Several reasons for this conflict have been suggested by researchers: a communication gap (Kaiser and King, 1982); misalignment of goals (Hartog and Herbert, 1986); credibility problems (Doll and Ahmed, 1986); and poor system design (Bostrom and Heinen, 1977). Others believe these to be merely symptoms of more complex problems, such as interacting individual, organizational, and systems factors (Markus, 1984). However, this research leaves it unclear what IS managers can do about user-IS conflict.

What *is* clear is that organizations are under pressure from global economic forces to rationalize their operations and computers represent one of the most significant means of doing this. Previously, computers mainly affected workers; today, it is business managers. Zuboff (1982) notes that the introduction of technological change is almost always followed by a period of conflict and upheaval as people and institutions struggle to come to terms with it. The period ends only when adjustment is completed.

The purpose of this chapter is to identify and explore the organizational conflicts at a management level in response to technological change. This chapter includes material from both IS managers and their user counterparts gathered during 150 in-depth interviews. It first looks at how user-IS conflict manifests itself in spite of the fact that overt conflict is generally frowned upon in organizations. Second, it examines these obvious conflicts to determine whether there are some common underlying sources of conflict. Third, it looks at the implications of this conflict for the future of the organization. Finally, it provides recommendations for managers interested in resolving or reducing user-IS conflict.

MANIFESTATIONS OF CONFLICT

At first glance, conflict in the user-IS relationship appears to be similar to that in other problematic business relationships, such as line versus staff, interdepartmental, and professional versus bureaucratic. Lack of trust and understanding, hostility, and frustration with the other group are typical of these relationships. These symptoms are certainly evident between business managers and IS personnel. Interestingly, however with IS, the conflict appears to be somewhat asymmetrical—users have more problems with IS than the reverse.

User-IS conflict is apparent despite the fact that negative attitudes are deplored in most organizations. The mutual lack of trust is evident. One user remarked, 'IS doesn't believe us when we give them answers.' 'Users often want to go their own way; they don't seem to trust us,' said an IS manager. A Director of Systems Development summed up the relationship as—'Users don't trust us; they feel we haven't delivered.'

Some IS managers believe that users are hostile because they instinctively oppose change and feel their jobs are threatened. On the other hand, business managers apparently feel that IS is not responsive to their needs and does not understand business needs. Senior executives' frustrations are clear . . .

> 'Our biggest problem is in understanding . . . IS people do not understand our requirements . . . IS people are 'tekkies' and don't understand business . . . IS doesn't have good interpersonal skills . . . they have a sort of arrogance . . . they tend to zero in on the technical side of things and live in their own world . . . They're full of jargon.'

These examples suggest that user-IS conflict is a very real fact of life in most corporations and a major obstacle to effective IT implementation. What makes user-IS relations stand out from other problem relationships in business is the fact that conflict appears between IS and almost all other departments in a wide variety of contexts. IS is largely considered a staff function, yet it has trouble with other staff functions in the user groups as well as with line functions. IS has conflict with groups that were both more and less professionalized. And finally, IS has conflict with many different corporate departments; in fact, we did not find a user department in our interviews where there was not some degree of conflict with IS. This suggests that conflict between users and IS is unlike other organization problem relationships, and that it is symptomatic of other deeper and broader sources of conflict between the groups.

SOURCES OF CONFLICT

Underneath all the complaints, there appear to be four main sources of conflict: decision-making; strategies for implementing information technology; the perceived lack of measurable benefits achieved by IS; and disagreement over the roles and responsibilities of IS and business in systems development.

1. *Who Makes the Decisions about Information Technology?*

While many business and IS managers would like to believe that IS is simply a service group, like telephone service suppliers, the relationship between the two groups is much more binding. Theoretically, an organization could turn to outside services to meet its IS needs, but in reality, this is not generally a viable alternative. Therefore, the majority of user managers are forced to go cap-in-hand to an IS group to get the systems they need. IS, of course, would not exist without the business it serves. Such enforced interdependence causes tension when it comes to decisions regarding IT. This fundamental conflict is further exacerbated by an IS vision of the organization that differs considerably from that of user management.

IS focuses on optimizing the company's use of data, systems, and technology: this involves streamlining or modifying business functions to take advantage of uniform computer systems. User managers have a different perspective: they feel that many seemingly anomalous situations in business actually make sense and that computer systems need to be more flexible and accommodating. Implicit in their argument is the feeling that systems should bend to meet the needs of business and not the reverse. One said, 'IS doesn't understand that business is more than changing the way we do things. IS thinks we should roll over and play dead and change.'

The possibility of a shared vision is further hampered by the fact that IS departments are often isolated and wedded to a different ethos. 'A company within a company,' 'an island,' 'a wonderful world' were terms used to describe IS. One senior executive stated, 'IS has a life of its own. They forget we're customers.' Another explained, 'They feel systems are ends in themselves.'

The isolation of IS is reinforced by the fact that IS people were almost never seen in the organization at large. Unlike people in other departments, IS people almost never went 'outside' to see what was happening and when they did, it was only to 'observe'; they did not get involved. Many users perceive this aloofness with hostility. One remarked . . .

'Until IS changes its *modus operandi* from [an] all-knowing occupant of [an] ivory tower and gets down into the trench and asks users what to do, rather than telling us what IS has determined, communications won't improve.'

Fundamental to the users' vision is a basic understanding of the nature of the business—something often (if not always) lacking within the IS department. Business people are in-credulous that IS can be so little involved in the business. 'They definitely feel the business is trivial' said one executive. Another commented . . .

'In IS, almost no one knows what is going on [in the business] . . . These guys come in and say "Let's spec the project" and they take half an hour to understand what a [common company product] is. The users find this difficult to tolerate. It gets the relationship off on a bad foot.'

IS managers regularly see themselves as salespeople for their own vision of the company. One IS manager described conflict resolution in her project. 'It's basically a selling job. You can usually convince [the users] of the IS solution if it doesn't create a problem. By and large, they go along with you.' In another company, the Vice President 'sold' his company management on the idea of implementing common systems with its corporate parent. 'This was going to happen sooner or later and IS would prefer to be in the driver's seat . . . This way we're in control.' As a result of this strategy, the business is facing many unpalatable changes and users are extremely unhappy. The IS manager in charge of the project remarked . . .

'The business people weren't fully aware of what this plan meant . . . No one had really thought about it . . . Now, the users don't know what is happening to them . . . They've lost the feeling of control . . . Someone else is pushing all the buttons.'

Overall, users feel that systems reflect the IS vision rather than their own. 'We're still fighting the old fashioned attitude that the user doesn't know what he wants; that his requirements are a *nice to have*' said a manager at a large corporation whose business depends on the new technology. '[They] pat me on the head and agree with me and expect me to be happy with anything that's delivered.' A vice president of IS summed up this attitude. 'We try to make the users happy but we won't give them whatever they want.'

Decision-making regarding information technology—what systems should do, and how business should use systems—is in the forefront of most conflicts. This issue is further complicated as information systems become fundamental to business strategies.

2. Different Strategies for Implementing Information Technology

IS and user managements' differences are also apparent in their approaches to implementing information technology. IS emphasizes moving resources out of the operational zone (i.e., where they are working on activities that will be complete within one year) into the tactical (two year) and strategic (five year) timeframes. In many companies, this approach involves modelling business processes and data that are or will be needed over the next few years and building corporate data bases. Once these have been established, IS contends that it will be possible to build systems that are flexible and much more responsive to business' rapidly changing needs.

Initially, users are often enthusiastic, if somewhat confused. It is easy to confuse a *strategic time frame* with a *strategic use* of IT. They are aware of the potential of IS and like the idea of integrated data and flexible functions. However, business managers have difficulty accommodating protracted planning and delivery horizons. A senior IS manager noted that users are keen on modelling at the start. But after about six months, when they see only a thick book of models they wonder when the system is coming. When told that models are not system requirements, their reaction is 'Why did you spend six months on models then? We need function!'

User management needs systems that support their own business plans which usually have a considerably shorter implementation cycle. Because IS prefers to focus on the broader, longer-term needs of the organization, users often become frustrated at the lack of short-term results. One manager complained . . .

'We're getting zero stuff right now . . . It's taking too long to establish the foundation and to develop strategic systems . . . The business isn't prepared to wait . . . We want the Corvette, not the garage, and we don't care what the garage looks like.'

The typical IS response is that it cannot 'sacrifice the future to save a particular function.' They also believe that the initial technical and modelling work lays the necessary foundation for systems that will ultimately prove to be strategically beneficial. The result of these conflicting planning horizons and orientations is the feeling by users that IS attempts to shape their wants, rather than designing systems that respond to their needs. For example, one IS department was trying to obtain its goal of a corporate data base by limiting the options it presented to users. When their choices are limited by an IS agenda, users have very little real say in determining systems strategies. It was therefore no surprise to find that most of this large-scale, long-term systems work is spearheaded by IS staff with minimal user involvement.

3. *Perceptions of IT Benefits*

Problems between IS and business are partly attributable to the fact that, while there is consensus about the necessity of IS, the benefits of information systems are long-term and/or difficult to quantify. In the past, information systems have made major contributions to productivity gains in business. One senior manager at a very large corporation said that it has been estimated that, without the use of the systems his company has installed since the 1960s, the business would now have to employ over a million people to do the same work! But as computer systems move into providing decision support or executive information, some managers are finding their benefits increasingly elusive.

The situation at one firm is typical. Management had pressured IS to complete and install over 100 computer systems over a two-year period. IS staff had worked long, hard hours to make it possible. Senior management was therefore shocked that, in spite of this activity, no measurable bottomline benefits were achieved anywhere in the company. Where had the antici-pated benefits gone?

Partial answers can be found in the way many of these systems were implemented. Some systems were imposed on users and were consequently ignored. Others are highly complicated to use. One manager explained that each branch of his organization had to be able to use over 40 different systems, each with its own security, logon, and data collection procedures.

Pressures on IS to produce may result in systems that bear little resemblance to the original concept. Target dates are established early in a system's life cycle and are politically very difficult to change. Thus, if a system falls behind schedule, the IS solution is often to cut function, sometimes without the knowledge of senior management. Often, after implemen-tation, it is extremely difficult to get any changes made, because the IS staff have been moved to other, high profile projects. A user commented, 'IS people wash their hands after their part is done and inevitably something goes wrong.' Therefore, some of the reasons systems fail to achieve their be-nefits are because the expected functionality was never delivered. Furthermore, because they look only at target dates and not details, this failure can remain a mystery to senior management.

Managers are also beginning to question the kinds of systems selected for development. What is the value of extra information or of a corporate database? While it may be 'nice to have' or ultimately mean more flexible systems, there seems to be no mechanism to determine if the cost—both in dollars and lost additional function—is justified by the benefits. A common complaint is that the hard dollar savings of IS projects are illusory, while IS expenses never cease to increase.

IS feels that many projects will provide the foundation for a whole new generation of systems. One IS organization has spent two years developing a corporate data base that users do not want. Another has spent half of its resources for the last four years converting to common corporate systems that will provide the users with less function than they currently have. In these companies, IS has convinced senior management to accept short-term pain for long-term gain. Notwithstanding the frustration of their middle managers at the lack of short-term results, executives accede to IS recommendations, because they sound plausible and because of an inherent belief in information systems, rather than because of any demonstrable benefits. Benefits are always 'around the corner.'

We saw a good illustration of this 'leap of faith' in a large company we visited. A division manager had been convinced by the Vice President of IS to implement a package of office automation technology which required considerable organizational restructuring and a major change in the relationship between management and support staff. He accepted the IS proposal despite the fact that support staff morale in the group where these ideas have already been implemented is the lowest in the company. His stated motive for imposing these measures, in the face of nearly unanimous opposition by his staff, was economic. While he is not sure what the payback will be, he believes that there *is* one. This situation was typical; user executives and IS were convinced that the benefits of computerization would ultimately materialize. User managers were sceptical and thus largely uncommitted to supporting IS projects.

4. *Responsibilities in Systems Development*

A curious feature of business-IS conflict is the general unwillingness of user managers to get involved in systems development despite the sincere desire of IS to promote user participation. IS managers constantly reiterated the message that a 'bad' user is someone who does not want to take the time to work with IS or to accept accountability for his or her responsibilities in systems development. A 'good' user is 'someone who does his/her homework . . . He/she understands the existing system, the data, and what it means.' Why then is effective user participation in systems development so difficult to achieve?

Senior users say they simply do not have the time to participate at the level IS appears to need. Many user managers feel that the responsibility for systems development falls squarely on IS. It is often difficult for the resource-constrained business side to free people to participate in systems development. The underlying message is that many senior users have little interest in IS projects. One manager in charge of a corporate data base project noted that users did not care about the project 'because it had low visibility to them [and because] our priorities are not their priorities.'

At lower levels of management, IS appears to be asking users to participate in ways that they find inappropriate. Users often lack the technical expertise to participate as IS would like. For example, users have trouble relating to conceptual data models and designing system test plans—activities which are often considered user responsibilities in IS development methodologies. Users in this situation have two choices. They can avoid participation as much as possible or they can become more technical.

Overwhelmingly, IS advocates the latter approach. With these more technical users, routine tasks can be delegated from IS to the users. To this end, many organizations have established small groups of user analysts whose jobs are to represent the business in the systems development process. Increasingly, these more technical users assist IS in evaluating work requests from their areas, coordinate user training, help with systems maintenance and supply the dedicated staff necessary for systems development projects. They are expected to be computer literate and to take technical training. In many companies, they are evaluated on their skills and abilities in using the computer tools at their disposal.

The technical education of users has caused some problems for IS. 'Because they have the skills, [some users] want to compete—to tell us how to do something and not what to do' said one IS manager. However, on the whole, these more technical users provide important benefits to IS. The efforts to educate users in technical issues stand out in marked contrast to the limited or non-existent business training that is usually given to IS personnel. It is rare to see any formal efforts being made in this regard. Where users have attempted such programmes, IS people are usually too busy to spend more than a few hours on such training.

User participation in systems decisions is now the rule rather than the exception. The quality of this participation is, however, problematic. The users who were the most enthusiastic and involved in systems work were generally those who were the most computer literate and technical. However, managers who are more business-oriented and less technical still appear sceptical of the need for participation and are reluctant to get involved. Perhaps user participation suffers most from this process of self-selection.

User responsibilities in system development are central to the dilemma facing modern business managers. They are caught between the more traditional ways of doing business with their emphasis on experience, judgement and intuition, and the newer, more analytical approaches to decision-making.

IMPLICATIONS FOR THE FUTURE

It is clear that IS and business managers generally have significantly different perspectives regarding many features of the computerization process. While immediate conflict is a natural outcome, it also foreshadows some longer-term implications for organizations and their management.

1. *The World Will be Seen in Shades of Grey*

As systems impinge upon management, what will be their impact on normal business practices? It is possible that the IS approach to work, which emphasizes means over ends may come to dominate in the organization. If so, standardized procedures, and predictable, quantifiable outcomes will come to be valued over individual judgement and flexibility. Indeed, some managers have become conscious of such changes in their ways of working . . .

> 'If you're not careful, a system paints everything grey . . . It makes everyone adequate . . . [With systems] some people who could have exploded the business have levelled out . . . systems can become the *raison d'etre* of a business instead of using them to support the business . . .'

Usually, however, managers are not always conscious of how their thinking is changing. A director who was radically restructuring his organization for a new system enthused: 'The beauty of this [new] approach will be that it's standardized. Now people all do jobs differently because the skills are not automated.' In short, it appears that individual judgement is becoming less valued than the ability to adapt to the system.

IS people have also observed these changes in business. One IS manager noted that he felt that user managers' knowledge of their business areas has actually declined over time. He suggested that once a function is automated, business people lose their understanding of it and 'become the system's slaves.' Another cited a case where the IS people had to refer to program code to answer a question about a company policy. The logic had been embedded in the code years before and no user could remember it. Once this happens, it becomes increasingly difficult for managers to control or guide the systems decisions that are made for their areas.

An IS executive voiced the heretical position that over time, systems which make or support management decisions may cripple managers' experiential judgement. As a result, information presented by the system which matches prevailing beliefs is presumed to be legitimate. Managers who lack the experience to evaluate information critically are led to make decisions that are not well thought out or indeed, misguided. In this way, some systems can ultimately work to a company's detriment.

The suggestion that systems encourage technocratic rather than entrepreneurial skills is unsettling. Yet as corroborating evidence, consider what management guru Tom Peters has to say about innovation in organizations:

> 'In the past decade we've flattened out corporate hierarchies, re-engineered companies to beat the band, emphasized Total Quality Management and dramatically reduced product-development time. Yet despite these revolutionary changes, firms, from banks to chemical companies, are offering their customers nothing better than look-alike, run-of-the-mill products . . . the very process of creating the modern corporation has blunted the taste for the off-beat . . . genuine innovation goes by the board. The management revolution . . . has produced a generation of gutless wonder firms and leaders so insipid as they are efficient.' (Peters, 1995)

2. IS Methods Will Influence the Organizational Culture

Typically, both IS and business managers talked not only about their different ways of thinking but also about their different attributes and skills. Business managers tend to have managerial and selling skills while IS people are more likely to be analytical and technical. The two groups are seen as representing different 'cultures' and group conflict was often described as a clash between them.

The notion that such differences are responsible for business-IS conflict has led some companies to try to change their corporate environments in order to integrate the groups. Executives, frustrated by disappointing systems results, sometimes believe that, by mandating change, they can signal the necessity for a change of culture and of thinking in their companies. In some cases, change is imposed by relocating some IS staff to the user groups in order to encourage the two groups to grow more alike and improve mutual understanding.

But while a new hybrid culture may be the goal of such massive upheavals, many believe that IS is proving to be the dominant strain. Some observers viewed the swing towards IS as fundamental. 'Previously,' said one senior IS manager, 'business plans have been the driving force behind systems plans in my company; now technology plans are pushing the business forward.' In other companies, change is happening in a more piecemeal fashion, but it is still being deliberately planned. Examples which were encountered include: pressure on middle level managers to 'stop managing people and begin to manage processes,' the erosion of managerial authority through important reductions in the clerical to manager ratio, and the requirement that managers perform their own data entry and maintenance tasks.

The changes in these companies are still too new to assess thoroughly but the intention is to revolutionize both the way in which business operates and the skills and responsibilities of management. Usually, the need to integrate IS and user groups is explained in terms of moving the technology closer to business' needs. It seems that few senior managers have fully grasped the implications of technology for managerial jobs, in terms of both content and skill requirements. When the cultural changes are complete, the hybrid offspring may look remarkably like its IS parent.

3. *Technology Will Constrain Organizational Needs*

It is often said that the spread of personal computers (PCs) will eventually free managers from their dependence on IS. As the use of PCs becomes widespread, many managers relish being able to produce a computer report (e.g., a spreadsheet) without reference to IS. Certainly, PCs, information centres, and other forms of user-friendly software have enabled business managers to exercise some control over their IS needs, for example, by accessing their own data without reference to IS. In some organizations, business departments have developed small groups of PC experts to develop management systems that would never get started if given to IS. Because these groups have often been able to respond quickly to business' needs, they have proved popular.

While user computing is growing dramatically, PCs and office systems are being increasingly integrated with other forms of systems. Therefore, control over these areas is becoming a significant issue. The most obvious way to assert control is through organization structure and formal rules and procedures. As an example, a formerly autonomous PC group was recently moved under the IS umbrella. Now any PC work has to be justified and approved on a Request for Service form. While the move was 'theoretically the right thing to do,' the former manager regrets it. 'There's not nearly as much inter- action [between the groups] as there used to be . . . and it's demotivating to both sides.' Most control the hardware and software that can be used. The majority of IS groups have already established controls over security, training, access to data, standards, appropriate uses of PCs, etc., all in order to protect their organizations from proliferations of non- compatible equipment and the inability to interconnect PCs to networks. Several companies have also installed PCs which do not have external disk drives, thus effectively limiting what the PC does to what it is allowed to do by IS.

Some writers have pointed out that control can also be exer- ted in more subtle ways. Markus and Bjorn-Andersen (1987) have noted that, in addition to the technical and structural controls which IS exerts over the *facts* of systems development (e.g., system design features, organizational structures, and IS policies), IS also influences people's values about and attitudes towards computing. By shaping what users want to do with computers, IS can exert *de facto* control over the nature of information technology in business without formal policies and procedures. They cite Lukes (1974) who writes . . .

'Is it not the supreme exercise of power to get others to have the desires you want them to have—that is, to secure their compliance by controlling their thoughts and desires?'

Analysis of business and IS conflict raises some disturbing questions about the role of IS in influencing managers' wants.

Was the administrative pool concept really chosen by business managers? Who determines the appropriate use of a PC? What effects do IS standards and strategies have over the type of systems that are developed or not? Does the use of decision support systems liberate or constrain managers in their jobs? These questions are current focal points of business-IS conflict. However, it is not difficult to foresee a time when such things as administrative pools, system selection standards, and decision support systems will become the accepted norm in business. If so, it is clear that IS will have had an important role in shaping the business environment in which it operates.

RECOMMENDATIONS FOR MANAGERS

How can organizations achieve a balance between reaping the enormous potential benefits of IS and becoming its slave? We found no companies which had found the ideal combination of structure, policy and management involvement. Yet, through our opportunity to look at both groups in depth, we can identify some approaches that contribute to an effective balance and can speculate how this balance might be achieved.

- **Make Users Aware of IS Implications.** If user management has problems with how IS operates in the organization, it must also bear a large part of the responsibility. The uses and impacts of IT are considerably farther-reaching than most business managers are prepared to acknowledge. Dealing with IS is not like dealing with other technicians or service people in the company, because IS personnel have far more scope to influence the direction of the company. Mistakes can also be considerably more costly. Thus, in order to achieve a balanced approach to computerization, users cannot ignore it. They must become more aware of the full implications of the decisions involved in developing systems. IS managers can work to help users become aware of these implications by, first, recognizing users' attitudes and, second, making implications explicit in their interactions with users of all levels.

• **Work with Business People as Peers.** Many IS people work hard at developing a corporate point of view. Most have considered the procedural and organizational implications of their work—at least as they see them. Yet, while they understand them, they are in no position to evaluate the costs and benefits of their decisions—either to the business or the people involved. Only a business manager can do this, and only if that manager understands the extent and nature of these decisions. The most effective systems were developed with users and IS staff who learned this lesson.

• **Familiarize Users with IS Methods.** At a middle and junior level, effective decision-making can only be achieved if user managers are familiar with systems development work. Users must be able to understand the IS environment and methods in order to review IS plans effectively. IS staff must provide them with opportunities to learn. This does not mean training them to become an IS professional, but rather it means ensuring that they can recognize IS issues and decisions which have become an important part of a manager's work.

• **Learn About the Business.** Additionally, IS managers must make an effort to learn about basic business concepts. This is rarely done, since most business managers find it incredible that someone could work for a company in a relatively senior position without absorbing its business. But this is exactly the case with IS staff. Business managers who take the time to provide orientation and training to IS staff find their efforts well rewarded.

• **Colocate Users and IS on Development Projects.** One very effective way to maintain the necessary level of business involvement and minimize conflict is to adopt a policy of colocation. This involves seating the fulltime IS and user staff together for the duration of a project. Colocation not only facilitates project-related communication between the two groups but it also encourages IS personnel to learn more about business. Colocation works especially well when the groups are in the business area or in a politically neutral venue. Business people are likely to feel less threatened by such an arrangement and senior managers can become more involved with their project.

- **Use Prototypes.** Another way to redress concerns about IS control and user dependence in systems development at this level is through the use of prototypes. Studies have shown that both users and IS personnel feel more satisfied with both the *process* of development and the resulting system when some form of prototype is used.

- **Work for a True Consensus with Senior Users.** At a senior management level, achieving a balanced relationship with technology is more difficult, because senior managers have more demands on their time and because the issues are considerably more complex. Most executives are involved in establishing systems strategy and project priorities. However, the effectiveness of this involvement is often questionable. Too often senior managers have the option of agreeing with IS plans or appearing backwards and unenlightened. In no companies did we find senior executives who felt especially comfortable with the way these decisions were made. However, the most dissatisfied executives were those in companies where there was no true consensus between business and IS plans. When strategies and priorities are imposed without the commitment of all parties, feelings of loss of control increase and with these come increased hostility and a much greater likelihood that goals will not be achieved.

- **Do Not Sell Technology.** Too often *strategy* is used synonymously with *state-of-the-art technology* or with IS' plans to sell its systems and capabilities. While technology may be a worthy IS goal in itself, it often does little to support the strategic needs of the business. These can be considerably simpler and less exciting to IS than all-encompassing plans. For example, installing a remote printer in every agent's office was one company's very effective yet technologically straightforward strategy to produce insurance policies faster and gain advantage over its competitors.

- **Evolve Technical Strategies.** Working together to find solutions that represent an effective marriage of business and technology usually means evolving towards the ultimate solution rather than trying to implement it all at once. In one case, an organization recognizing that its corporate data bases were some years away from implementation, created a method of extracting data from various system files and putting it in a data base for use by all areas of the company. Although this was a technologically awkward solution, it addressed the business' need for information immediately, while the ultimate data bases are being modelled and built.

In these examples, everyone understood that technology was beneficial to the company. Thus, a partial solution to the question of the benefit of IS is to ensure that it is used to meet real business problems and strategies. Often these uses are not developed in the boardroom but discovered on the front line. Because of this, one organization has decreed that all of its management personnel, from the president down—IS included—must work in one of its branches for several days every year. In this way, it hopes to keep everyone's focus on the ultimate reason for systems.

- **Avoid Creating Technical User Groups.** On a broader scale, senior business managers must guard against turning themselves or their organizations into mini IS groups. The technocratic perspective is not a substitute for entre-preneurial and people skills. Over-reliance on systems can be dangerous to effective decision-making. Too often, systems are seen as the only appropriate solution to a business problem. While systems are certainly necessary to an organization today, senior managers must leave no doubt in their subordinates' minds that individual initiative is valued in all aspects of business. Business people need to be encouraged to look for non-technical solutions to their needs. Ironically, many IS personnel are more aware of the limits of technology than business management. Thus, IS may also be useful in determining areas where technology would *NOT* be helpful.

CONCLUSION

In *The Technological Society*, Jacques Ellul (1964) laments the inevitability of the rule of *technique* or the technologically rational approach to all aspects of our lives. In our work we have met many managers who favour the technological imperative—the idea that it is technology that is driving the business. Some managers feel that this is the necessary price to be paid for modernization and keeping their business competitive. We have also seen companies where IS is kept under tight control. They have rejected the long-term promises of IS and insisted on demonstrable benefits before approving systems. In these companies, IS is under control, but it may also be underutilized, because potential business opportunities are limited by the fear of IS.

As the roles and responsibilities of IS in the organization change over time and people adapt to new ways of working, the particular causes of conflict between IS and user managers will change also. But conflict will remain as long as IS continues to challenge older sensibilities; only its sources will change. In the longer term, conflict will ultimately fade as the technological transition recedes into the past and with it the sense of psychological crisis. But by then, the organization, with its goals, beliefs, behaviours, and values will have changed. What that organization will look like depends, in large part, on how business and IS management responds to the issues facing it today.

In general, business management has stepped back from making informed decisions about IS. IS has moved into the vacuum not out of a conscious desire to grab power, but to get these decisions made. As a result, many IS values and beliefs have been planted within the organization. Managers need to understand that these changes will be the real impact of IT on the organization and to ask themselves if they are really willing to pay the price for their lack of involvement. If their answer is no, they must begin to make a conscious effort to reassert business leadership in the use of IT.

4
Marketing Information Systems
. . . And Getting it Right

INTRODUCTION

Marketing the Information Systems function internally in organizations is a reality for IS managers—whether they like it or not. While IS managers would like to believe that increasing use of information technology is somehow inevitable, in fact, most IT use in organizations is the result of a deliberate, strategic choice to use it by management. Current research has shown that both the amount of IT used in organizations and the way it is used are largely dependent on internal organizational factors, such as management's perceptions of the importance of IT (Busch et al., 1991). Thus, IS managers who wish to see their organization benefit from IS capabilities and skills must market themselves in much the same way as any other business.

Unfortunately, marketing conjures up negative connotations for many IS managers to whom marketing is the art of tricking the unwary into buying or using what they don't want or need. They feel that formal marketing should not be required since, if their product is good it will sell itself. Yet, as any good marketer will tell you, even good products can fail if they are not targeted to the right audience or if inaccurate information is circulated about them.

Other IS managers feel that the last thing they need is **more** marketing. 'I can't even keep up with the existing demand,' they groan. 'Why should I market IS? The media is doing it for me!' These managers are generally overwhelmed with demands for products or services that are the 'flavour of the month' with the media gurus or certain vendors. Yet, this is a marketing problem as well. If business managers don't trust or appreciate what their IS function **is** doing for them, or if it is not addressing their real needs, they will naturally become anxious when they learn about what others are doing and begin to pressure the IS department for something more or different. The reality is that marketing is an integral part of any product or service.

If anything, the need for marketing IS products and services is actually growing over time. There are several reasons for this. First, unlike other organizational functions, such as finance, or sales, the IS function in many organizations is still not well understood and consequently under-appreciated. Second, increased economic pressures on organizations have caused them to carefully examine what they are spending on IT, and the IS function is being called on to justify its existence (Richmond et al., 1992). Third, the IS function is being challenged to take on a major role in re-engineering the organization and to act as a change agent to make organizations more competitive (Hammer, 1990). In each of these situations, the IS function must demonstrate that it has the skills and the capabilities to do the job, i.e., market itself.

WHAT IS MARKETING?

The concept of marketing is based on the philosophy that:

> '. . . achieving organizational goals depends on determining the needs and wants of target markets and delivering the desired satisfactions more effectively and efficiently than competitors' (Kottler et al., 1988).

Marketing must be differentiated from **selling**. While selling starts with the company's existing products and calls for selling and promoting them to achieve profits through increased sales, marketing starts with the needs and wants of the customers and calls for the integration of all activities that will affect customer satisfaction. Profits are achieved through customer satisfaction, not necessarily through increased sales. Effective marketing ensures that the product or service being offered for sale satisfies the needs of the target audience in a number of ways such as: function, quality, price, and packaging. To do this, a good marketing strategy will first begin with a detailed analysis of the target audience involved: What are their needs? their goals? their capabilities? How much can they afford? What do they like?

Next, a marketing plan will assess the product being offered for sale. Is it what the target audience needs? Will it help them achieve their goals? Enhance their capabilities? Can they afford it? Can they visualize themselves using it? What is the demand likely to be? Professional marketing companies do extensive market research in this area to prevent costly errors. Stories about companies that think they have a product that will be used in one way but which actually appeal to a totally different segment of the market, abound in marketing literature. In short, effective marketing involves the creation and im-plementation of a thorough plan for bringing a product or service to the attention of the right target audience.

HOW THE IS FUNCTION MARKETS ITSELF

An assessment of the current ways that the IS function currently markets itself demonstrates just how much it has to learn about marketing. Typically, the IS function has focused its efforts on selling IS products and services. Following this generic strategy, IS managers are exhorted to **educate** business managers—informing them about IT, showing them how IT could be used more effectively, and teaching them basic IS skills (Sprague and McNurlin, 1992). Improved **communication** between IS staff and business managers has also been presented as a means of marketing IT and IS skills. While each of these are useful as general means of enhancing awareness in a business, as marketing strategies, they leave a lot to be desired.

This generic approach to marketing IS (i.e., educating and communicating) makes at least three assumptions. First, it assumes that the organization consists of a single, homogeneous group of customers who have a similar need for, and interest in, information technology. This is a clear fallacy. As we have noted above, the use of information technology in a business is a strategic choice based on a management's perceptions and the business of the organization. Organizations in information-intensive industries are more likely to make IT use a priority than resource-based organizations. Similarly, individual business units may be more or less knowledgeable in, or concerned with, IT issues.

This approach to marketing also assumes that IT is a homogeneous product and ignores the variation in type and quality of products and services offered by IS departments. It assumes that the match between the product (IT) and organizational needs is present, and that all that is necessary is to promote (i.e., educate and communicate) the product to the customer (business). A related third assumption of this approach is that the price and packaging of the product is appropriate. Again, it does not take into consideration that the wide variation in these features may affect how IT and the IS function is viewed in the rest of the business. Without a good knowledge of the target audience and the product being offered, it is very difficult to match price and packaging to organizational needs.

In short, marketing efforts of IS departments are seriously hampered by their limited understanding of the marketing process. This chapter tries to develop a better understanding of what IS marketing should be. It first looks at how the IS can identify its target markets and their needs. Then, strategies for each of these markets are developed including: marketing objectives; what approaches work and don't work; what aspects of IS need to be sold or don't need to be sold; who the target of such efforts should be; and what success criteria should be used.

TARGETING YOUR MARKET

Abraham Maslow proposed that people are motivated by a desire to satisfy a **hierarchy** of five types of needs: physiological, security, social, esteem, and self-actualization (Thierauf et al., 1977). Individuals first focus on meeting their most basic needs (e.g., for food, shelter, security) before addressing more abstract needs (e.g., for education, satisfying work). It is only after lower level needs have been met, that humans become concerned with addressing their higher level needs.

If an individual's needs are not met, he or she will experience increasing amounts of tension and frustration. A common reaction to this frustration is hostility against the source of the frustration. Maslow also pointed out that if lower level needs stop being met (e.g., as in a natural disaster, or a war), then the individual will cease striving to meet higher level needs and will re-focus on meeting his or her survival needs.

This concept of a hierarchy of needs can be adapted to organizations to help target the IS marketing effort.

Level I Needs: At the most basic level, organizations require a **competent** IS function. This function must demonstrate that hardware and software will be available, data will not be compromised, reports and services will be reliable, and changes made will not cause problems when implemented. These needs parallel Maslow's physiological and security needs in individuals. Organizations are so highly dependent on such basic competencies that if these are not present, senior executives (like persons who are denied their basic needs) will tend to take extreme measures to get what they need. Hence, many IS executives find themselves in the 'revolving door syndrome' and plagued with 'outsourcing' demands.

Level II Needs: When its basic needs for competent IT service have been met, organizations need to know that their IS function provides services that can assist it to meet its business goals. The IS function must show that it can deliver high-quality and cost-effective systems. **Credibility** is therefore the second level in the needs hierarchy. This need could be considered to be equivalent to an individual's social and esteem needs in that an organization looks for an IS function it can trust and respect and which will trust and respect it in turn. Until this need is satisfied, IS managers will find that their strategies and plans will be held up to scrutiny in various levels of the organization and a certain degree of scepticism will exist between the business and the IS functions.

Level III Needs: Finally, organizations need a **committed partner** with which to make strategic and structural decisions at the most senior organizational echelons. To satisfy this third level of need, the IS function must demonstrate that IT is an integral part of business strategy and problem solving and that the IS function can bring useful and beneficial skills to the executive offices. This need is equivalent to an individual's need for self-actualization, defined as 'realization of one's capacities and potentialities by achieving a stated goal' (Thierauf et al., 1977). At this level, the IS function is called upon to be proactive, to show that it is more than a service—that it can be a dynamic and equal partner in the company. Until the IS function has been admitted to this partnership, there will continue to be a gulf between the IS function and the rest of the organization which will hamper the full realization of the organization's potential.

As with Maslow's hierarchy, an organization's needs must be met, and continue to be met at lower levels before the organization can be expected to consider higher level needs. While this fact may appear self-evident, it is often forgotten by IS managers trying to keep up with the latest trends in information technology and its implementation. For example, IS management at one company we know was having great difficulties getting the Executive Committee to accept its systems plan. It could not 'sell' the committee on the need for this plan and couldn't understand why everyone seemed so hostile to it. What the VP of IS did not see was that recent operational problems in which the organization's data had been seriously corrupted, had compromised the executive's willingness to agree to **any** IS plans. In this case, the IS function had failed to meet the organization's need for basic IS services and attempts to address Level II needs with a systems plan were not received favourably.

If an organization's needs are not met, it will experience a considerable degree of frustration which may turn to hostility if needs remain unresolved for a period of time. For example, at another company we know, a moratorium was declared on all development and 'unnecessary' maintenance while the entire IS department worked on developing a corporate data base which had been declared strategically important by the IS function. Managers were furious because no work was being done to address their current business needs and the IS department was rapidly losing the credibility it had worked so hard for. In this case, failure to continue to meet lower level business needs, while trying to address higher level needs, resulted in a very swift descent down the hierarchy.

WHERE YOU'RE GOING DEPENDS ON WHERE YOU ARE

Clearly, different IS departments will sit in many different positions in this organizational hierarchy of needs. Indeed, in any one organization, the IS function may be meeting the needs of certain organizational sub-units quite differently. At each level, the products and services the IS function must create and market are different. Thus, developing a marketing strategy for an IS department first requires an assessment of its strengths and weaknesses mapped against the organization's (or the sub-unit's) needs. The questions in Table 4.1 should help IS managers assess which level of organizational needs they are currently meeting. These will, in turn, provide a platform from which to approach higher level needs. Marketing strategies for addressing each level of needs are outlined below and summarized in Figure 4.1.

Table 4.1. *Assessing IS' Strengths and Weaknesses*

Circle the number in the **YES** column if you can definitely agree
with the statement. Answer **MAYBE** if you partially agree or
if you are not sure and **NO** if the statement does not fit your
organization. Then add up your total score.

	YES	MAYBE	NO
Our CEO considers IT an integral part of his/her business strategy.	10	5	0
Our middle level business managers are strong supporters of information systems.	10	5	0
The IS department consistently meets its commitments to users.	10	5	0
Our CEO is very knowledgeable about IT.	10	5	0
IS systems and services are considered high quality by the business.	10	5	0
Our service levels are consistently high.	10	5	0
The IS department is consulted about most business decisions.	10	5	0
Users believe the IS department's delivery of systems is acceptable.	10	5	0
Employees from the IS department are actively recruited by other areas of the business.	10	5	0
Current IS management is highly regarded by the business managers.	10	5	0

Total Score: _____

0–39 Points: Your IS organization should focus on meeting
Level I business needs (competence).
40–69 Points: Your IS organization is considered competent,
but Level II needs (credibility) still need to be addressed.
70–100 Points: IS is both competent and credible in your
organization. Level III needs (partnership) are where your
marketing strategies should focus.

	Level I Business Needs	Level II Business Needs	Level III Business Needs
Objectives	Establish IS Competence	Build Credibility	Develop Partnerships
Audience	IS Staff & Operational Managers	Business Managers	Executive Committee & Board of Directors
Strategies	• Discipline & Controls • Damage Control	• 'Hug' Your User • Make it Easy to do Business with IS	• Use IT to solve business problems • Show how IT is integral to business strategy
Pitfalls	Promising more than IS can deliver	Trying to direct business strategy using IT	Automating processes, not re-engineering
Timeframe	Less than 1 year	Medium term: 1–2 years	Longer term: 2–5 years
Success Criteria	No news is good news	IS is consulted about business decisions	IS is at the decision-making table
IS Role	Service Provider	Consultant	Team Player

Figure 4.1. A Three-tiered Marketing Plan for IS

Marketing at Level I:
'Would You Buy a System from this Organization?'

Approximately 25% of all IS organizations are still trying to deliver basic IS services to the business and establish their competence. Because they have been unable to deliver consistently high levels of service, security, integrity, or other basic deliverables, IS departments at this level are usually on probation within the firm. As a result, the IS function's role at this level must be as a *service provider*. Attempts to lead and direct the organization will be given short shrift. IS managers in these situations tend to have an extremely short tenure and therefore need to effectively market themselves and their function quickly. Progress should be visible within one year.

Marketing Objectives: Establish IS as a competent function—with competent management that delivers on its commitments, provides consistently high service levels, and produces adequate systems.

Audience: IS staff and front-line users.

Marketing Strategies: The primary focus should be internal. The IS manager needs to identify key problem areas and establish effective and visible discipline and controls that will deliver the needed services. Staff may need improved education—for both technical and personal skills. The manager's focus should be on building a demonstrable track record in the problem areas.

Outside the IS department, the IS manager should become actively involved in damage control. He or she should develop and sell an achievable turnaround strategy and promote it to users who are most affected at all levels. If failures occur, they should be clearly acknowledged and quickly addressed. Progress and successes should be effectively communicated to users and IS staff.

What Won't Work: promoting the need for more automation; marketing IS as a strategic resource; promoting IS solutions to business problems; selling projects that are not immediately achievable; promising more than can be delivered in the short term.

Success Criteria: Managers will know when they've achieved success at this level when their phones stop ringing with complaints.

**Marketing at Level II:
'IS for Sale—Who's Buying?'**

Probably half of all IS functions are striving for credibility within their organization. While they have established their basic competence as service providers, business managers are still uncertain as to whether the IS department should be a *trusted consultant*. At this level, managers raise questions about the quality of the systems produced and the high cost of IS services. While the IS function is no longer on probation, business managers need to be reassured with visible short- and medium-term results that demonstrate its ability to assist the organization to achieve its goals.

Marketing Objectives: Establish IS as a credible organizational function through the development of high quality systems and services that meet real organizational goals and through building the confidence of middle level managers in IS.

Audience: Business managers.

Marketing Strategies: Focus on delivering high quality systems and customer service to the organization. The IS function must align all aspects of its operation with these goals. Wherever possible, it should make it easy for business managers to work with the IS department. Externally, this means listening to the customer more, providing support to the core business first, acknowledging mistakes, and designing service teams to deal with the business. These strategies attempt to eliminate or reduce the frustrations of dealing with IS bureaucracy at all stages of system development, implementation and operation. At this level, as well, IS management can begin to promote cross-pollination between the IS function and the rest of the organization where staff is exchanged for development or where staff is co-located for a project.

Internally, quality and customer service should also be a focus. IS management needs to articulate and implement a strong commitment to these goals. IS staff need to be trained to develop a customer service orientation, both as individuals and as teams. A key feature of this strategy is the redesign of management controls and rewards to support these goals. Frequently, IS managers speak about high quality service while continuing to monitor and reward other skills. Similarly, IS management controls and tools can hinder efforts to promote customer service and send contradictory messages to staff and customers. A thorough assessment of each of these aspects of IS management is therefore essential.

Finally, IS managers need to continually measure their results with their customers, ensure that successes are communicated to them, and in all ways deliver on commitments.

What Won't Work: promoting the need for more automation; long-term state-of-the-art systems with a long-term payback; using IT to direct business strategy.

Success Criteria: IS will know it has succeeded in establishing its credibility within the organization if it is consistently consulted about business decisions.

Marketing at Level III:
'Trust Me, I'm an IS Specialist'

When the IS function has established itself as a credible entity within the organization, it still has to satisfy one more important need: for a partner to help realize the organization's overall goals. The marketing strategies of the 25% of IS departments at this level need to take a radical reorientation. While previously IS management emphasized responsiveness to the business, now it must take more of a leadership role. Once it is being consulted about business decisions, the IS function must demonstrate that it can offer more than high quality systems and customer service. It now must show that it has the skills and capabilities to work with the business as a *team player* at the highest executive levels to direct and guide the organization. Now that the IS function has the trust of the business, it can and should take more risks to develop longer term projects.

Marketing Objectives: Develop commitment among executives to form a partnership that makes full use of information technology and IS skills to achieve organizational goals.

Audience: The Executive Committee and Board of Directors.

Marketing Strategies: IS management's primary focus should be on showing how it can help solve high-level organizational problems. The integration of IS strategy with business strategy is crucial. One way of doing this is through the development of new products or services using IT. Another way is to demonstrate how substantial operational efficiencies can be achieved through business re-engineering. A third way is to show how IS staff can contribute to a business unit through their skills and knowledge. By communicating and demonstrating what IT and IS staff can bring to the organization at the most senior levels, the IS function will enable the organization to reach its maximum potential.

At this level, education of the executive in information technology issues and increasing executive awareness of IS potentialities can be an effective marketing approach. The CEO needs to see that use of IT is fundamental to the development of the organization. To support this approach, wherever possible, IS staff and organizational managers should be cross-trained at all levels. All staff should be encouraged to look for better ways to address problems rather than simply automating existing processes. Successes in this area should be communicated widely throughout the organization, but particularly at senior levels.

Internally, IS managers must never forget to satisfy the organization's lower level needs while addressing business problems. Because solving high-level problems is more attractive work than maintaining service levels on core business systems, it is tempting to neglect the latter while focusing on the former. This usually results in retrogression in the needs hierarchy. To guard against this possibility, junior IS staff must continue to emphasize quality, customer service, and accuracy in their work. If IS managers lose this focus, they will soon lose their organizational partners as well.

What Won't Work: Justifying the IS function—management already views it as a valuable service; not taking risks; automating processes, not re-engineering; promoting technology answers without recognition of the human and cultural elements of the problem.

Success Criteria: True partnership will be reached when IS managers and business managers jointly reach decisions and solve organizational problems.

CONCLUSION

This chapter has tried to show that while the IS function doesn't need to **sell** itself to the organization any more, it does need to **market** itself, and do it much more effectively. Since marketing is a process of identifying and satisfying needs, IS managers cannot promote particular IT strategies and plans without reference to how well they are meeting the organization's needs at present. We have suggested that these needs can be placed in hierarchical order and that the IS function must develop a plan to meet these needs in the same order. When marketing is approached in this step-by-step fashion, the IS function and business gradually build a relationship of respect and trust, which form the basis for a committed partnership between the two. This, in turn, enables an organization to achieve its maximum potential.

Executive Interview:

Ken Smee
Executive Vice President
The Royal Bank Group

What is the role of information technology at your organization?

The Royal Bank has made and is continuing to make rather significant investments in information technology. Obviously, we believe these investments will prove to be beneficial. What is important to realize, though, is that this is not a case of technology driving the business. In fact, it is just the reverse. Many, if not most, new initiatives for technology arise within the various business units. If these units do not see the benefit in the technology, they will not request it. And, of course, they are the ones who must pay for it. This forces the alignment of IS with the business.

Would you say that the Royal Bank is striving to be a 'leader' with technology?

Without appearing to be evasive, I would say that our investment in information technology is always considered within the context of business opportunity. So to say that we are consciously trying to lead or follow really blurs the issue. Our goal is quite simple—we use technology to enable us to lead with offerings to our customers. We are careful to market test new technology so that we have solid evidence to suggest that our customers are ready for it. If we feel that the timing is right, then we will introduce a new service or product. So, as appropriate, we 'lead' with technology in that sense. But, I just would not want to leave you with the impression that technology is driving the business. That is not what is happening.

Do you find the concept of 'marketing IS' relevant for your company?

Absolutely. It is right on the mark. I might disagree with your assertion that IS has failed to market its services though. I think IS has perhaps failed to consider its activities as marketing activities. This has meant that we have not taken advantage of some well-established marketing concepts. The hierarchy of needs concept is particularly relevant. It is useful because it explains a lot of client behaviour and at the same time suggests the best approach. Marketing depends on client response. Sometimes I find clients (and by that I mean business units) want to hear advice from us and sometimes they want to give orders. If you think in terms of the hierarchy of needs, their behaviour becomes more clear. When they want you to mainly take orders from them about what it is they want you to build, that suggests you are at Level I. If your credibility has been shaken, they are not going to be very interested in hearing from you about how you think they should run their business.

Can you explain how the hierarchy of needs works in your organization?

Well, first of all, I feel that too many of our IS people assume that they are at Level III when dealing with their clients with the result that they do not understand why things are happening the way they are. I think that different parts of our organization are at different levels, they have different strengths and weaknesses, and we have to relate to each individually. This is what the chapter suggests.   We can never afford the luxury of ignoring the Level 1 demands even though we may consider ourselves at a higher level. If we have a glitch in a production system, then it is difficult to enter into conversations with that particular line of business about strategic partnering. I think that a lot of marketing, as it is referred to in the chapter, relates to client relationships and client relationships are grounded in the IS–business alignment. This alignment of IS and business seems to be a hot topic judging by the frequency I see it presented at conferences.

Tell us about the alignment of IS with the business at The Royal Bank.

We have worked hard to align technology with the business. Technology represents a large component of our business plans and because we chargeback, the business units bear the cost of technology. In some business units, the IS portion of the budget can be as much as 12% of operating costs so it is taken very seriously. The business plan is the focal point—this is where the alignment occurs and this happens throughout the organization. The decision to invest in technology is not some edict from on high—the decision to invest in technology is taken in all parts of the organization within all lines of business. If the business does not feel that the case exists for a new technology, then it is not likely to be pursued. The plans prioritize the need for technology and thus dictate its introduction.

What role does IS play in these activities?

IS works very closely with each business unit. In fact, our IS organization is organized to mirror the business unit organization, e.g., the treasury systems group does work for treasury, and the retail banking systems group does work for retail banking. This enables IS groups to learn the business by working with the same business unit over time. We feel that this strengthens the alignment between IS and the business and builds a level of understanding and trust between the groups—all part of marketing. We like to think of the relationship as one of partnering. It is up to the business to determine the appropriate usage of information technology but they cannot do this alone. IS must determine the feasibility of various technological solutions and work with the business units to decide the most appropriate way of delivering the technology. Obviously, the better IS understands the business and the better grasp the business units have of the technology, the better this alignment works.

What services does IS market?

Working directly with business units is only part of the picture. The IS function must take a leadership position when it comes to technology. IS must set directions for the organization *vis-à-vis* technology particularly with respect to computing platforms, communications, networking, and data. IS must establish the standards to be followed by the organization, ensure compatibility and security of data, systems, and architecture, and perform basic research into emerging technologies. It is vital that our organization adopt certain standards and adhere to them carefully in order to achieve a high level of integration across functions. The sharing of information allows us to build additional value into our products. IS plays a huge role here. This is where a lot of our marketing efforts are channelled.

You mentioned marketing efforts. Can you identify some specific actions you have taken to market your services to the organization?

That is a little difficult, since I would like to think that everything we do in IS is aimed at strengthening the alignment of IS with the business units. A lot of what we do is not obvious—not identified as marketing *per se*. We survey business units on a regular basis to find out what characteristics of the things that we do for them are important and what characteristics are less important. We want to know how we are doing especially on the important characteristics. This sort of feedback is valuable to let us know how good a job we are doing and where we can improve. As you point out in the paper, getting feedback from your clients is crucial in order to market to them successfully.

I have already mentioned the planning processes in place within the organization. These are really marketing activities because we work out together what it is we should be doing to satisfy the clients' needs. This enhances the mutual understanding which we see as very important for us in the long run. One of the more visible efforts at marketing has been our technology 'open houses.' These are held periodically and are used to demonstrate various uses of emerging technology within the bank. It is a chance for employees to see what is being tried in other parts of the bank. We think that this is a very successful way to educate employees in an informal setting. Most importantly, it is hoped that people will discover new uses of these technologies in their own areas which will result in savings or perhaps new products and services for our customers.

When you speak of new technology, do you see any limits to how fast and how much technology people can absorb?

The rate of assimilation depends on a number of factors. If we are trying to roll out changes which involve all branches across Canada, then we cannot always move as fast as we sometimes might like. In smaller business units, we have the flexibility to introduce technology much faster. As I mentioned earlier, the customer is critical in all of this. If our market testing suggests that customers are reluctant to use a particular technology, then that obviously will affect when and how we choose to introduce it. Sometimes the customer is ready before we are. In that case, and if the payoff is high, we would likely introduce the technology as quickly as possible. Being early to market carries its risks so that is why we are careful to test technologies with our customers.

As with your hierarchy of needs, not all areas of the bank are uniformly eager to assimilate new technology. There are some areas which are slower than others. But this is a result of our planning process—if the business units do not see the benefit in the technology and since they are paying for it, it might not be implemented as quickly as we may think it should. I guess that is where successful marketing comes in.

We have discussed some strategies for marketing IS. Will these have an impact on IS personnel?

Definitely. The decision to integrate technology with a business unit sets the tone for the business relationship. In order to do this successfully, you need more than technical skills—you need business skills and people skills. We have recently instituted a project management development programme with courses and training in such areas as relationship management, people management skills, establishing expectations with the client, as well as other programmes. We feel that these are necessary for all IS employees. It is an investment in our personnel and in our future. These skills play a critical role when it comes to forging ties between IS and the business units. We feel that these efforts have been very successful for us. Again, successful marketing reduces in large part to managing client relationships—negotiating agreements, establishing requirements, managing expectations, delivering products and service, and evaluating outcomes.

Do you think this chapter outlines an effective strategy for marketing IS?

It is a good basis for assessment of the relationship between IS and the business units of an organization. It invites you to go through a process of 'self analysis' to determine which level you are on with respect to a particular client. Then, if your objective is Level III, you should be able to determine where you are now and what things you need to do to get to your target level. It gives us a different way of thinking about what we are doing and what we want to do. It provides a base from which we can improve. We can certainly gain by adopting some concepts from marketing theory. Many of your suggestions are valuable. I would like to see us recognize that we are involved in marketing and use that to guide our relationship-building activities.

The concept of 'client' needs to be refined somewhat. Our clients are typically business units, but business units are a collection of individuals—not a single person. This makes the relationship a little more complex than you suggest. More recently, we have had lots of discussion about this matter of who is the client. In a very real sense, our 'true clients' are the customers of the bank. We would like to think that IS is in a partnership with the business unit to market to the end customer. Some would argue that you cannot be in a partnership with a business unit and at the same time treat the business unit like a client. It makes for some interesting discussion and lively debate. While sometimes I wonder if it is only semantics, it does suggest different approaches to doing business.

As a final question, what challenges lie ahead for IS?

Certainly one of the major concerns (or challenges) is how to measure the benefits of our investment in information technology. In the past when something was automated, you could see the benefit and you could measure it. Getting tangible measurable benefits is different when you are using information technology to empower knowledge workers. We have been reading in journals for some time now that the productivity of office workers is actually declining. Maybe we are not measuring the right things. For instance, much of our technology is being applied at the customer interface. If we offer you a car loan, we can measure how long it takes to finalize the loan with and without the system and come up with an ROI calculation. What is not so easy to do is to assess how much the customer values the fact that we knew all about her relationship with us by being able to extract data from our other systems. I guess if business moves to our bank, we can assume that we are adding value for our customers, but there are lots of other factors influencing that behaviour. Market share increases are only a partial measure of the benefits of information technology. You also have to make a profit to stay in business! In this competitive market, the days of soft justification are gone. Costs must be lowered, and this has to be demonstrated. We need methods to assess the true benefit of our investment in information technology.

THE ROYAL BANK GROUP

The Royal Bank Group is among North America's largest providers of integrated financial services with more than 9.5 million personal and business clients. It ranks first among all financial institutions in Canada in stock market capitalization and total assets, and first or second in almost every type of financial service provided in the Canadian market, except insurance. Its services are provided through one of the largest banking networks in the world—almost 1600 Canadian branches and special business units, over 3900 banking machines, 442 self-serve account updaters and almost 30,000 point-of-sale merchant terminals. It carries on investment banking activities through RBC Dominion Securities Inc., Canada's leading investment dealer.

Outside Canada, Royal Bank Group operates in 32 countries through more than 90 business units. These units deliver corporate banking, investment banking, treasury and capital market products to institutional clients, and private banking services to high-network individuals. Royal Bank also operates a well-established retail franchise in the Caribbean. Its global reach is further extended through correspondent banking relationships with 3500 of the world's top banks in some 180 countries.

PART 2

Managing the IS Organization

5

Re-tooling Information Systems:
A New Vision for IS

INTRODUCTION

Faced with the profusion of information technology, the information systems function within the majority of organizations is entering a period of unprecedented change and upheaval. This situation is further complicated by the growing centrality of IS to its host organization. As a result, many organizations are under severe pressure to change and IT is seen as a major force in an organization's ability to adapt (Senn, 1991). As one IS manager put it: 'IS is on the critical path for almost everything these days.' This has led to a spate of advice about how IS management should be leading the way with strategic systems and corporate re-engineering plans (Hammer, 1990).

Building an IS function to handle these complexities represents a formidable challenge. It is evident that a more sophisticated mechanism for delivering IS to the organization is now required. Like the process of retooling an outdated factory to produce products faster and more efficiently, the IS function must undergo a change that is no less comprehensive if it is to fulfil its organizational mandate. The cost of this retooling will be substantial, but the risk of not doing so is increasing inadequacy and eventual obsolescence.

Retooling requires a new vision for IS—a blueprint for change. This chapter sets out to identify and articulate such a future direction for the management of information systems.

A NEW VISION FOR IS MANAGEMENT

To identify the emerging trends critical to the future of IS in organizations, each Forum member was asked to outline trends in his or her organization in a number of key areas including: functions, organization, critical topics, staffing, and goals. To help them put the issues in perspective, members were asked to discuss where their organization was ten years ago, where it is now, and how they foresee it changing over the next five years.

The results of this exercise were both illuminating and surprising. A decade ago the biggest concerns for IS were systems development, operations management, and vendor relationships (Ives, 1991). Today, these items are still IS responsibilities, but the list has grown to include: data management, end user computing, communication and personal computer technology, education and training, managing emerging technologies, consulting, corporate architecture, strategic systems, and systems planning. In the near future Forum members felt that these items would continue to be important but system integration, network management, and electronic data interchange, as a minimum, would be added. This 'add-on' growth in IS responsibilities explains why the IS function is becoming more complex and difficult to manage.

To accommodate these pressures, Forum members agreed that the IS function's vision of itself and what it can do for the company must change over the next few years. In the process, almost every aspect of IS management will be affected. Table 5.1 presents a summary of this new vision by outlining ten critical areas where it was felt that IS management must change. Each area is discussed in detail below.

IS Mission. Previously, the IS department's key task was **technology management**—to control the diffusion of IT through technology and systems planning. In the future, while these will continue to be important tasks, the focus for IS management will shift to facilitating **corporate change**. Information technology has now evolved to the point where it is available to those who want or need it. Having the technology *available* is the first step—making the technology *work* for you is the next step. What organizations need in the coming decade

Table 5.1. *The New Vision for IS Management*

	1980s View	**1990s View**
IS MISSION	Technology Management	Corporate Change
IS FUNCTION	System Automation	Corporate Re-engineering
IS MANAGEMENT	Reactive	Proactive
IS SELF-IMAGE	Service Provider	Facilitator
EXTERNAL CONTROLS	Balkan States	Federated Republic
INTERNAL CONTROLS	Metrics	Impact
STAFFING	Specialists	Skilled Generalists
SYSTEMS DEVELOPMENT	Structured	Evolutionary
HARDWARE/ SOFTWARE MANAGEMENT	Planned	Confused
IN THE WORKPLACE	Office Automation	Automated Office

is assistance in making the technology yield competitive organizations which are flexible, cost efficient, and service-oriented.

As the primary IS mission evolves away from technology management, IS management must broaden its focus to include the cultural and political implications of IT. The corporate changes that the company will require will threaten the existing corporate culture by challenging personally-held *fiefdoms* and by interfering with the currently comfortable *status quo*. Thus, they are likely to be unpopular despite high-level executive approval. IS management, having spent the last two decades keeping up with technology, may find itself outmanoeuvred in a high stakes game of corporate politics. As we move into forward, it will be people, not technology, that will be the main stumbling block to IS achieving its mission. Since IS managers often have limited training in this area, they will need expertise in the areas of organizational design and organizational behaviour to assist them in making this transition.

IS Function. Business systems automation was the job of the IS department in the 1980s. Applications were designed to assist functional areas to do their work. Specialized personnel—business analysts—were developed who had functional business knowledge, and efforts were made to ensure that the IS staff who worked on these systems had a good knowledge of the business area. To promote this orientation, funding was often allocated on a functional basis (i.e., so much to financial systems, so much to marketing systems, etc.). In addition, IS departments were often organized functionally. As the eighties progressed, it became clear that even within functions, systems were not communicating well and so functional architects were created to help design common data structures and bridges between systems that would encourage system coordination.

Today, functional system automation is not enough to justify the enormous costs involved in information systems. Over the next few years, the IS function will be asked to create corporate-wide applications to improve work processes on a scale paralleling those realized when manual operations were first automated. Companies will be looking to 're-systemize'—to change the fundamental ways in which work is done—by eliminating processes altogether, by simplifying them dramatically, by integrating them with related processes, or by restructuring them. Properly done, this **corporate re-engineering** is predicted to help organizations achieve quantum productivity increases by eliminating departments, by reducing staff, by cutting layers of management, and by identifying functions as unnecessary (Hammer, 1990; Senn, 1991).

Because IT will play a significant role in this re-engineering process, the IS function may find itself in an adversarial position with the very functional areas with which it sought to align itself in the 1980s. Forward-looking managers may wish to take this into consideration in structuring the IS organization appropriately to achieve the systems synergy that will underlie the profoundly different ways organizations will operate in the future.

IS Management. In the last ten years, IS has worked extremely hard to improve its image with its users. Responding to user criticisms that it was inflexible and bureaucratic, IS organized itself to be **responsive** to users' needs. To this end, a wide variety of customer service functions were created within IS, e.g., the 'help' desk in operations, the information centre to support end-user computing. Some departments even reorganized to move key systems staff physically into the user areas so they could become more client-centred. Some companies appointed users to head their applications development areas. Methodologies were implemented that emphasized that it was the *user* who specified the system requirements and made the business decisions involved; IS merely implemented them. In general, IS management's overriding philosophy was to appear responsive to its users and their needs.

After a decade of work to become responsive, many IS managers may feel dismayed to discover that it is not going to be effective in the future. Now, the IS function must be **proactive**, not reactive. It will need a vision for how systems can help the company and then market that vision to the rest of the company. IS management will be a catalyst for corporate change, not a weathervane that responds to corporate conditions. User requests that simply 'put wheels under existing functions' will be resisted. This is not a prescription for IS management to return to its 1970s style of superiority and inaccessibility. The new IS function will have to retain its people-orientation but marry it with solid leadership skills. In doing so, it will have to work hard to sell what IS can do for the rest of the organization. Catalyst, visionary, leader, salesperson . . . these are the management styles that will be needed to cope with new IS challenges and opportunities.

IS Self-Image. The IS function's image of itself will have to change as well. Until recently, it has seen itself as a **service provider** to the business community: it is responsible for user satisfaction, for supporting business strategies; and for providing access to the users' data. As users become more computer literate and computers become more user-friendly, however, this role will no longer be necessary. Instead, the IS department will become a **facilitator**, providing the business community with the tools to fulfil most of its own information needs. This concept may appear to threaten the very existence of the IS function and, indeed, if the IS function fails to change, it may. Yet it can also be an appealing prospect—a new order where users can create their own reports or change report formats or data fields. Instant user satisfaction! A precise marriage between business needs and information systems! Enabling users to meet their own information needs can eliminate many of the headaches that currently afflict the user–IS relationship such as time delays and errors (see Chapter 8). As a facilitator, the job of the IS function is to provision and consult. In short, users' new abilities and responsibilities can be very liberating to IS, freeing it of much of the drudgery it has assumed over the past two decades and enabling it to meet the enormous new challenges that now face it.

External Controls. IS management may shudder at the loss of control that is implied in the image shift outlined above. Until now, the IS department has been the conduit through which all information and most technology flowed to the users.

In the process of serving the users, it also ensured that standards and controls were maintained. But, in practice, as the 1980s progressed, standards and controls became somewhat illusory. The IS function dealt with each user department separately, negotiating different arrangements and tolerating others. When they got frustrated with the controls imposed on them, some user departments simply made an 'end run' around the IS department. Few users saw the reasons for controls and standards. Most saw them as a means of propagating more bureaucracy. By the end of the decade, IS controls within the rest of the company could best be described as **'balkanized'** with the IS department struggling to impose order on a variety of user departments, each determined to go its own way.

Along with the new IS function's self-image will come more effective means to ensure that everyone follows the same rules. The new IS function has recently been referred to as a **'federated republic'** (Holland, 1991). That is, the IS function of the coming decade will operate much like a country of united states. Within individual departments (states), users will be relatively free to make IT decisions. However, as soon as they use the corporate infrastructure (e.g., the national highway system), they must follow corporate standards (laws, quality control levels, security). Establishing this infrastructure of data and communications will be expensive, and the IS function must protect and maintain it for use by the company as a whole. Its challenge now will be to establish the necessary cooperation and harmony among the departments so that each will be able to see the benefits of adhering to the standards and of belonging to a 'republic of IS.'

Internal Controls. In the past, the productivity of the IS function was increasingly put under a microscope. Fed-up with the *laissez-faire* management of the seventies and expensive systems disasters, executives decreed that IS work had to be brought under control. As a result, systems organizations focused on **'metrics'**—function points delivered, lines of code, delivery on time, and delivery within budget. As a corollary, users became responsible for determining systems requirements, theoretically to ensure that the systems met their needs. With the separation of the responsibility for system development into metrics (IS) and requirements (users), no one took personal ownership of both. This led to some very poor systems since project leaders focused primarily on ensuring their measurements looked right and not on whether the system was useful. Management's message was clear: effective IT was IT under control.

In the past few years, many executives have begun to question the value of their investment in IT (Oman and Ayers, 1988; Roach, 1989; Strassmann et al., 1988). It is not enough to simply deliver systems. These systems have to be shown to be truly beneficial to the organization as a whole. In the future, the IS function will be under increasing pressure to demonstrate its bottom line **impact** and will be held responsible and accountable for its results. Management's new message will be: effective IT is IT that benefits the organization.

Staffing. Ten years ago, operations staff represented a declining but significant proportion of IS personnel (McKeen et al., 1990). The decade's emphasis on IS productivity has resulted in a steadily declining operations staff as day-to-day computer operations become more and more automated. Among other IS staff, however, more and more skilled **specialists** were developed. As the technology became more complex, the IS function responded by creating experts: in data, networks, hardware, software, communications, and applications develop-ent. Each area of expertise was sufficient unto itself and was characterized by a general outlook that there was a 'right' way and a 'wrong' way to do things.

Staffing the IS function will continue to be a challenge. On one hand, operations staff will continue to decline, while on the other, pressures will be maintained to obtain the best people for the other areas of IS. These pressures will be substantial because, at present, it is increasingly obvious that existing IS staff lack the necessary skills. In the future, IS staff will have to function effectively with increasing degrees of uncertainty in their work. Since technical skills will have a reduced half-life, a specialty will no longer be the sinecure that it once was. Change will be the only constant and to succeed, staff members must be able to adapt. Effective IS staffing strategies will look for **skilled generalists**: people who have a good knowledge of the technology (and what it can do) combined with a good knowledge of business. IS staff will then have to be able to apply these general skills in specific, specialized situations, adapting themselves by learning whatever tools and techniques are required.

Systems Development. In the 1980s, systems development was **structured**. Almost all organizations adopted some form of life-cycle approach. Teams dedicated to a particular system were established and user participation was strongly encouraged. The result of this careful methodical approach to systems development, was . . . careful, methodical systems. While the structured approach was designed to address the imperfections of an *ad hoc* style of systems development, it also created huge bureaucracies—sign-offs, hand-offs, phase-end reports—that slowed many systems projects to a crawl.

In the last few years, organizations have become impatient with both the process and the result of these approaches. It is extremely difficult, if not impossible, to capture a system's requirements effectively, encase them in concrete, and expect them not to change. To compete effectively, organizations need shorter delivery times and more flexible systems. To accommodate these needs, much of structured systems development will become extinct. In its place, a new **evolutionary** style of systems development will become the norm. While systems will be part of a larger, corporate plan, they will be developed in smaller pieces and in shorter time-frames. Team staffing will become more dynamic with 'virtual' teams being formed and disbanded as necessary. In fact, the only constant team members will be the users who will be the owners of the system and who will actually develop large pieces of it themselves with high-level, user-friendly tools. Because the IS function will be focusing on developing infrastructure and identifying and selling corporate level re-engineering opportunities, systems (that is, functional systems) will be much less important IS activities in the future, with IS team members acting as consultants and facilitators rather than systems developers.

Hardware/Software Management. In the past, technology has been a relatively stable entity. Hardware was mainframe-based and could be **planned** and managed. There were a limited number of hardware vendors, and companies tended to establish long-term contracts with a few of them working to maintain good relationships to ensure service and to facilitate capacity planning. Hardware was important and it tended to garner the lion's share of the technology manager's attention. Beside it, software was a relatively trivial item. Costs were lower and switching packages was a practical option, if a better package came on the market.

Today and in the foreseeable future, technology selection will be very frustrating and **confusing**. The proliferation of hardware available and the increasing number of vendors mean that a technology manager is going to have to run hard just to keep up. On the positive side, unit hardware costs are likely to continue to decline, and international alliances and standards will mean that hardware will become more interchangeable. Software will gain in importance over this decade. Software costs are expected to escalate dramatically once a company has locked itself into a particular software technology. Selecting appropriate software and managing the vendor relationship will be the challenge for the next five years.

More and more, information technology decisions will affect the direction and profitability of the firm significantly, and as a result, become more and more visible. This means that the IS function will have to do an effective job of monitoring and selecting emerging technologies—which ones will best suit the business needs? which can be made available to the company? how will emerging technologies affect business strategies? When is the best time to integrate these technologies into the existing platform? Faced with such uncertainty, astute IS management may be wise to adopt a *hedging strategy* with regard to hardware and software management. That is, rather than investing in a single technology, organizations will invest in multiple technologies. This strategy keeps options open and is most appropriate where universal standards are lacking and/or technologies are not yet mature. Because of the impact of inappropriate technology decisions and the visibility of those involved, the pressure on the IS function will be enormous.

In the Workplace. In the past decade, **office automation** was introduced gradually into much of the workplace. Electronic mail, calendaring, and word processing were made available to office workers. By now, almost everyone in the organization has access to these tools through a PC or a mainframe terminal. But, still in many organizations, these tools have not yet worked their way into the fabric of daily office life. Over the next few years, as people gain familiarity with the tools, as new graduates familiar with technology arrive, and as tools become more effective and user-friendly, office automation will become the only way to do business, as essential as paper and pencils and the telephone are now. Then the **automated office** will have been achieved.

For the IS function, the major challenges of the automated office will be threefold. First, it will have to keep up with the increasing demand for computing power that is associated with 'wired-up' users. Many organizations have recorded a quantum leap in usage about three years after office automation is introduced. Second, the IS function will have to be prepared to establish and maintain a technology policy that integrates the automated office as **the** sole delivery mechanism for systems to users. In the past, office automation has been seen as something apart from other information technology. In the future, it must be at the centre of the IT infrastructure being created. Finally, IS management will have to develop a workbench of tools that makes a wide range of IT available to users as a matter of course. These will include common software packages as well as other software that is developed in-house. Determining and developing the tools that will enable users to use technology most effectively, and providing tools at a reasonable cost will be no simple matter. However, as the automated office becomes a reality, it will be the cornerstone of the survival of the IS function within the organization.

CONCLUSION

This chapter has outlined a vision for an IS function that is radically different from that of the previous decade. Reorienting and restructuring most IS departments to face the future will be a daunting task. Organizations and people tend to resist change and accommodate it best in small doses. For this reason, IS organizations that were successful previously may be at the greatest risk in the next decade simply because their success may cause them to resist making changes by subscribing to the maxim 'If it ain't broke, don't fix it.'

However, change is a process that can be managed and directed. It will be most effective if management has clear goals and can communicate its vision effectively. In the world of information technology where change is accelerating on a daily basis, IS management must provide some means of integrating and accommodating these changes in a coherent fashion. Does this retooling of IS mean something as radical as shutting down the factory while all the old equipment is moved out and the new equipment is moved in? Probably not. More likely, it will mean continual pressure from IS executives to change, accompanied by a clear picture of what needs to be accomplished in many different areas of IS, and an effective bridging strategy to get there from where they are at present.

The vision of the IS function we have outlined is exciting but what will happen to the IS organization that does not change? It will not immediately disappear. Companies will still need good, old-fashioned systems for some time to come, so the traditional IS organization will still be around. But, over the next decade, as the changes in IT that we have identified come to pass, traditional IS departments will become increasingly unnecessary to the rest of the organization. As users become more able to help themselves, traditional IS will be in less demand. Then, IS will lose its position as a leader and its position in the organization will become less and less central. Gradually, its functions will be subsumed under the aegis of other departments until IS becomes simply a provisioner, providing computing power to the rest of the organization . . . much like any other utility does today.

As we move ahead, IS management must decide where their organization should be by the end of the century. If they wish to become a utility manager, the way is clear . . . keep on doing what you have always done. However, if they want to help shape a more competitive organization, then they must be prepared to retool for the future.

6
Re-engineering IS:
The Experts Look at Themselves

INTRODUCTION

Re-engineering the organization has been the focus of much attention in the last two years. Organizations of all sorts have been urged to re-examine what they are doing and to determine whether it is really necessary, the value it adds to the corporate bottom line, and whether there is a better or simpler way of accomplishing the same objectives. The goal of these efforts is to achieve dramatic improvements in organizational performance, resulting in cost savings, time savings, better customer service, higher quality products, in short, a more effective organization.

It is well-accepted that information technology plays an important role in enabling and supporting the re-engineering process. But what of the information systems function itself? Is it designed to deliver IT most effectively? Are all parts of it really necessary? For many years, users and business executives have been asking these questions of IS, but for the most part, have received very few answers. However, in today's challenging economic and competitive marketplace, even IS is not immune from the re-engineering process. As some IS managers have found out, those who do not respond to these challenges may have the issue decided for them. It is not difficult these days to find organizations where the IS function was 'outsourced' when an external competitor demonstrated it could do the same job for less money.

Can IS re-engineer itself to achieve the dramatic changes in its own operation that companies are coming to expect? This chapter looks at how the re-engineering 'experts' of the organization might re-engineer their own function—IS. In order to force Forum members to challenge their own assumptions about the work of IS, we chose a 'stretch' objective for this re-engineering exercise which would encourage them to look beyond traditional solutions. We asked each member: 'What would your IS function do if forced to respond to a 20% budget cut this year?' While a cut of this magnitude was designed to simulate a crisis within which re-engineering could be fostered, we cautioned members that re-engineering requires two other prerequisites:

- a bold vision of what the IS function should be/do;
- discontinuous thinking that recognizes and breaks away from the outdated rules and fundamental assumptions that underlie IS activities (Hammer, 1990).

THE REALITY OF RE-ENGINEERING

The results of our re-engineering exercise were mixed. Our experts had a harder time looking inward than most IS professionals have looking at other functions in the organization. The re-engineering process is not nearly as straightforward as management consultants would have us believe. Overall, our members were proud of what they had achieved with their organizations and found it hard to believe that any magic answer could be found that would lead to the desired result.

Their difficulty illustrates the first reality about re-engineering: re-engineering is NOT a magic answer. It is a lot of hard work that causes considerable organizational disruption. It also drives home a practical point about how hard it is to be objective about one's own organization. The tendency is to protect and support it, rather than challenge and question it. While this does not invalidate the re-engineering process, it underlines the serious problems that will face anyone who attempts it.

A second reality of re-engineering is the difficulty of breaking away from traditional solutions. Although we had set our target in financial terms, members were cautioned against excessive attention to cost reduction alone when re-engineering because it results in tradeoffs that are usually unacceptable to stakeholders (Davenport and Short, 1990). However, when confronted with a cost-reduction objective, most of our members proceeded to address ways to reduce costs, rather than take the more roundabout ways of identifying a vision and challenging their assumptions about work. Thus, re-engineering is counter-intuitive to traditional management techniques.

Some of our members also had difficulties identifying the fundamental assumptions of IS work. Very few questioned the work they were doing at present or considered the value particular functions added to their organization. This illustrates yet another reality of re-engineering. Some managers felt that questioning the work their organization did was part of an ongoing and continuous process of improvement, not a one time only activity. Most effective IS organizations, they believed, were *always* questioning the assumptions on which their work was based. Other managers disagreed. Particularly in organizations where costs were completely charged back to users, they felt there was a tendency to accept high overheads or administrative functions because these costs are buried in the chargebacks. The reality of re-engineering is that challenging our assumptions can be threatening and makes even the best managers distinctly uncomfortable. The implication is that if certain aspects of work can be challenged, then managers have not been doing their jobs effectively.

A final reality of re-engineering is that it is actually a mixture of three distinct processes. In Chapter 2, we suggested there were three basic re-engineering activities—each requiring a different approach and attempting change in a different manner:

Organizational Re-engineering involves modifying the organization to make it a more coherent business by adding or deleting core functions from it.

Business Re-engineering is somewhat narrower in scope. It attempts to re-establish 'natural entities' by linking related processes and activities together. While doing this, the re-engineering process questions and challenges assumptions about the most effective means of accomplishing a given goal.

Process Re-engineering concentrates on making processes more efficient. Here, the emphasis is on process simplification, streamlining activities to make them run smoother, reduce paperwork, improve quality, and improve response time.

Our managers found that in practice, effective re-engineering involved addressing each re-engineering activity in turn. A thorough re-engineering of IS first involves an evaluation of what business IS is in and the vision for IS in the company. It is critical that organizational and business level re-engineering take place before process re-engineering occurs. Streamlining processes before they are redesigned makes little sense because processes may be eliminated or radically restructured during the business re-engineering activity.

PRACTICAL STRATEGIES
FOR RE-ENGINEERING IS

In spite of the difficulties of this exercise, our Forum members came up with a number of practical suggestions for managers wishing to re-engineer their IS function. While it is expected that considerable cost savings could be realized for a company by some of these strategies, they are not quick fixes to a difficult problem. Re-engineering is not an approach for the weak-stomached. While the payoffs can be high, the stakes are high as well. These strategies are meant as a guide to stimulate and direct the re-engineering process. They are not a substitute for the insights, ideas, and experiences of IS management.

1. *Re-engineering the IS Organization*

- **Outsource Non-Core Functions.** The functions of IS vary widely by company, but our experts felt that managers should consider eliminating the functions from their organization that are both straightforward and not central to the main business of IS. They suggested outsourcing (i.e., hiring an outside company) for most data entry functions. As well, small to medium organizations should seriously consider outsourcing operations as well. Newer approaches to operations have led to considerable savings in this area, but only if companies are large enough to take advantage of the economies of scale that are available. All companies should take advantage of outsourcing services that can be shared, such as communications, to a third party organization which can offer subscribers the benefits of bulk purchasing.

- **What is the Business of IS?** A key function of the IS organization is its development and support activities, it appears. Therefore within this area, companies should question where the boundaries of its IS organization should be drawn. Some companies include business analysts within each user department. Others consolidate them all within the IS function. Arguments can be advanced for each perspective, but the key question that needs to be asked is: Is IS in the business of providing technology and technological advice or is it in the business of providing business systems solutions to business problems? If it is in the business of providing technological advice, then many business analytical functions can be shifted to business groups. However, if it is in the business of providing system solutions, then it is highly questionable whether replicating analytic functions in user areas is the most effective way of delivering this service. Companies should seriously question the value of decentralizing their analysts and consider alternative ways to address user concerns about keeping analysts knowledgeable about the business.

- **Use Outsourcing Effectively.** Once core IS functions have been determined, management should selectively use outsourcing to handle staffing peaks and to supplement staff where specialized skills are required. While development is a basic IS function, outsourcing can be used appropriately in this area to reduce staff overheads and numbers of permanent staff. When staff with specialized knowledge are required, savings can be realized by recognizing the lack of competency in a particular area and supplementing it temporarily from the outside, rather than trying to hire expensive specialists.

2. Re-engineering the Business of IS

• **Build a Clear Vision of Your IS Organization.** After the core IS functions have been identified, a key step in the re-engineering process is to delineate a vision for the IS organization as a whole. This process starts at the corporate level when key questions about what IS should be doing are addressed. It continues within IS itself as senior managers clarify a coherent vision for their organization.

How important is this vision? Consider two different visions of IS that are current in the industry:

Vision #1. IS should *contribute to* the business' profitability and service goals through building, promoting and effectively using a responsive IT infrastructure.

Vision #2. IS should *be responsive to* users' needs through building, promoting, and effectively using an IT infrastructure.

The differences between a **proactive** (Vision #1) organization and a **reactive** (Vision #2) organization are substantial. If these visions are effectively implemented in two IS organizations, they will result in two markedly different approaches to IT delivery. Properly articulated, a vision can be a powerful message to all IS staff about how business is to be conducted. Sadly, many IS 'visions' have deteriorated into meaningless, toothless mission statements full of 'motherhood' statements that cannot be effectively implemented.

Implicit in the re-engineering process is an 'apolitical' or 'egoless' approach to redesigning IS. The crisis precipitating the re-engineering process is critical to this step. Only if the entire function is threatened will managers start thinking as a team and stop protecting their roles. One Forum member told how some of his group of IS specialists served much the same function as another group of specialists in another part of the organization. He remarked that he and the other manager involved would never have had the motivation to merge the two groups, resulting in a 20% staff reduction, without the serious economic recession that has brought the existence of his entire company into question.

- **Map Strengths on to this Vision.** With the overall IS vision as a guide, the management team needs to identify IS strengths and core competencies and how they contribute to this vision. Strengths that do not complement it should be challenged. It is unfortunate but true, that many IS organizations have bought into specialized visions for a particular aspect of IS that do little, if anything to further the overall organization's vision. For example, an IS organization may have a very strong data modelling and architecture group but this may only have a tangential impact on the overall goals of IS. In assessing strengths, management must be brutally honest and willing to break away from prevailing industry thinking. What is the point of a group of highly paid, highly trained specialists who may do excellent work but who have a vision of IS that is substantially different from that of the overall IS organization?

- **Get Tough with Sacred Cows.** Another area in which management must be brutal is in addressing 'sacred cows.' You will know you have hit upon one of these when others react in horror at the thought of questioning its purpose. A large number of administrative overheads probably fall into this category. As we have noted, organizations that charge all their costs back to groups of 'captive' users are particularly susceptible in this area. This is because there is little motivation to challenge these functions. For example, project control reporting could easily be a sacred cow in many organizations. Many developers spend a significant amount of their time each week reporting on the work they have done. Much of what they are reporting may not benefit the user or the project in any way, but may be designed for the sole benefit of justifying IS' existence. Another sacred cow may be the amount of time spent on training staff. While project control and staff training may be desirable in themselves, how much is necessary and how and when it is required may be very appropriate questions. Too often, IS management tends to take a broad brush approach with such issues, instead of using a more finely tuned approach that delivers the necessary amounts only when needed.

- **Look for Embedded Assumptions.** Many assumptions about IS work may be embedded in other activities and not immediately apparent. This is why it is important to challenge and explore every aspect of IT delivery. For example, one of our members told of how certain forms of history collection were discovered only when the chargeback mechanism was challenged. When the details were explored, it was determined that months of history data were saved for users on online storage. When consulted, users stated that they rarely, if ever needed to access this data and that online storage was unnecessary. Cheaper means of history storage resulted in savings for both the users and IS. This story underlines the importance of getting into enough detail to really understand what is occurring. It is all very well to say that history collection is essential, but to question what is being done, how it is being done and how much of it is being done, truly challenges assumptions about this process.

- **Welcome Comparisons.** Previously, many IS organizations have reacted protectively when users announce an external IS provider would be able to provide the same service for less money. Typically, IS managers will begin to list all the benefits they provide that the external provider does not. From a re-engineering perspective, this is missing the point.

As Michael Hammer (1990) notes, it was only when Ford saw how their competitor, Mazda, handled its accounting paperwork, that it realized what could really be done in automating its accounting function. One of our members told of a user who was being charged six times the amount of money by her in-house IS function than it would have cost to go to an outside provider. No amount of internal benefits are worth this much. True comparisons with other service providers force IS managers to face realities in their own organizations. They can also be a learning experience if IS managers use these facts to force change on their own organizations. In fact, part of the re-engineering process should be a close look at how competitors and other companies operate their IS organizations.

- **Reintegrate Natural Entities.** Previously in business, functional groups were created to handle different pieces of a customer's needs or a product's development. Unfortunately many of these have added little to a company's overall product or service. In many cases, they actually decreased productivity and service because work had to be handed off between organizational units, thus increasing the likelihood of error. The elimination of such hand-offs and the reintegration of natural entities such as a 'customer' or a 'product' are the main goals of re-engineering (Huff, 1992). This is why many companies are rapidly moving to put functional pieces back together either organizationally or through the use of a computer system that enables a composite view of an entity.

In IS, the natural entity is the system. In the past 20 years, systems development has become increasingly fragmented as maintenance and development were separated; analysis and programming were separated; and numerous pieces of the development effort were farmed out to specialist groups, such as security, system audit, quality assurance, data administration, development centres, operations analysts, system testers and the like. Each of these groups has created hand-offs by developing their own standards, bureaucracy, and paperwork. The elimination of as many of these hand-offs in systems development as possible is probably the biggest single activity that managers can undertake to re-engineer IS.

• **Remove Artificial Barriers to Productivity.** In addition to functionally separating systems into pieces, IS has also created artificial barriers to productivity through the use of complex system development life cycles and project control techniques. While methods and controls can be an important component of productivity, many may actually be lowering productivity by what they are measuring. As Goldratt and Cox (1984) point out in *The Goal,* certain accounting measures of productivity that have been well-accepted in manufacturing firms, can actually decrease throughput and increase inventories, resulting in poor bottom-line performance.

An example of this could be two traditional IS measurements of performance—schedule and budget. Many IS organizations have worked long and hard to ensure that all projects are completed on time and on budget. Yet users still express dissatisfaction with systems developed in this way. A closer look at how these measures are implemented reveals why. IS managers often cut functional pieces out of systems that look like they are not going to meet their target schedules and budgets. The result is systems that do not meet users' needs (Barki, 1992). If all that is being measured is how much got done in a particular time or budget, what is the real value of these measurements? When re-engineering IS, managers should pay careful attention to the bottom-line goals of their organization and use only those measures that actually contribute to these goals.

3. *Re-engineering IS Processes*

Process re-engineering is probably the most straightforward part of the re-engineering effort because it is the one IS professionals have been trained to do. This step in re-engineering is an important one because there are significant benefits to be gained from traditional approaches to work simplification and streamlining. However, it must be re-emphasized that process re-engineering should take place *after* organizational and business re-engineering because it does not challenge the rationale for doing the work, only the ways work is done.

Forum members had numerous suggestions for achieving substantial cost savings within IS. These have been grouped into three major categories: Operations and Equipment, Applications Development, and IS Management.

A. *Operations and Equipment*

- **Mainframe Equipment**. Mainframes can be expensive to purchase. Many companies therefore choose to lease them. However, purchasing a mainframe can be cost-effective if one of two strategies are followed: buy high/sell high, or buy low/sell low. New mainframes tend to maintain their value during the first three or four years. Thus, companies can recover much of the cost of a mainframe by reselling it before prices fall. Conversely, many older mainframes can be bought extremely inexpensively and may be more than adequate for an organization's computing needs. To take advantage of these cost curves, it is important to monitor the market value of mainframes and to decide which strategy of equipment replacement to pursue.

- **Equipment Utilization.** With effective capacity planning, an organization can save a considerable amount by operating its mainframes and DASD storage at close to 100% utilization. Whereas this used to be an impossible target, improved operating systems have meant that organizations can expect more from their equipment. Upgrades should be carefully planned so that the organization utilizes all available machine power before a larger machine is purchased and yet does not run out of capacity.

- **Follow Best Practices.** Many advances in operations management in the past few years have led to substantial efficiencies in computer operations. At present, the average operations organization spends about 60% of its budget on equipment and 40% on people. The most efficient operations organizations spend about 80% on equipment and 20% on people. There is currently substantial expertise available in streamlining operations and it is reasonable for IS organizations to aim for this 80/20 balance in their operations. The ultimate objective of a cost-effective operations organization should be no people. IS organizations should invest in the proven technology available in this area to achieve this goal.

- **Reflect True Costs in Chargeback.** While this would seem to be axiomatic, in many organizations the true costs of a system cannot be accurately determined because chargeback mechanisms are sometimes adjusted for a number of reasons. Where this is the case, it is very difficult to identify problem areas in operational systems because comparisons are impossible to make. This problem is exacerbated where comparisons with outside suppliers are being made. Charging algorithms should be a true reflection of the costs of doing business and always reflect system usage accurately.

- **Standardize Platforms.** One of the largest expense factors for many operations groups is the requirement that it operate from numerous software platforms. One manager noted that he was managing four data base packages and had to have 15 people to maintain them. Our experts recommended that IS select a standardized software platform from which all systems should operate. This platform should provide options but limit the amount of infrastructure required to maintain it. Systems which use non-standard platforms should have a 'sunset' clause to ensure they are migrated on to this platform within a reasonable time frame.

B. *Applications Development*

- **Invest Wisely in Technology.** While there is considerable technology available to make computer operations more productive, there is little comparable technology for applications development. Current development tools can promote productivity but, as we point out in Chapters 10 and 11, they are not a panacea for systems development productivity problems. Similarly, it is not always appropriate to invest in the newest technology for systems solutions. Often, proven technology is more cost-effective to implement. New technology may be more appealing for IS staff but unless the benefits are obvious for the business, it does not make sense to use it.

- **Adopt a Single Application System Image.** With more and more users being required to use multiple systems, many organizations have found that it saves both developer and user time to adopt a single system image, i.e., a standardized look and functionality for all systems. This simplifies the development effort in many areas. Screen designs are easier and common data elements are used across systems. In addition, access to systems is standardized and function keys are the same. A single system image also promotes shared program modules. The benefits of this approach continue after implementation since users need less time to learn the system.

- **Investigate Packages.** Many IS staff and users unfortunately consider that packaged software is always undesirable since they could do a better job. As a result, many hours are spent modifying packages that are bought or developing systems for which packages are readily available. One of our Forum members noted that this attitude was 'crippling' IS productivity. Many hours have been spent developing 'gold-plated' solutions to business problems, instead of considering whether the missing functionality in packages is truly necessary.

- **Rationalize Systems.** Just as a standardized computing platform can reduce operating costs, standardized versions of systems can reduce applications development costs. One manager noted that her organization had paper, mainframe, PC, and pen-based versions of certain forms. Changes were correspondingly costly to make and were also limited by some of the media involved.

C. *IS Management*

- **Eliminate Fixers.** Many organizations have staff devoted to fixing things that go wrong. This is particularly true in operations where 'expediters' are used to ensure that operational errors are fixed quickly. Typically, some systems cause significantly more problems than others. Often, however, no one ever gets at the root causes of the problems so they keep occurring over and over again. Our experts recommended a careful analysis of these problems. Efforts to correct their causes should result in the elimination of fixers on staff. Similar studies should be made in any part of IS that feels it is necessary to employ fixers.

- **Empower Staff.** IS bureaucracy and management structure can prevent staff from doing their jobs most productively. If staff have to consult with management before making most decisions, or if staff are kept waiting while senior managers make decisions, they are not being productive. As we discuss in more detail in Chapter 10, many organizations have found that creating a corporate culture of ' do it yourself ' where staff have the ability to make decisions without management approval have substantially improved productivity.

- **Value Long-term Staff.** IS staff are highly mobile and every time a staff member leaves, he or she takes with them, not only technical skills, but accumulated and valuable knowledge of business practices, systems, and procedures. One manager suggested that the reason why the Japanese are more productive than North Americans is that their employees stay with them much longer. He has calculated that the turnover in his organization costs the company millions of dollars in retraining and lost knowledge. If IS management can retain its staff longer, then it may reap significant benefits from the intangibles that long-term staff bring to the job.

CONCLUSION

Restructure IS to focus on its core competencies; rethink the work that IS does; and ensure that all work is done as efficiently as possible. Will these result in a 20% decrease in the IS budget? We would have to answer yes and no. These changes will have a huge impact on how work is done in IS and should result in a significant productivity increase. However, re-engineering will have little impact on the large percentage of the IS budget that is composed of equipment and tele-communications. Some reductions can be achieved in these areas, but the IS manager is limited in the extent to which these can be re-engineered. While re-engineering should by no means ignore these areas, it will be difficult to obtain savings in such fixed costs. However, substantial savings should be realized in areas where management has more direct control, i.e., systems development and operations. Regardless of the exact amounts saved, the re-engineering exercise will encourage IS management to approach their own organizations with the same objectivity as they approach other functions in business. If IS management can rise to the occasion and overcome some of the more difficult personal and political problems inherent in re-engineering, we believe that IS and its users will be pleasantly surprised with the results.

7
Managing the IS Infrastructure

INTRODUCTION

In the past few years, a cadre of IS specialists have been created to support the enterprise and the IS function in many companies (see Table 7.1). These specialists usually have particular skills to assist with one aspect of system development (e.g., system integration testers) or to support developers and users in doing their jobs better. Unfortunately, it is unclear whether in fact these specialists do positively affect IS productivity or quality.

Recently, many organizations have begun to question the value of this 'IS infrastructure' and its benefits. It was developed to improve productivity, upgrade IS skill levels, encourage integration, and ensure standards. However, with the recent interest in re-engineering, IS executives are being forced to ask if many of these specialists truly add value to the development process. Users have been complaining for years about the high degree of bureaucracy and the long development times involved in many IS projects. Has the IS infrastructure been responsible for these? Are there other ways that IS goals such as standards and improved skill levels can be addressed without creating such overheads? To date, IS managers have found very little that has a significant productivity impact in the development area. Is there a lever to the productivity problem to be found in addressing the IS infrastructure, thereby streamlining the development process and eliminating hand-offs?

This chapter looks at the composition, function and contribution of the IS infrastructure to organizations. Causes of problem infrastructure are then discussed. The remainder of the chapter explores effective infrastructure management and alternative ways that IS goals could be addressed without creating the overheads involved with these infrastructure groups.

Table 7.1. *Types of IS Infrastructure*

Clerical	Secretarial, reception, supplies
Librarian Services	Maintain documentation and records
Information Centre/ End User Support	Office automation, E-mail, user id's and data access
Training	Provide/acquire technical training
Personnel	Recruiting, staffing
Planning and Budgeting	Chargeout, capital reporting
IS Accounting	Track and reports expenses
Strategic Planning	Develop information system plans
Business Area Analysis	Establish general business requirements
Audit	Assure data integrity and accuracy
Quality Assurance	Ensure quality standards
System Integration	System testing, JCL
Security	Security standards, ensure adequate security

Table 7.1 (*continued*)

Project Control	Monitor project milestones, time
Data Base/ Data Administration	Data base design, data modelling, corporate data models
Documentation Services	Assist with project documentation
Forms	Design and supplies
Methods	Standards, practices, procedures
Development Support	Productivity tools, coaching, internal systems and procedures
Technical Planning	Hardware and software acquisition, technical architecture, capacity planning
Systems Programming	Software installation and maintenance
Technical Support	Support existing technical platforms

WHAT IS INFRASTRUCTURE?

Imagine you are a general of a large army that needs food and supplies. How are you going to get it to them? Modern armies have created specialized quartermaster units whose responsibility is not to fight but to ensure that front-line troops get what they need when they need it. As we all know from history, no army can afford to be too far from its supplies or it will be courting disaster. Yet, quartermaster units that limit or slow access to supplies through bureaucracy or incompetence, can also lead to calamity. In short, to be effective, a delicate balance must be maintained between the two units.

This analogy illustrates a key type of infrastructure in IS organizations: *logistics*. The 'troops'—development teams— need the support of specialized services on a periodic basis. Logistical infrastructure includes: clerical and librarian services, budgeting, accounting, forms design, operations 'help' units, data administration, system programming, and development support. Without many of these services, the quality and effectiveness of the development effort could deteriorate over time simply because developers would be spending valuable time trying to deal with the matters addressed by these groups.

Another type of infrastructure common in IS organizations is: *directional*. Not only do development teams need support groups, they also need to have a good idea of where they are going. Just as railways need groups of people to survey and lay down tracks before they can become operational, so IS needs to have people planning its direction; hence the creation of architecture, strategic planning, standards and business analysis groups. While it is highly desirable to have a clear direction, problems can arise when too much effort is expended in track-laying. Just how far ahead should the planning horizon be? Is it sensible to be surveying and laying track for an intercontinental rail network when there are only resources to use a few hundred miles of track? IS planning groups have been criticized by some for being so far removed from current reality that their plans are really worthless to the organization. Yet, clearly some overall direction for the IS function is necessary if there is not to be a proliferation of platforms and systems all trying to accomplish the same things.

Finally, a certain amount of infrastructure is necessary for *organizational health*. Here, an analogy with human body fat is useful. Fat serves many useful purposes. In fact, the body operates best with a certain degree of fat. Problems only arise when the fat accumulations represent a high proportion of normal body weight. Then, fat becomes an inhibitor of health and it is desirable to get rid of some of it. In the same way, even the leanest organizations could use some 'fat' or infrastructure. Management is a classic example. It provides the excess resources to cope with unexpected problems or change. However, too much 'fat' causes the organization to become top-heavy. And if there is too little, the organization's vitality could be sapped.

THE ROLE OF INFRASTRUCTURE
IN IS PRODUCTIVITY

Clearly, infrastructure can be either good or bad for an organization. All Forum members believed that at least some infrastructure was essential for an effective IS organization. But problems occur when managers attempt to control infrastructure. Like compulsive eaters, they need to 'cut down' but cannot stop eating altogether. All too often, IS tends to treat infrastructure management like a crash diet: slash away at the fat when budgets are tight; pack on the excess when more money is available. Like the 'yo-yo' dieter, a lot of effort is expended but nothing gets accomplished.

Before infrastructure can be effectively controlled, its role in IS productivity needs to be understood. As we have seen, infrastructure in organizations can both enhance effectiveness and diminish it. In IS, infrastructure can be a productivity enhancer in a number of ways. It can:

- **Be a source of necessary expertise and skills development.** In the fast-moving field of information technology, certain skills can be in high demand at any one time, especially until a large number of individuals have received training and experience in a particular area. Infrastructure can provide a means to spread a small amount of expertise over a large number of people and projects, and at the same time facilitate a skills transfer to those individuals and groups.

- **Provide 'just-in-time' services in a cost-effective manner.** Certain services, such as clerical, personnel, or training are only needed for a short period of time within a system development project. Effective infrastructure groups can provide these services when needed on an ongoing basis to a number of projects.

- **Act as a catalyst for cross-divisional solutions.** In the reality of organizations, certain essential IS projects may never get completed (e.g., corporate data bases) because no 'user owner' is willing to promote or pay for them. Internal IS infrastructure groups can identify and champion such projects for the benefit of the organization as a whole.

- **Enable IS to respond quickly to technical or organizational challenges.** It is not infrequent that IS functions are expected to 'drop everything' and deal with the latest crisis. Infrastructure groups can act as a source of resources that can be quickly and effectively directed to deal with such matters without detracting from the overall development effort.

- **Establish organizational standards.** IS must operate within certain standards that ensure that systems will integrate with each other and meet all corporate and legal requirements. Identifying these standards is an important cross-functional job that provides direction to all development groups.

- **Evaluate complex issues and facilitate managerial decision-making in these areas.** IS work is highly complex in many areas. Effective infrastructure can provide guidance and direction to managers who must make difficult technical and organizational decisions.

On the other hand, infrastructure can also sabotage and frustrate efforts to improve productivity. It can:

- **Increase the number of 'hand-offs.'** When certain portions of system development work are handed off to infrastructure groups in IS or in the user community, time is spent in such things as: formal report-writing, meetings, examining work done to date, and getting knowledgeable in the decisions to be made. As hand-offs increase, so does the time spent in these transition activities which do not directly contribute to projects' output.

- **Diminish quality.** Infrastructure can counteract efforts to improve quality in two ways. First, infrastructure groups can make poor decisions based on their own perceived needs and not those of the larger group. For example, a data base administration group can impose detailed procedures and standards that need to be completed for a project sign-off. While these may ensure that all existing and potential data needs are addressed they can also represent a major barrier to completing small maintenance and enhancement projects on time. Second, poor quality decisions can be made based on imperfect information because the infrastructure group(s) involved do not have the comprehensive knowledge of a project team.

- **Increase cost.** Infrastructure is overhead and must be portioned out to users of IS services. Infrastructure that becomes entrenched in the organization, or that exists to serve itself, can be very costly because it never goes away. In addition, with every hand-off, direct project costs increase with time spent on transition activities when the project is handed off and when it is handed back.

- **Confuse accountability.** As more groups get involved in creating a system development project or making an IS decision, there is a greater chance for problems to arise over who was responsible for what. Thus, not only can infrastructure result in poor quality decisions, it can also mean that those responsible do not have to live with their consequences. Finally, infrastructure enables individuals to point fingers at each other if poor decisions are made and means that no one is ultimately responsible for the work that is done.

- **Decrease flexibility.** As infrastructure and hand-offs increase, a project's and an organization's ability to adapt to new challenges diminishes proportionately. Changes must be approved by many groups and go through many procedures. Thus, it is not at all unusual in some organizations for simple maintenance changes to take weeks or months to get implemented because of all the steps and double-checks that must be completed. While this may be one way of avoiding potential implementation problems, it may not be an effective way to run a business or to respond to business needs.

A clear direction, effective logistical support, and a vital healthy organization able to adapt quickly to new demands are what every organization is looking for. Unfortunately, infrastructure often ends up costing too much, decreasing flexibility and becoming entrenched in bureaucracy while reducing quality. How does this happen?

WHAT CAUSES PROBLEM INFRASTRUCTURE?

1. **Organization Image.** In the 1970s and 1980s, IS was structured according to a mechanistic image of how organizations work. This meant there was a heavy emphasis on creating clearly defined groups that would accomplish key portions of the overall IS work in much the same way as parts of a machine have specific functions that each contribute to the total output of the machine. Following this model, many companies created a wide variety of IS specialists to support IS development and operations (e.g., development support, system integration, quality assurance). With a mechanistic structure, development teams ' handed off ' portions of their system to specialists who ensured that systems contained certain key features (e.g., quality, auditability, security). The mechanistic design of IS it was felt, enabled IS to operate in a rational and efficient manner. Unfortunately, while these organizational models looked good on paper, they soon led to a number of undesirable consequences. As the number of hand-offs between groups increased, costs went up and quality and flexibility declined (Morgan, 1986).

2. **Risk Aversion.** In organizations where success is rewarded and failure punished, a culture of risk aversion develops that reinforces and promotes the development of infrastructure. In such organizations, employees become defensive and unable to tolerate high levels of uncertainty.

This leads them to want to 'tie things down' and 'be on top of the facts' which in turn leads to the creation of infrastructure groups that will manage and control the risk (Morgan, 1986). As infrastructure increases, hand-offs increase and with these come more 'politics,' i.e., exposure of one's errors to others. And so the cycle of infrastructure building continues (see Figure 7.1).

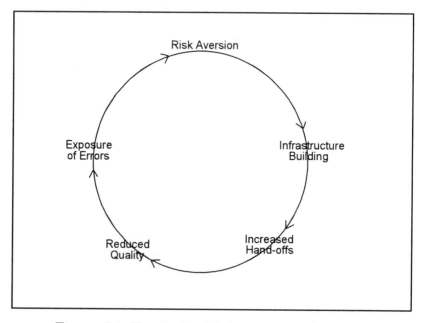

Figure 7.1. *The Cycle of Infrastructure Building*

3. **Size.** Infrastructure tends to increase with the size of the organization. In most organizations, it increases and decreases in proportion with the rest of the organization. However, size can complicate the effect of infrastructure because the hand-offs involved tend to become bureaucratized. That is, in smaller organizations, where the infrastructure is embodied in individuals or within teams, the amount of infrastructure and its costs can be kept to reasonable and effective levels. Communication is generally more direct and the people involved in the infrastructure functions have a clear, strong picture of their mission relative to that of the rest of the group. This miti-

gates against the erection of bureaucratic barriers and ensures that members of the infrastructure see directly how they are contributing to the overall output of the project or the IS function in general.

Problems tend to arise when infrastructure becomes enshrined in separate groups, departments or business units. Separate infrastructure units tend to lose sight of the overall purpose of their work, and replace it with their own goals and objectives. These tend to be self-serving and not necessarily related to the overall goals of the larger IS unit. Excess 'fat' tends to accumulate in these types of infrastructure groups because they develop their own bureaucracies and system of hand-offs internally which requires additional people.

4. **Groupthink.** A final cause of infrastructure stems from organizational mindsets that prevent individuals or groups from viewing their function in new or different ways. 'We've always done accounting in this fashion' or, 'We couldn't do without a planning function' are examples of groupthink in action. Entrenchment of infrastructure units in the organization mindset enables them to grow unchallenged. Such mindsets tend to develop when individuals and organizations feel threatened. This causes them to tighten up on their practices, intensifying rather than questioning their nature and effects (Morgan, 1986). It is this groupthink mentality that writers such as Michael Hammer (1990), are asking managers to address through re-engineering.

EFFECTIVE INFRASTRUCTURE MANAGEMENT

Forum members agreed that delivering infrastructure in a modern IS organization should involve two complementary management activities. The first is designed to identify and reduce excess or harmful infrastructure. The second addresses improving ways to deliver essential infrastructure to the organization.

What is the Right Amount of Infrastructure?

How do you know whether you have the right amount or type of infrastructure? How can a manager decide which infrastructure is good and useful and which is detrimental to IS productivity? Here are some guidelines for making these important decisions:

1. **Assess your infrastructure units.** Do you have separate groups, business units, or departments devoted to certain infrastructure activities? A good rule of thumb is that the higher their level in the organization, the more hand-offs and bureaucracy will be associated with the activity. As hand-offs increase, costs will increase, and flexibility decrease. A good way of reducing the negative impact of infrastructure therefore is to integrate infrastructure units more tightly into the organization. For example, if there are separate business units devoted to testing, they could be made groups associated with development areas or integrated into project teams themselves.

2. **Make infrastructure groups self-destructive.** One of the most effective means of controlling infrastructure is to create it for a limited time period only. Perhaps a special group is needed to provide expertise for a new technology or prepare a plan. Creation of an infrastructure group can be a good way to accomplish these specific tasks. However, when the task is accomplished, the group should cease to exist. Including a 'sunset clause' in the formation of a new infrastructure group is the best way to ensure that it works its way out of a job.

3. **Practice deliberate discontinuity.** This is the process of continually challenging the existence of particular groups and functions. According to Forum members, managers should always be 'poking, prodding, and taking things out of the infrastructure.' One of the most dangerous features of infrastructure is its tendency to become entrenched in the organization. With deliberate discontinuity, infrastructure is never given a chance to get that way.

4. **Add money, not people.** One organization we know practices a policy of 'unyielding' infrastructure containment. Their management states: 'You can have money, but not people.' This enables IS to supplement staff with consultants when resources are needed for certain infrastructure functions, but prevents the organization from growing to support infrastructure. According to the IS manager, this policy changes the way infrastructure is viewed in the organization and ensures that the costs involved in supporting it never get buried in overhead budgets. This policy also prevents the 'yo-yo' syndrome of adding and laying off people depending on the budgets available.

5. **Never integrate what is with what might be.** A corollary to the policy of infrastructure containment is to keep existing activities and functions separate from new activities. Too often, old functions get rolled into new infrastructure groups as a way of logically connecting similar activities. The problem with this is that old and new activities get justified together instead of being examined and evaluated separately. Managers should first attempt to fund and staff new activities by freeing up resources from existing functions. If this cannot be accomplished, staff should be added only if the new function can justify an increase in headcount.

6. **Use your instincts.** Sometimes, managers ignore their instincts and maintain infrastructure groups long past their usefulness because of concerns that eliminating these groups will be unpopular. Other times, managers create infrastructure groups because they feel such groups may protect them from failure. Managers should set aside such 'political' considerations and ask themselves: what is the real value of this function to the company? If the value is not clear and quantifiable, chances are the benefits of creating or keeping the function will not outweigh the disadvantages.

Improving Infrastructure Delivery

In the 1990s, with organizations under increasing pressure to become more flexible and productive, managers have been searching for alternative approaches to accomplishing work. Newer theories of how organizations work have caused IS managers to realize that the mechanistic model is not the only method of delivering essential infrastructure functions (Morgan, 1986; Senge, 1990). Once unnecessary infrastructure has been eliminated, the organization can still fall prey to the 'yo-yo syndrome' when management attention is focused elsewhere unless new methods of infrastructure delivery are put in place. To address this concern, managers should consider some of the following new organizational models when designing infrastructure delivery mechanisms:

1. **Reduce individual exposure to error.** Just as hand-offs are created by risk averse behaviour, they can be reduced by newer ways of dealing with uncertainty in a more constructive manner. Error and uncertainty are inevitable in the complex and changing IS environment. Legitimate errors (as opposed to mistakes that could and should have been avoided) can be used to the advantage of the organization rather than buried or hidden as they tend to be in more traditional organization structures (Morgan, 1986). Some companies have implemented this philosophy as a policy of joint responsibility. The management team is jointly responsible for the success of the entire function. If one manager is in trouble, everyone else is expected to pitch in. One manager cannot succeed if the others fail. While this may seem to suggest that individual effort is not rewarded in this system, companies that have tried it believe that 'the cream rises to the top,' while overall quality is improved.

2. **Aim for a holographic organization.** Rather than a machine with many specialized parts, newer images of organizations suggest that the most flexible model of organizational structure is the brain. Theorists point out that while parts of the brain are specialized, if one part is

injured, another part can take over from it. Thus, parts are both specialized *and* generalized. In an organizational context, following this image suggests that companies should aim to develop multi-functional individuals who can self-organize to cope with the demands they are likely to face. Even though it requires some redundancy of skills, this type of organization structure has many benefits, largely due to the fact that people are more involved with their work because they are able to solve problems and implement actions.

Gareth Morgan (1986) suggests that in a holographic organization, wherever possible individuals should be multifunctional, but where this is not possible because the skills involved are so complex (as is sometimes the case in IS), teams should be made multifunctional. 'Organizations can be developed in a cellular manner around self-organizing, multidisciplined groups that have the requisite skills and abilities to deal with the environment in a holistic and integrated way.' The holographic model would suggest that as much as possible, infrastructure functions be embedded in development teams where skills exchange would be enhanced.

3. **Establish a learning organization.** Peter Senge (1990) notes that organizations that have learned to 'enhance their capacity to create' will be in the best position to prosper over the next few years. He and other theorists stress that this type of organization is much more than the simple 'feedback loop' on which many organizations are now structured. True learning must emphasize knowledge of the 'big picture' and how the pieces fit together. This is one of the reasons why Japanese management techniques, which have been so effective in recent years, emphasize such a broad dissemination of potential management decisions and policies in the organization. They believe that this consensus practice ensures that all aspects of a decision are examined and that through exploration, effective actions will emerge (Ouchi, 1981).

These principles have a fundamental impact on the design of infrastructure delivery. Rather than isolating infrastructure groups where they cannot see how their work contributes to the whole, the learning organization model would encourage their integration within larger IS units that focus on the overall goals of the function. It is only when this larger system is understood, that the operating assumptions of infrastructure activities can be effectively challenged and practices improved.

4. **Practice Minimum Critical Specification.** Managers and organizational designers have traditionally felt it desirable to define organizational structure and functions as clearly as possible. Newer management theories state that if less structure is imposed, the capacity for self-organization, adaptability and flexibility is encouraged. Morgan (1986) suggests that a manager should specify no more structure than absolutely necessary for a particular activity to occur. Leaving roles ambiguous and overlapping can create an environment where inquiry, rather than predesign is the main driving force.

   This is not an argument for organizational chaos, but rather for self-organization. If individuals and subunits use their autonomy to find appropriate ways of interacting with each other, it is suggested that they can develop a remarkable ability to find novel and increasingly progressive solutions to complex problems. Interestingly, if this practice is followed, hierarchical structures do emerge. They will just not be the same ones that would have been imposed by an organizational designer. In other words, if infrastructure is allowed to emerge through self-organization and consensus, rather than being created by edict, it will be more effective and more flexible.

5. **Outsource.** Finally, organizations should consider outsourcing some of their infrastructure. There is nothing wrong with using outside groups to provide certain specialized services. This is a particularly effective way to provide expertise in new technical or development techniques where support is required for a limited period of time. However, outsourcing may also be effective for support that is needed on an *ad hoc* basis, such as training.

The costs involved in outsourcing these services means that more scrupulous attention will be paid to their value on an ongoing basis, and this will act to limit their growth.

CONCLUSION

This chapter has explored the value of infrastructure to the IS function. Contrary to popular belief, the existence of IS infrastructure is not necessarily a recipe for increased bureaucracy and decreased flexibility. Infrastructure plays an important role in ensuring that vital support is supplied to system development teams and that effective coordination and direction is available to IS as a whole. Without infrastructure, productivity would soon decline as individuals and groups each attempted to replicate the work of others.

However, while some infrastructure is desirable and necessary for optimal productivity, current methods of organizing and delivering it may actually be counterproductive. Structures that encourage a large number of hand-offs or that fail to question or challenge existing infrastructure lead to a build-up of bureaucracy, and a decline in quality and flexibility. Thus, infrastructure problems tend to be the result of management policies and organizational structure rather than inherent in the infrastructure itself. Attention to these, rather than the traditional approach of 'slashing away at the fat' during lean times will be a more effective method of keeping infrastructure under control and should yield improvements in productivity, quality, and flexibility.

8
Human Resources Management for IS

INTRODUCTION

In 1990, the Ministry of Employment and Immigration Canada commissioned a study[1] to examine the IS human resource issues and opportunities in Canada. Results from the 'in-house' software sector (i.e., IS professionals working within organizations whose primary goods and services are non-IT) published in 1991 found the following:

Characteristics. The typical IS worker is a male, in his 30s or early 40s, who may or may not have an educational background in computing and may have performed a variety of functions, not necessarily related to computing, during his working life.

Functions. The functions performed by the in-house

---

[1] The study was conducted by Peat Marwick Stevenson & Kellog assisted by Abt Associates of Canada and IDC, Canada. Guidance and management of the project was provided by a Steering Committee co-chaired by the Canadian Advanced Technology Association (CATA) and the Canadian Information Processing Society (CIPS). The study was sponsored by Employment and Immigration Canada and published in December 1991 under the title 'Software and National Competitiveness: Human Resource Issues and Opportunities—Executive Report (IM-180/2/92).'

software worker tend to reflect the traditional systems development life-cycle of design, development, implementation, testing, documentation and maintenance. Typical job titles include 'programmer,' 'systems analyst,' 'maintenance,' and 'end user support,' as well as 'project manager.' While some organizations have a broader vision of IS functions, encompassing 'business analysts' who work in the various line-of-business units to ensure that the applications developed provide strategic advantage to the operations of the business (including the use of joint application design techniques (JAD), the use of PC-based computer-assisted systems engineering (CASE) tools, and a much broader use of PCs in general), the majority of in-house software workers perform functions relating to the development and use of systems which operate in a mainframe computing environment.

Knowledge and Abilities. The typical IS worker has knowledge relating to hardware, operating systems, programming languages, other proprietary applications including database packages, project management and personal/communication skills, higher level research skills, and business acumen. The majority of these skills reflect the traditional mainframe and minicomputer environment.

Demand. Total employment of in-house software workers, as of 1990, was approximately 100,000 with a projected growth rate of 5% annually (which has fallen dramatically since the 1980s). Growth in specific organizations is likely to be quite varied. Increasing demand for other skill sets, and techniques related to new methods of systems development, is projected, rather than an increase in sheer numbers. The rise of information engineering techniques and the need for increasing interaction between the traditional IS organization and the other business units, have caused a skill gap among those mid-career professionals who have spent their entire careers as in-house software workers. The study therefore found that the technical knowledge of many of these workers is rapidly becoming obsolete and they have inadequate business-related skills to compensate.

Supply. Despite a full existing complement of mid-career professionals, supply problems exist due to inappropriate skill sets. Universities and colleges are seen as 'adequate' in terms of supplying generally acceptable candidates.

The study concluded that there is a skills crisis, which if not addressed, will create a large set of workers whose skills are irrelevant. The plateauing employment projection combined with the increasing staleness of the skill sets held by many IS workers is producing a difficult challenge for IS managers.

In order to understand the human resource management (HRM) issues facing IS, this chapter reviews the current context of HRM in IS. It then examines current practices in: skills assessment, recruitment of personnel, training, career progression, team-building, and measurement as they pertain to IS. Strategies for effective HR management in IS over the next few years are presented at the end of the chapter.

THE CONTEXT OF HRM FOR IS

The challenges facing the IS profession are further complicated by the context of IS work in the 1990s. The group looked at three which, while not unique to IS, have a considerable impact on how IS works:

Job stress. The economy is in recession and the road to recovery is proving to be long and steep. At the same time, regulation, deregulation and reregulation are combining to change the rules of competition. In short, the economy is undergoing significant upheaval and the fight for survival is fierce. This has placed IS under increasing pressure to bring systems to market in the shortest time possible and as cheaply as possible. At the same time, IS budgets are undergoing severe scrutiny by the business. Everyone is being asked to 'do more with less.' Cost overruns and project delays are no longer tolerated by the business. This alone has introduced severe levels of stress on IS workers. Coupled with the threat of job loss, the situation can be debilitating. While an appropriate level of stress can encourage people to attain higher performance levels (i.e., 'good stress'), extreme levels of stress brought about by worries of employment, for example, rapidly erode performance (i.e., 'bad stress'). Stress is a fact of life—the challenge for IS managers is to maximize the first while minimizing the second.

Conflict. All too often, IS managers are faced with conflicting organizational demands. For example, efforts to delayer organizations often come into conflict with traditional employee motivation techniques which rely on regular upward advancement as a means of employee recognition. Similarly, management's recognition that certain employees are redundant conflicts with their demands for employee loyalty. How do organizations instill feelings of loyalty in the face of downsizing activities? Organizations find themselves under concurrent pressure to 'promote women' while 'delayering management' or to produce 'strategic impact' while providing 'short-term gains.' This results in increasing levels of conflict and confusion about how people should be managed within IS.

Change. Perhaps nowhere within the organization is the rate of change more noticeable than in IS. Change is constant—only the rate of change is variable! IS professionals are under pressure to learn more, faster. Much of this pressure to change arises from IS internally as new technologies appear at an unrelenting pace. However, increasingly, pressure is originating in the business side of the organization. Users, exposed to 'solutions' in trade journals, make demands on IS to reproduce those solutions in their company. Certainly there has been a barrage of arguments recently for organizations and IS to 're-engineer' (Drucker, 1993; Davenport, 1993; Stewart, 1993) or reinvent whole new ways of doing business. In fact, some gurus believe that incremental change is suicide—only massive change brought about by questioning the very basis of the organization will result in the necessary quantum leaps in productivity necessary for survival!

In short, IS professionals appear to be 'running as fast as they can' while simultaneously receiving the message that productivity must increase and skills must change with training budgets reduced or constrained. Conflicts such as these—while not unique to IS—cannot be ignored by IS managers for in spite of many technological improvements, it is still people who must work *with* the technology to deliver productivity. Coupled with the increased need for IS in organizations, the management of the IS resource takes on critical proportions. In the next section, we examine six specific issues for HRM that must be understood and addressed by managers if IS is to continue to prosper.

CURRENT HRM PRACTICES IN IS

To assess the effectiveness of current HRM within IS, each Forum member was asked to comment on six specific aspects of their practices.

1. **Skills Assessment.** There was general agreement that it is necessary to know what skills will be needed in the future if we are to decide who should be hired, retained, promoted, encouraged, and discouraged. Interestingly, none of the companies had done such an assessment. For most, the skills they identify are technology-oriented and do not address other skills needed by IS professionals. Such skills are the easiest to identify as well as to justify. The group felt that it was critical to maintain high technical skill levels among IS professionals, sometimes just to keep ahead of the users (see also Todd et al., 1993). Not all technical skills are in demand however. Group members felt strongly that most companies possess adequate skills in large mainframe technologies (e.g., host systems, DB2), traditional systems development (e.g., methodologies), project management (e.g., methods, procedures), communications (e.g., RJE, CICS), POS (e.g., terminals, software).

   The need for additional or enhanced skills appeared in three areas: the first was predictably in emerging technologies (e.g., open architectures, client/server) and newer methodologies (e.g., RAD, iterative, object-oriented), the second (and only slightly less predictably) was in consulting/business skills where the group members felt that improvements in general business knowledge, analytical skills and judgement (i.e., more broadly based skills) would be beneficial to their organizations. Finally, it was felt that a skill that has become important is the employee's ability to work in an environment characterized by change. The term that was used to describe this skill was 'change ready'—indicating that the individual would respond positively to change. It is in these areas that companies need to do a more thorough assessment. Not only do companies need to know who has the requisite technological skills, but they must also make efforts to assess and appropriately value business and analytic skills and to identify who among their staff are most able to change and adapt to newer ways of working.

2. **Turnover and Recruitment.** Acquisition depends on turnover. This has been extremely low recently—certainly below 10% and as low as 1 or 2% in some companies. This, in and of itself, represents a significant problem since without turnover, there is not enough new blood to drive new ideas. This is the flip side of the problem IS had in the 1980s (i.e., excessive turnover) which was equally damaging. IS managers attempt to balance the inflow and the outflow so that there is a constant fresh supply of new talent in the IS pool but both situations pose significant problems for effective IS management. Currently, managers are concerned with the lack of staff movement and the attendant aging of the core base. In other words, turnover is a problem because it simply is not happening.

    However, in spite of low turnover, IS organizations need new skills. The shortage of certain technical skills means that it is a 'seller's market' for people with these skills and organizations often find they must pay exorbitantly to attract such individuals. Identifying and hiring people with the right skills mix therefore is a serious problem for IS managers, even when job openings occur.

3. **Training.** The need for continuous training of IS staff is well established. While there appears to be a trend toward

more technical training, IS management is not looking for narrow technologists. Rather, most companies are striving for the holistic developer and generalist who has some technical specialty. This apparent conflict reflects the relative ease of imparting technical skills, as opposed to business or communication skills. It also underscores the need to identify the 'right' people for technical training (i.e, those who have these other skills) who will most be able to make use of their new skills in the future.

Companies' training philosophies have undergone a significant change in recent years. Their objective is to provide a cost effective and flexible training programme that fosters continuing productivity improvement rather than training for training's sake. Management is becoming an 'education partner' not an 'education provider.' At least one company now ties training with promotion—that is, the onus is on the employee to acquire the necessary training in order to demonstrate mastery of the skills required for career advancement.

Companies use a variety of training methods depending on what is available and what is being taught. Methods include: computer-based training, classroom lectures, workshops, 'lunch and learn' sessions, mentoring programmes, external conferences, seminars, and user groups. While ongoing training continues to be viewed as critical in IS, companies are increasingly aware that current training methods leave much to be desired. They are beginning to recognize that training is not a binary proposition (i.e., you are trained or not trained) but a continuum (Yourdon, 1993). Trained staff are merely ready to be apprentices on a project and are nowhere near mastering their new skills. Organizations are starting to structure work in recognition of this knowledge and to realize that the definition of training must include substantial on-the-job training as well as classroom experience. This new perspective on training puts the onus back on management to support their classroom-trained employees with practical work.

4. **Career Progression.** IS career progression is a problem area due to the slow market, low turnover, and the

delayering of organizations. One manager characterized the problem at his IS department as follows:

'IS is top heavy with managers . . . salary and status remain tied to organizational level . . . IS personnel can no longer depend on growth for advancement. . . clearly, a new approach is needed.'

Many organizations maintain dual career streams—one managerial and one technical. Managers focus on managing people (setting goals, coaching/mentoring, developing staff, etc.) while individual contributors focus on applying specific skills (business, application design, technical support, etc.) to projects. With career advancement and salary increases slowing over the past few years, managers recognize that motivation will have to come more from the job itself and from 'softer' rewards such as lunches and dinners, recognition in company newsletters, kudos from the boss, etc. However, the group recognized that significant cultural and structural changes were necessary in the area of career progression.

5. **Team Building.** A significant amount of IS activity occurs within teams. Because this was seen by the group as an area in which current management practices are lacking, it was singled out as an area where managers should focus their efforts. Many of the problems in teams relate to HR practices and mindsets that are focused on the individual rather than the team. For example, how should team members be rewarded?—as individuals, or as part of a team? How do you solve the implicit conflict of rewarding 'team players' individually? Are teams more effective than individuals? In all tasks? What is the best size of team? Should teams be self-managed? How do you do this? Can we identify 'team skills' and train for them? How do we build cohesiveness? and What are the roles of leadership and responsibility within the team?

6. **Measurement.** Measurement remains the 'bugaboo' of HRM. Although group members were confident they could

evaluate staff according to traditional measures (such as delivery of systems on time, within budget, and fully functional), they felt that the measurement process lacked many necessary features for the future. Questions regarding the individual's place in the team have already been addressed, as have problems concerning 'flexibility' and other such non-quantifiable skills. Members were especially concerned with the quality of the appraisal process which often lacks input from peers and customers, and with the difficulty of assessing staff skills. Annual appraisals tend to focus on performance over the most recent three to six months which may be unfair to some workers. Peer comparisons with managers sharing information about staff in different areas help in the evaluation of personnel. It remains difficult to assess how good staff are relative to the competition, although hiring experienced people does provide some comparison.

MANAGING IS HUMAN RESOURCES MORE EFFECTIVELY

Developing new HRM strategies for IS is critical given the increasing challenges and pressures on IS staff and its management. IS managers have a responsibility both to the organizations they work for and to the people who work for them. Developing and motivating people is the key to improved productivity and effectiveness but often managers find themselves impatient with these longer-term strategies and seeking 'quick fixes.' It is far more effective to develop a cohesive strategy for change that (a) evolves current HR practices into more useful and effective practices, given current and future IS needs, and (b) links these strategies to tangible deliverables, e.g., quality. The group came up with several recommendations in this area:

1. **Manage Your Turnover.** As stated earlier, turnover[2] is a

---

[2] We use the term turnover to mean 'regrettable' turnover. There is always some turnover that is not regrettable—a 'self-correcting hiring error' by another name! One company has chosen to look at 'retention' instead of

problem both if it is too low or too high. Currently, IS faces stagnation due to low turnover rates, but a few years ago it was the reverse resulting in significant talent loss. Members agreed that a turnover rate of between 5 to 10% was desirable to balance between the two extremes. Companies should therefore monitor and manage their turnover actively to keep it within these boundaries.

Given the current economic climate, managers must seek to increase turnover and thereby create openings in IS. One company does this by requiring its senior IS managers to spend a considerable amount of their time trying to place their *best* IS people elsewhere in the organization! The logic is straightforward. By placing their best employees in the business side of the firm, these individuals are kept within the firm and become valued IS assets over time because of their background in IS. We all know the value of an educated user! These staff are replaced by new recruits which allows personnel to be moved to growth technologies, services or businesses. While this strategy must be carefully managed to maintain an effective balance, over the long term, the benefits of this are easy to see. In some organizations, it might be modified by enabling the secondment of IS personnel to business departments as a temporary measure.

Another IS manager used the significantly lower turnover in his shop to increase the overall business knowledge and experience of his staff. As a result, he is able to rely more completely on these staff and thus get more accomplished both personally and organizationally. Both of these organizations monitor and manage turnover to achieve their desired ends. IS managers who simply accept current turnover rates as inevitable may miss key opportunities to benefit their organization.

2. Learning . . . not Training. When there was a limited,

'turnover.' This focuses on the positive side of personnel and causes you to concentrate on proactive steps of acquisition, grooming, promotion, and enhancement of your best people. Focusing on turnover causes you to concentrate on losing people (good or bad) and taking reactive steps to redress turnover.

stable set of identifiable technologies, training was manageable—that is, IS personnel were allotted a given number of training days annually (on average, this might be approximately 200 hours but traditionally, heavily skewed in favour of new recruits) and these days were spent predominantly on courses. However, times have changed. As we point out in Chapter 14, new releases arrive frequently, new methodologies must be introduced as do new technologies, new development tools and packages. Training will have to change to accommodate this new world.

Training will have to become an ongoing affair—not a planned, packaged, 'let's collapse it into a few days a year' approach. IS professionals must learn continuously as opposed to being trained periodically. They no longer have the time to paw over long racks of manuals or spend time in courses for technologies they might not use for two years. Learning has to be delivered just-in-time. Skills must be taught exactly when they are needed, not a year (or even six months) in advance.

Along with this type of learning, individuals must take the responsibility to manage their own development and, in fact, their own career. Organizations must provide the opportunities and the encouragement for this process, but the motivation must come from the individual. One company has developed a catalogue of courses and skills in several categories that are required for 'certification' at a particular career level. These categories are also part of the individual's appraisal, thus linking skills development and evaluation more closely than they have been previously.

The new emphasis on learning means that individuals must have better access to it. New technologies such as learning software, video courses, and formal and informal mentoring programmes should all be part of IS management's HR toolkit in the 1990s. Recommended skills development programmes should be created for all levels and these must be closely linked to more comprehensive skills assessments—both globally (through needs projections) and individually (through appraisals). Companies must develop programmes and inducements through such methods to encourage individuals to learn continuously throughout their careers.

3. **Balance Your Workload and Resources.** In the face of ever-tightening and limited human resources, it is not always possible to produce higher and higher quality products in shorter and shorter time spans. IS cannot be 'all things to all people.' The realities dictate that IS will have to work smarter not harder. This means that work and resources will have to be rebalanced. And some tough decisions regarding what can be done and what cannot be done must be taken. As a partner with business, IS must assume a more active role in deciding what systems and technologies make most sense for the organization. As a partner too, IS can explain the tradeoffs and options and together decide how to work smarter.

One rather dramatic approach is to ask users to rank order their current job requests and then cut the bottom 30% off this list. Taking a proactive stance and removing these requests frees up IS resources to tackle high priority issues and growth technologies. We know that the existing IS workload is enough to keep everyone working to capacity (or slightly beyond). The only way to redirect the IS effort is to first reduce the workload and then reassign IS personnel to the key areas identified.

Another way of working smarter is to question whether all expertise must be in-house. Many companies are beginning to outsource certain activities or hire consultants for startup technologies. This approach differs in that it frees IS staff to be assigned to key projects while not forgoing any existing projects. It is also a more expensive approach as compared to simply cutting projects. Out-sourcing, however, is a complicated managerial decision and needs to be dealt with thoroughly.

4. **Build Effective Teams.** Most IS work is team-based and, as a result, IS professionals spend a significant portion of their daily lives working within the team framework. It follows that building effective teams should have a dramatic effect on IS personnel and their productivity. Unfortunately,

most teams are formed with very little thought or understanding as to what constitutes an effective team.

Peter Drucker (1993) has identified three different types of teams:

- **The Baseball Team.** Members of this team play *on* the team but they do not play *as* a team. Each member plays a fixed position and members tend to stay in their respective positions. This type of team has great strengths in situations where members can be given specific tasks of their own, can be measured by performance scores for each task, can be trained for each task, and where the rules are well known and stable.

- **The Symphony Orchestra.** Members of this team play *on* the team and they also play *as* a team. Like its namesake, the team requires a 'conductor' and a 'score' and endless rehearsals to work well. Unlike the baseball team, this type of team has great flexibility if the score is clear and if the team in well led. It can also move very fast.

- **The Doubles Tennis Team.** This type of team has to be small (i.e., seven to nine maximum). Each member has a 'preferred' rather than a 'fixed' position and members cover for one another. They also adjust themselves to the strengths and weaknesses of each other. According to Drucker, a well-calibrated team of this kind is the strongest team of all. Its total performance is greater than the sum of the individual performances of its members, for the team uses the strengths of each member while minimizing the weaknesses of each. But the team requires enormous self-discipline. The members have to work together for a long time before they actually function as a 'team.' Another model of this type of team is the 'jazz combo.'

Drucker points out that one of the major differences among the different types of teams is the way in which the players receive their information. On a baseball team, each member receives information appropriate to his or her task, and receives it independently of the information the team-mates all receive. In the symphony orchestra, the information comes largely from the conductor who controls the 'score.' In the doubles tennis team, the players get their information largely from each other.

Many IS projects use the baseball team approach where individual members each perform specific tasks suitable to their positions. This works well with large teams where the game plan (i.e., the technology, the methodology, and the specifications) are well understood. However, problems arise when greater flexibility is required. It is no accident that many organizations are now looking for analysts who can programme and programmers who can analyse. Having team members who can 'play more than one position' makes the job of the project manager, or conductor, considerably easier. However, the role of the project manager required to 'orchestrate' the system development process becomes pivotal.

Neither baseball teams nor symphony orchestras, however, are particularly conducive to innovation and creativity. If you know exactly what you want to build, then both approaches will guarantee delivery. On the other hand, if you are trying to stimulate new and different solutions, where you do not have a clear statement of objectives and deliverables, then the doubles tennis team may prove to be the better choice of team style. According to Hammer (1990), attempts to re-engineer the organization using linear thinking and established procedures are guaranteed to fail. Because of their structure, neither the baseball team nor the orchestra approach work very effectively in these circumstances.

To produce new, creative, synergistic, and perhaps *ad hoc* thinking, a team structure is required where members play off each other's strengths and in doing so, reinforce each other's efforts. In such teams, members with particular strengths may lead for a while and then let others take over (Stewart, 1993). It is time IS rethought the way teams are formed, rewarded and reinforced. No single type of team is superior in all cases and attempts should be made to create differing types of teams for different activities and to match these with different management. For example, self-directed teams must be given greater levels of empowerment and responsibility, and measured on product not process. Team goals, team measures, team accomplishments, team rewards, and team skills should all be given greater attention instead of individual skills.

5. **Pay for Performance . . . Promote for Potential.** If an employee is a superior performer at his/her present job, he/she should be paid for his/her performance. The problem arises when we 'promote for performance.' The implicit assumption is that if the employee is good at this job, then he/she will likely be good at the next job. Based on this assumption, we have tied pay and promotion together. Unfortunately, the result is frequently that we take the 'super-star' and turn him/her into the 'also-ran.' The danger here is that we try to make our best sales people into managers, our best designers into administrators, and our best programmers into project managers. The link between pay and promotion needs to be broken. Promotion must be based on potential to satisfy the particular tasks that are part of the next job. The identification of the tasks and competencies of the job are discussed below.

Individuals have expected to be promoted up through the ranks simply because money and status were associated with level within the hierarchy. With many organizational levels being removed, individuals can now expect to stay at each level much longer than ever before. Therefore, we need to motivate and reward individuals separately from promotion. One manager put it this way: 'IS professionals should receive satisfaction instead of status and should receive pay for contribution instead of level.'

This means that we will have to be more creative in terms of rewarding individuals and team players. Certainly, recognition for individuals who consistently deliver high quality service is a good start. Other softer rewards including gestures like lunches and dinners, recognition in company newsletters, kudos from the boss, and company achievement awards are also effective. Whatever the type of recognition, IS management must take steps to ensure that IS personnel are able to clearly link actions with rewards. These actions must be achievable by personnel given their individual skill level, otherwise they will rapidly become discouraged. IS personnel must be aware of their inventory of skills and be given clear guidance regarding the specific skills they require in order to contribute more effectively to the organization. Obviously this will require a substantial degree of coaching and development on the part of supervisors and managers. There is also every reason to believe that individual members can assume a more direct and hands-on role in managing their own careers and should be encouraged to do so provided the proper systems are in place. Given the financial investment in IS personnel, the length of time it takes to differentiate the top performer from the mediocre performer, and the fact that IS is a people-intensive activity, it behoves IS management to take the time and money to recognize and reward their personnel appropriately.

6. **Identify the Requisite Skills.** Technical skill requirements are easy to identify and, by and large, they are easy to acquire by means of courses (e.g., in-house, outside, self-study, etc.). Identifying the required skill requirements for less technical aspects of the IS business is less tractable. The area of project management is a case in point. We are capable of identifying our successful project managers. We have a pretty good idea of what they do and what makes them successful. Where we fail is in training potential project managers. This often happens because IS has not articulated exactly what the project management skills are and how they are best learned.

One company has started a quality programme focusing on project management. Project management was a logical starting point because of the key role it plays in IS activity. With their project management development programme, five competencies have been identified: business management, technology management, process management, team management, and self-management. Within the teamwork category, for instance, ten specific skills have been identified. These include team building, participation, cooperation, consensus, responsibility, helping others, critical feedback, identity, commitment and sharing success.

Five courses have been offered geared to each competency with course credits earned and a professional certificate programme in place to recognize mastery of each of the competencies. This means that IS personnel develop a 'profile of competence.' The advantages of this are many. IS employees now have knowledge of specific competencies that they have or are working on—that is, each employee manages their own competency profile. Employees can be rewarded for competence as opposed to level and status. Because of the individual competency profiles, teams can be formed based on a strategy of optimal competency mix. Perhaps most importantly, this brings a level of professionalism to the workplace that has been lacking in the non-technology aspects of the business.

7. **Motivate through Challenge.** The ability to motivate and reward IS personnel is no longer possible by promoting up through the ranks of management (for the reasons previously discussed). Some organizations will see this as a handicap—others will see this as an opportunity. In order to see how this might be seen as an opportunity, we need to understand the nature of IS personnel.

Research (Couger, 1990) has shown that IS professionals have the highest *growth need strength* (indicating that they have a high need for personal growth and development) and they have the lowest *social need strength* (indicating that they prefer to work alone) of 500 different occupations! Couger concludes that 'programmers and analysts are not antisocial; they will participate actively in meetings that are meaningful to them but their high growth need also causes intolerance for group activities that are not well organized and conducted efficiently' (Couger, 1990). This result explains a significant portion of personal experiences in IS!

Relative to the rest of the organization, this puts IS in an enviable position. To be specific, IS personnel have a built-in predisposition to respond to challenge. Given this, the task of management then becomes one of creating tasks that are interesting and demanding and to which IS personnel will respond. We have already mentioned some of the ways in which this might be done such as assigning IS personnel to challenging growth technologies, services or businesses and seconding IS personnel to high profile business initiatives. Successful companies will be those that seize this opportunity and use it to convert their IS departments into dynamic, challenging, invigorating, and rewarding places to work despite the harsh realities of the 1990s.

CONCLUSION

The study cited earlier painted a very pessimistic picture of the IS industry. However, our Forum members did not seem to share this 'doom and gloom' attitude. The group would acknowledge, however, that the IS function is likely at a junction point in its development. Certainly, things cannot continue as they have in the past. The demand for increased productivity, for more for less, for higher quality faster, and for new technologies to be introduced seamlessly into businesses suffering constrained financial resources, places the management of human resources in IS in a critical position. Fortunately, tough times are also times for innovation. In this vein, this paper has attempted to address these HRM problems in IS by seeing them as opportunities. Hopefully, some of the ideas and strategies presented here will guide the management of IS towards a better future.

Executive Interview:

Kamil Khan
President and CEO
Bell Sygma Inc.

This section outlines a vision for a new kind of IS organization. What is your vision for IS at Bell Canada?

Before I answer your question, I must tell you a little about Bell Canada and its strategic direction because IS is one of the key players in the company's future plans. Bell is the most effective and efficient telephone company in the world, but we are under many external pressures to change and continually improve. For example, we are committed to price parity with US business rates by 1996. Internally, we must improve the speed with which we introduce new products and services and do this with ever fewer resources. My vision is for a different kind of IS organization at Bell—for a total corporate function responsible for all of the company's infrastructure and for an organization that is much more closely aligned with company strategies than we have been in the past.

How are you implementing this vision?

We made a business proposition to the corporation a year and a half ago about how IS could assist the company to become more effective and efficient and transform the way Bell

Canada does its business. I told our senior executives 'To go from the Bell of '91 to the Bell of '96, here's what's required.' With this strategy document, we attached detailed costs and benefits and a macroeconomic statement for the company. In other words, I showed them how IS can improve the company's balance sheet and income statement.

This kind of vision has to be backed up with metrics. We did just that . . . we described how the company is now and how it ought to be and attached costs and benefits to each major functional area. I worked with our clients on plans to accomplish these changes. Then I said, if we are going to tackle this large amount of work, I am going to need a more effective organization structure, so we have a fighting chance of success.

How does your new IS organization work?

Well, for one thing, the name of my organization is now Operations Development, not IS. I used to be an IS guy, but I 'saw the light.' My organization now has total responsibility for building the corporate infrastructure required to run an effective telephone company. This is an end-to-end function handling: policies, strategies, planning, funding, systems, methods, training, documentation and programmes, whether mechanized or not. My group is now made up of people from both business and systems. For example, our Consumer Sector group consists of 278 people: 132 are business analysts, 66 are from engineering and research; 45 are systems people; 31 provide information access; and four are from network services. At the beginning of 1991, we took about 1700 systems people and over 1000 business/methods people and created an organization to transform the way Bell does business.

Does this mean you have eliminated users?

We have moved all of the users who used to be responsible for problem solving, non-computerized procedures, and business plans and strategies into this new organization. We still meet with the line users regularly as part of our business planning networks that exist for all functions of the company. However, it is our job to manage the strategies and to cause the transformations to occur—whether it is in floor space or working hours or systems. Inevitably, non-technical issues are closely linked to technical issues these days.

Users of systems still exist and they will, as you suggest, have to become more sophisticated. In fact, I think your picture of the user of the future is too simplistic. Our future users are going to have to be multifunctional—able to access and manipulate large chunks of data, using a natural language of some sort, in order to do their work. It is not going to be as simple as just moving data fields on a report. Future users will also have much more flexibility and capability with both data and systems than they currently do now.

Was it difficult to sell this vision to your non-IS colleagues?

It did require a leap of faith on behalf of my colleagues who had to throw all these people into my organization. This is a large power base and they would not have done it if they did not believe it was required, that it was not in the best interests of the corporation, or they did not have respect for my people. We are being viewed as an investment, not a cost. The biggest problem my colleagues had was within their own organizations. There did not seem to be the same kind of conviction back on the ranch. Their staff was much more apprehensive about this new organization. This was not a credibility problem, but more fear of the unknown.

You have noted the need for more flexible systems in the future. Does your new organization help you to achieve this?

Absolutely. We have a much better integration of functions and systems now. We used to have two players at every party. Now one person is multifunctional and responsible for everything right down to middle-level management. Hand-offs between user groups and IS are almost totally eliminated. We now have a common view and my guys are delivering a customer view, not simply a systems view. The time savings are dramatic. For example, a major system change that was requested on September 27 will be in production on 5000 workstations by October 19. The difference is that now when system changes are discussed, there is only one person handling every aspect of them and there are no extensive discussions before decisions are made; no back and forth meetings between the user group and IS and whatever other groups there are involved. We handle every aspect of the change. This new organization has been successful beyond our wildest expectations.

What about the cost of all this infrastructure you are building?

First, you cannot justify building this infrastructure on a project by project basis any more because so much of it is used in many functions and in many ways. It can only be justified at the corporate bottom line. At this level, I can articulate the benefits clearly enough to say that a dollar invested in me this year will yield the company 70 cents in benefits per year for the next five years. I have the details to support this in the form of strategies and savings for each function of the company. This is why I am responsible for getting the funding for our plans, not our clients. Our clients agree only on the deliverables and at certain key checkpoints.

A second aspect of the cost of the infrastructure is that you cannot resystemize everything. You will never get funded for it. The key to economical transformation is to reuse and rework as much of the installed base as possible—even if it runs on technology that is not your first choice. In many cases you have to bolt together pieces of old systems with a new user interface that makes the complexity and heterogeneity of the platforms opaque. Then you can gradually add functionality. This is what you meant when you stated that systems development in the future should be 'evolutionary,' not structured. Ideally, software should be like 'Lego' where you slot pieces in and out of systems as necessary.

How are you staffing your new organization? What new skills will you need?

We believe that our people are one of our best assets, comparable to few in the industry. One of my key jobs is to create an opportunity for their continued growth and prosperity while achieving our corporate mission. However, if you asked me what new skills I need to add right now I would say: re-engineering, process mapping, benchmarking, security, and inter-enterprise knowhow. IS organizations that do not include business people should also seek to build up a significant knowledge of the business within IS through an interchange of resources.

Traditional IS organizations are missing something because they are too incestuous. I do not want to restrict entry into it nearly as tightly as we have done in the past. I think we need to hire a better balance of people—of the pure sciences and the liberal arts. I want a mix of sexes, skills, and ethnic groups. With globalization, you never know when certain backgrounds and abilities are going to be necessary. Then, it will be our job to build the specific skills these people will need at Bell, such as those I just mentioned.

How are you handling the issue of hardware and software complexity?

You have noted that the outlook for the future in this area is confused and I agree. However, it is only a small group in any organization that needs to be confused. For the rest, the connections should be 'Any to Any,' i.e., any hardware and software should connect to any other. It is the job of the small group to make these connections transparent to users and to customers. You cannot build systems in isolation any more. This is why the infrastructure is so critical. All systems must connect to everything: data, terminals, networks, lines.

Will your retooling strategy work for all IS organizations?

A key factor in our strategy for IS was the level of mechanization at Bell and the high degree of knowledge of IS capabilities amongst our senior management. (Our President is the former Vice President of IS.) And, there is probably a difference by major industry segments about what will work for IS. If IS is simply going to be used for administration, as in some manufacturing or natural resources industries, then it should expect to be shunted off to the side of the organization somewhere. But IS guys cannot sit around either, saying 'I'm the IS guy and I want to be involved.' This is not a right . . . You have to demonstrate why you should be at the table making corporate decisions.

Do you think this is an effective strategy for retooling IS?

It is a reasonable assessment of where most companies are and where they are going. Many of your points are bang on. However, for those companies that want to deal with inter-enterprise systems and which have a high degree of customer interaction, I believe that IS must go even further than you suggest. It must transform itself into more than IS . . . into a total infrastructure group, as we have at Bell.

What final recommendations do you have for today's IS managers?

First, I would tell them that they are capable of doing a whole lot more with their organizations than they are doing today. Second, they must articulate the benefits of their organization at the level of the corporate bottom line. If they cannot demonstrate that they are providing good corporate worth, they should ask to be removed and outsource their entire operation. You conclude that many organizations, particularly successful ones in the '80s, will resist change. I would like to tell those IS managers that if they do not change, and change dramatically, they will be dead meat.

BELL SYGMA INC.

Bell Sygma, a premier provider of telecommunications operating solutions worldwide, is one of the largest information technology (IT) and network management service companies in Canada. A wholly-owned subsidiary of Bell Canada, Bell Sygma provides IT solutions for Bell Canada use, develops IT related products for Bell Canada to offer its customers, and markets Bell Canada's telecom operating systems and expertise to telecommunications companies around the world. The company is currently playing an integral role in Bell Canada's Business Transformation journey through the provision of tools, processes and expertise.

Bell Sygma has experienced rapid growth not only on the Canadian home front, but internationally as well. Bell Sygma participates in the dynamic global market by providing high value business solutions to telecommunications companies who need to improve their ability to compete. Their competitive advantage in this fiercely competitive market is the experience, depth and scope that has been acquired through Bell Sygma's long-term relationship with Bell.

Founded in 1993, Bell Sygma is a part of the Bell Canada Enterprises (BCE) group of companies, which includes Bell Canada, Bell Canada International, Nortel, Bell Mobility and Bell Northern Research. Bell Sygma's team of over 4000 highly skilled professionals are located throughout the Americas, Asia Pacific, Europe and the Middle East, and has engagements in Latin America.

PART 3

Managing IS Performance

9
Benchmarking IS: How Does Your Organization Rate?

INTRODUCTION

In today's difficult economy, companies are reorganizing and streamlining wherever possible in order to save money and attract customers. This new corporate emphasis on better organizational performance, i.e., both productivity and quality goods and services, challenges all parts of an organization, including IS, to make improvements in what they do and how they operate. This is easier said than done and many organizations are having difficulties knowing where to start, what to do, and what their goals should be. Organizational learning and change are the hallmarks of business in the 1990s and the starting point for this effort is the collection of accurate and adequate information and its appropriate analysis.

It is not surprising therefore that comparison, measurement, and evaluation have become something of a preoccupation in many businesses in recent years. The US National Quality Institute (which establishes the detailed criteria for the Malcolm Baldridge Awards), suggests there are three components of effective information and analysis which act as the 'brain centre' driving the corporate improvement effort, regardless of a company's organization or structure (Baldridge Criteria, 1993):

1. scope and management of quality and performance information;
2. collection, analysis, and use of company-level data, including: customer data, operations data, and linking performance data to overall financial performance;
3. competitive comparisons and benchmarking.

These criteria can also be used by individual corporate subunits to determine how well they contribute to overall quality and performance.

One organizational subunit receiving a considerable amount of executive attention in this regard is Information Systems. Many companies are looking to information technology to help them support corporate restructuring, but to do it with increasingly fewer resources. Unfortunately, IS has also been an area of the company that has been extremely difficult to measure and evaluate. IS also continues to have a credibility problem in some organizations where executives believe that IS has contributed little or nothing to the corporate bottom line (Roach, 1989). As well, there are still many users who tend to feel that IS service is lacking or could be bought cheaper elsewhere. With IS budgets coming under closer and closer scrutiny, IS itself is placing new emphasis on measurement to demonstrate its contribution to overall corporate performance, both through quality services and systems and through its ability to do so cost-effectively.

In order to explore and assess what IS organizations are doing to evaluate and compare themselves, Forum members examined the measures they use to understand and assess their own procedures and performance and how they compare their overall performance to others. In addition, they described what they would like to know about how other IS organizations work. This chapter looks at the three components of information and its analysis outlined above from the perspective of the IS department. It summarizes what IS functions are doing to assess and analyse their organizations and makes suggestions about how the measurement and evaluation of IS both internally and externally could be improved.

SCOPE AND MANAGEMENT OF IS INFORMATION

Forum members indicated they collected a wide assortment of statistics and qualitative data for their own internal use. The list in Appendix A gives a compilation of measures they collect regularly. Each organization has its own set of measures and comparative practices which bear little resemblance to any others. Some make customer satisfaction surveys a focal point of their efforts, while others do little or nothing in this area. Some have extensive and comprehensive programmes of evaluation; others are relatively haphazard about data collection. Some relate measures to bottom-line benefits; others track individual statistics only without linking them to any larger context.

Accurate and appropriate data is a prerequisite for any successful internal or external programme of measurement and evaluation. Current IS measurement practices are problematic in three ways:

1. **Information Gaps.** Most organizations do not track progress in one or more of the following key areas essential to monitoring quality and operational performance improvement (Baldridge Criteria, 1993):

   - customer-related information;
   - product and service performance (i.e., systems and operations);
   - internal operations and performance;
   - supplier performance;
   - cost and financial information.

2. **Lack of Standards.** IS measurement suffers from a lack of standards in almost all areas. Current measurement practices are characterized by a general lack of agreement about what constitutes appropriate data. As a result, with the exception of some performance measures in operations, very few statistics are comparable from organization to organization.

3. Difficulty in Collection. Much data collection in IS organizations imposes a serious burden on staff already under pressure to complete their work. As a result, accuracy and scope of data collection are often hampered. For example, determining the function points associated with a system to estimate a system's benefits is an extraneous task that does nothing to further the development process.

Altogether, the gaps in what is measured, the lack of standardized measures, and the difficulty of producing measures, suggest that IS organizations need to seriously examine what they measure and how they do it in order to obtain the type of data they need to improve their performance and quality and to make it demonstrable to their business management.

LINKING DATA TO PERFORMANCE

IS functions need to measure their performance for three reasons. First, such information can be an aid to credibility, reassuring senior managers that their IS function is performing efficiently, effectively and is continually improving. Second, it is an aid to productivity improvement, demonstrating trends over time and identifying areas where improvement is necessary. Finally, it can be the catalyst to organizational transformation, supporting company and functional review, action, and planning. The key to achieving each of these is demonstrating the link between the data collected and functional and corporate performance.

This link can be made most easily at present in the operational performance measures many companies collect. Response time figures, turnaround time, workload figures, and recovery times can be monitored over time and are important reflections of service to the company. Each of these, in turn, relate to broader measures of organizational performance, since operational systems support so many corporate functions. For example, monitoring calls to the 'Help Desk' can identify the quality of the services provided and can highlight important operational and system problems.

Unfortunately, all too often these measures are collected and used only in isolation. One large company is proud of its efficient Help Desk but fails to analyse the problems reported to prevent them recurring! Other companies monitor system availability statistics to two decimal places for each piece of their network. However, because for the business, 'availability' is a function of all parts of the network working together, these do not reflect the actual availability of computer services to users. Thus, while IS managers collect a large amount of data that accurately measures the efficiency of IS operations, they often neglect to interpret these data to make the necessary linkages with IS performance and quality. Additional analysis of these measures could yield more valuable information about the IS function and its impact on corporate performance.

In systems development, the link between measures and performance becomes even more tenuous. All too often, in IS as in other parts of the organization, measures assess what can be measured rather than what should be measured. Organizations then often end up collecting data about the wrong things and the resulting information can actually detract from overall effectiveness simply by putting management's focus on the wrong things (Goldratt and Cox, 1984). For example, calculating measures such as Return on Equity (ROE) or Return on Assets (ROA), for a project, do not reflect all the many and varied impacts systems can have on an organization and may result in the wrong systems being developed (Markus and Soh, 1993).

Problems with the meaningfulness of some of the measures used also prevent clear linkages with performance from being made. Do executives care that dollar sales per gigabyte of storage are increasing? What does this mean to the company's bottom line? Business people often complain that IS statistics tell them little about what they really need to know. For example, chargeout rates broken down by type of hardware and software may be meaningful to IS professionals, but to business people they are not figures that are intuitively easy to understand or that translate on to any yardstick they are familiar with.

Even simple descriptive measures can be difficult to interpret without the link to performance. As a Vice President of IS remarked 'Is it good or bad if IS expenditures per employee are increasing?' Measures such as staff counts, or budget break-downs, are useful only if clearly associated with measures of organizational impact. If we knew that increasing the development component of the IS budget was associated with increased revenue or decreased staff counts, then such data would be useful. On their own, they tend to be meaningless.

Linking IS measures to broader contexts of functional or corporate performance is an essential component of effective measurement. At present, while a considerable amount of information is collected by IS organizations, efforts linking these data to such broader contexts are largely missing. While poor measures and gaps in measurement undoubtedly limit management's ability to do so, it remains equally true that little effort is made to connect existing measures to larger contexts of understanding within IS or the organization. In short, as one senior IS manager noted, 'We have lots of measures, but very little context.'

COMPETITIVE COMPARISONS AND FUNCTIONAL BENCHMARKING

Benchmarking, or comparing your organization to others, is a strategy that addresses many aspects of organizational performance. At minimum, benchmarking can provide senior management with the assurance that the costs of their information systems function are not out of line with those of other organizations. But the true benefit of benchmarking is that it challenges managers to keep up with the best practices in business and to continuously improve their productivity. For example, finding out that Mazda could deliver accounting services using a fraction of the staff used at Ford, made Ford management realize that it had to totally rethink how they did this part of their business (Hammer, 1990).

Comparison in IS is still rudimentary. Amongst Forum participants, only one organization undertook a formal benchmarking study on a regular basis (although others were investigating doing so). While almost all companies compare themselves to others, this is usually done in an informal manner. Some of the methods currently used include:

- **Asking around.** IS managers go to conferences and trade shows on a regular basis. Part of the benefit of these is to learn informally from the other participants about what they are doing and how successful it has been.

- **Visiting other companies.** Many IS managers try to visit similar companies with whom they are not in competition to see what applications and practices they are using.

- **Vendors.** Vendors are often a good source of comparative information about the operation and deployment of their own equipment and software because of their knowledge of what goes on in other companies.

- **Joint Projects.** Some industries (e.g., travel) have the opportunity to collaborate on joint projects which enable participants to see first-hand how other companies work.

- **Industry Organizations.** Some industries have associations which collect and disseminate statistics on and to member organizations (e.g., the Life Office Management Association—LOMA).

- **Benchmarking Services.** Some companies hire professional benchmarking consultants to survey their organizations and compare them with others in the service's data base.

It is difficult to tell just how helpful these comparisons are. The problem with the first four of these methods is that they are so highly anecdotal that, as one IS manager stated 'No one really knows who's winning.' What are the factors associated with superior performance? It is difficult to compare oneself to industry leaders because there is no clear way of identifying who the leaders are and what made them that way.

Industry organizations and benchmarking services try to rectify this situation by collecting quantitative data for comparison purposes. While these services provide useful information they each have certain limitations. Industry organizations are limited to single industry members inhibiting functional comparisons in other types of companies (see below).

Benchmarking services are limited by the scope and quality of their data bases. For example, the service used by one group member had only three firms from the same industry in their data base.

Comparisons and benchmarking let companies 'know where they stand' in the larger business community. IS organizations could benefit substantially by undertaking more formal comparisons with other companies. While many problems with comparative data do exist (especially problems with imprecise definitions), there are few that could not be addressed if IS management were to manage measurement practices as carefully as they do other aspects of IS work.

ESSENTIALS OF EFFECTIVE MEASUREMENT

IS managers are more in agreement about what they would like to see. Forum members came to a general consensus about the features of an effective measurement and benchmarking programme. Together, these should form the basis of any organization's efforts to compare themselves internally or externally.

Relevance. A recent survey of CEO's and other top managers (IS and business alike) revealed that when assessing IS performance, they are seeking answers to three fundamental questions (Wilson, 1993):

1. How well are we doing the things we are doing now?
2. Are we doing the right things?
3. Are we positioned to compete in the future?

The most important test for any measure is whether or not it helps to answer one of these questions.

Use of the Same Yardstick. One of the benefits of benchmarking services, according to one manager, is that they force everyone to use the same set of measures. These then enable comparisons to be made. IS managers tend to see many of the problems associated with using common measures (e.g., problems with common definitions, poor data collection) and none of the advantages. While such measures may be imperfect, the use of common measures not only makes comparison possible but opens the door to greater and greater refinements of these measures, thus improving the quality of measurement for all.

Functional Benchmarking. In the past, when companies undertook external comparison they focused on their direct competitors. This was difficult since competitors are unlikely to share information with each other. Today, there is new recognition that value can be gained from comparing similar **functions** in a variety of different industries and this information is much easier to obtain. For example, companies have compared order-taking processes from several industries (Wiesendanger, 1992). While there are many differences in the process of ordering a pizza and that of ordering cable TV services, there are also many similarities and much to be learned. IS itself is one function that can be benchmarked in this manner. While there are many differences in **applications**, the **processes** involved in developing, installing, and operating those applications are fundamentally the same regardless of the industry. It is thus an ideal candidate for functional benchmarking.

Internal and External Comparisons. As the Baldridge criteria note, it is important to assess the IS function in both ways. Certain measures, such as network availability, or benefits achieved, are essential for monitoring performance and quality internally. Others, such as descriptive statistics on costs and headcounts, are more appropriate for external comparisons. Finally, some measures such as customer satisfaction or development effectiveness, can be used in both ways.

Future Focus. While statistics can assure management that it is operating efficiently and effectively in the past and present, the future dimension should never be forgotten. While it would be impossible to measure the future, interpretation of current data, as well as data-gathering, should not disregard analysis for the future. This is where many current practices of trend analysis fit in. Documenting and assessing industry-specific IS practice and technical trends, and how well your company is positioned *vis-à-vis* these, is an essential component of measurement.

However, managers should be warned against too-facile acceptance of 'what everyone says is coming.' One IS Vice President noted that one survey showed substantial agreement amongst IS managers about how they would be managing in the year 2010. The only problem was that no one knew how to get there from where they were at present! While visions for the future are important, practical assessments about what to do in the short and medium term and how to evaluate success, are a necessary measure for companies and their management.

THE TOOLS OF EFFECTIVE MEASUREMENT

Effective measurement for IS requires the use of appropriate tools designed to support each other. Good data is the result of properly-designed measures, that is, they are well defined and reflect what they are supposed to measure. In IS, different types of measures provide different types of information to management.

Contextual Measures. Since IS measurement is an art, not a science, understanding as much as possible about the organization and the management of a company and its IS function is essential to the proper interpretation of data. Contextual data provide important clues as to the reasons for certain findings. They assist the analyst in interpreting findings and determining their relevance to the organization. (Some examples of contextual measures are given in Appendix A.)

Diagnostic Measures. Rather than collecting a complete cornucopia of data on a regular basis, diagnostic screening measures give a general picture of IS performance and quality in key areas. Just as certain medical tests screen for a range of health problems, in IS certain measures of quality and performance can highlight problem areas and the need for further study. The use of a series of diagnostic measures on a regular basis would eliminate the need for the massive ongoing data collection activities that are often a significant part of IS work. (Some suggested diagnostic measures are listed in Appendix B.)

Analytic Measures. Where problems or superior performance are identified by diagnostic measures, more detailed analytic measures can be applied to discover the reasons why. Analytic measures focus on particular areas, and while detailed, are only used at certain times, rather than on a regular basis. They focus a spotlight on one area of the organization for a limited period of time only. When performance improves, analytic measures are disbanded. One organization has used this approach successfully in tuning its production systems to run more efficiently. They focus detailed analytic measures on one system at a time to achieve substantial operating improvements. When these are achieved, attention shifts to other systems. Analytic measures can be varied according to the problem. Because such data are short term, they can and should be organization and situation specific.

Longitudinal Measures. Any IS manager can tell a dozen 'war stories' of the business problems caused by IS. What they also recognize, however, is that most of these problems are short term only. Projects can get delayed at a point in their schedule and still finish on time. Systems can experience problems on installation, causing users to curse and gnash their teeth, and still benefit the company in the long term. Companies that invest heavily in one large system may show no return on their investment until the system is fully operational. Thus, measures of performance and quality that rely only on one 'snapshot' of the organization, can be subject to numerous errors of interpretation. In order to capture a true picture of IS performance, it is necessary to have measures that represent a series of pictures over time. Only then will trends and consistent performance be apparent.

Intuitive Measures. Effective measures are those that others can intuitively understand. IS organizations have a tendency to create new and esoteric measures that senior management cannot relate to anything in their experience. Intuitive measures make this connection naturally for the reader. The best measures are therefore those that are expressed in terms well known in business, such as 'sales' or 'revenues.' More complex measures should be left for detailed analysis only.

Qualitative and Quantitative Measures. Statistics can only tell part of any story. Illustrative stories, quotations, explanations, descriptions, opinions, and feelings each have a place in assessing IS performance. While statistics are important measures because they lend force and credibility to any assessment, understanding of what these figures mean can best be gained by qualitative support. Managers are also cautioned that many so-called quantitative studies do not capture objective reality but reflect subjective feelings, or worse, are designed to reflect back what the survey authors want to hear. Client surveys are a good example of this. Qualitative supporting material for statistics such as '67% of users stated they are satisfied with IS services' could help illuminate what IS is doing well and where it still needs to improve. Very often statistics leave out much of what can be learned. Ideally, therefore, a mix of measures should be used, particularly where such 'soft' measures as customer satisfaction or system performance are involved.

AN ACTION PLAN FOR EFFECTIVE MEASUREMENT

While most IS organizations claim they want effective measurement, many simply are not prepared to put the effort and 'think time' into doing it properly. Effective measures need not be time consuming to collect (indeed they should not), but they do require refocusing of attention about what to collect and careful thought about how to interpret the findings. These are the facets of measurement that are most often given shortest shrift in IS today. For managers short of time, professional researchers or measurement services can be employed, but participation in the process is essential. If your organization truly wishes to create effective measurement practices, the following action plan should be your guide.

1. **Make a Commitment.** As noted above, much of the best information is derived from longitudinal data, collected over a series of years so trends can be perceived. Management must make a commitment to collect data in the beginning, even if it does not realize substantial benefits immediately. A commitment to accuracy must be made as well. The 'garbage in, garbage out' maxim applies in this field, as in many others.

2. **Select and Develop Measures.** Many IS managers have deplored the lack of good measures that accurately reflect performance and quality. Yet IS managers are in an excellent position to develop better ones. Look for measures that relate directly to what you want to discover. Test them with the people who will be providing the data, and be prepared to make revisions. (You seldom get everything right the first time.) Assess the validity of measures by collecting qualitative data in addition to statistics. One organization began to poll all of its outlets on a random basis to see whether their systems are working, because traditional system availability figures contrasted with user complaints of system downtime. This measure has yielded useful information on system availability and, in turn, has developed into a much more meaningful measure than those generated by the Operations department.

3. **Focus on Diagnostics.** Rather than measuring everything, managers should focus on creating and capturing diagnostic information. This will reduce the time involved in data collection. Management should look for and ensure that relevant measures are developed. (See Appendix B for a suggested list of these measures.)

4. **Look for Gaps.** Make sure your measurement programme covers the five key areas identified by the Baldridge criteria, namely, customers, products and services, internal operations and performance, suppliers, and cost and financial information.

5. **Share with Other Companies.** Look for opportunities to work with other companies to share common data and to develop industry standards for measurement. Business and industry organizations (e.g., The Conference Board, CIPS, SIM, LOMA), benchmarking services, and universities are all doing work in this area.

6. **Integrate Findings.** Much information is lost due to the failure to carefully assess the data that is already collected in IS. Rather than a series of isolated reports on various subjects (e.g., customer satisfaction, comparison with other organizations, descriptive statistics), try to link all information together with the three questions senior managers are asking (see above). Then, try to describe what is known from a variety of sources under these broad general questions. For example, in addressing the question, 'Are we doing the right things?' look at corporate performance measures as they relate to IS, what customer surveys say, and trends in key diagnostic measures over time. The more data can be integrated, the more you will find that the context of the results will appear. Anomalies and corroborative evidence will also become obvious.

7. **Interpret Results.** The interpretation of the findings in any measurement programme is critical. One manager expressed concern that measurement results were often used to divide employees rather than motivate them. Any suggestion that a measurement programme will be used to evaluate individuals or even teams will ensure that people will find ways to subvert the process. Ideally, therefore, findings should be kept at the level of the IS function (i.e., the whole function, as well as development and operations), rather than broken down by team or individual. Areas should be challenged to pull together and support each other, discouraging finger-pointing.

   A second facet of interpretation concerns understanding negative findings. It is natural to react to such results with rationalizations and justifications about how one's own organization is 'different.' Such reactions will defeat the purpose of any measurement programme. While it is appropriate to explore if errors in understanding or measurement were made, managers should also be asking questions about what they can learn from the findings.

8. **Analyse.** While measurement programmes do reassure senior management that their IS organization is well managed, the true benefits to the company as a whole come from the problem areas that are discovered. The analysis and resolution of problems is therefore essential to an effective measurement programme. Analysis of most problems should have both a quantitative and a qualitative dimension, and should be addressed in a positive, non-judgemental manner. Where benchmarking has revealed significant divergence from best practice, site visits should be arranged. Again, keep in mind what can be learned from different industries. Detailed measurements should be undertaken both to explore the problem and to reassure management that it has been effectively addressed.

CONCLUSION

This chapter has addressed the topic of IS measurement. IS managers are committed to measurement for many reasons: organizational credibility, effectiveness, efficiency, and general improvement. While some may question the benefits or accuracy of certain measures, most IS managers do not want to eliminate measurement from their organizations. Instead, they want better information—more accurate, easier to collect, better interpretations, and clearer definitions. In spite of all we do not know about how to measure IS, each of these is achievable at present. While there are gaps in measurement practices, these are fewer than most managers realize. The true key to effective measurement is quality, not quantity. Making use of the data already available (with judicious pruning and additions), more effective integration and analysis, as well as a long-term commitment to internal and external measurement, will yield results. Like so many other things in IS, good measurement derives from good management rather than a single magic answer.

APPENDIX A: LIST OF MEASURES CURRENTLY USED IN IS

I. Corporate Context
- Company Size (assets, customers, employees, locations)
- Industry
- Head Office Size
- Sales
- Sales per Employee
- Competitive Environment
- Organization Structure
- Reporting Structure
- Morale Index

II. Overall IS Performance
- IS Costs
- IS Costs per Corporate Revenues
- Technology Costs per Corporate Revenues
- Total Benefits Achieved
- Total Sales per MIP
- Total Sales per GB
- IS Salary Cost as a % of Sales
- Time-to-Fill Hardware/Software Orders
- User Satisfaction (competitiveness, expert support, fulfilment, reliability, responsiveness, ease of doing business, partnership, overall satisfaction)
- Achievement of Service Agreements
- End User Support Survey
- Executive Satisfaction
- Employee Satisfaction

III. Descriptive Information About IS

A. IS Costs
- IS Budget as a % of Net Sales
- IS Budget versus Actual Costs
- IS Budget as a % of Total Expenses
- IS Salaries (permanent versus contract staff)
- Overtime Costs
- Cost of Benefits

- Training Costs
- Total Staff Cost as a % of IS Budget
- Hardware Costs
- Hardware Maintenance Costs
- Software Purchase Costs
- Software Rental Costs
- Communications Costs
- Disaster Recovery Costs
- Total Equipment Cost
- Capital Expenditures
- Expenditures per IS Employee
- Expenditures per Company Employee

B. Human Resources
- Total Staff
- Total Contractors
- Total Management and Administration
- Total Development Staff
- Total Operations Staff
- Total Technical Services Staff
- Total IS Staff as a % of Total Employees
- Hours of Training
- New Hires
- Terminations
- Absences
- Moves
- Promotions
- Resignations
- Skilled Staff (numbers trained to use CASE, methodology, GUI, Code Generators)
- Tool Usage (numbers using CASE, methodology, GUI, Code Generators)
- Staff Hours (charged, not charged, by phase, development, maintenance)
- IS Skills
- IS Job Descriptions

C. IS Context
- Reporting Structure
- Application Packages Used (number, variety)

- Hardware Platforms (number, variety)
- Tools Used
- Portfolio Assessment (age, complexity, platform)
- Degree of Centralization (processing, report distribution, location of help, staff, LANS)

IV. Operations Performance
- Number of MIPS
- Gigabytes of DASD
- Lines Printed
- CPU Hours
- Equipment Installs, Moves, Removes
- Capacity Utilization (CPU, DASD, Tape, Printers)
- Workload per MIP (Batch, online, interactive, DASD, output, time of day)
- Response Time (network, CICS, TSO, VM)
- System Availability Poll
- Availability Levels (by equipment, network)
- Production Hours per Year
- Turnaround Time (batch)
- Meantime to Recover (minutes/outage)
- Cost Allocations (CICS, TSO, batch, DASD, printing, forms, leases, people, testing, telecommunications, equipment)
- CPU Cycles per Business Transaction
- Help Desk Productivity (calls handled, total calls, length of call, by time of day, abandoned calls, time to answer)

V. Development Performance
- Function Points per Work Month
- Delivery-on-Time Trends
- Deliverables (completed, not complete, not started) for service requests, new projects, production problems
- Function Points per Person (cost, for in-house development, for packages)
- Time to Market
- Development Budget as a % of Maintenance Budget

VI. Project Information

A. Project Performance
- Benefits Delivered
- Function Points Delivered
- ROI
- Impact on Market Share
- Impact on Strategic Direction
- Work Value Assessment
- Alignment with Business Objectives
- Number of Changes
- System Performance
- Number of Abends and Reason
- Production Hours per Year
- Number of Work Requests
- Number of Hours on Post-Release Problems
- Number of Changes per 100 Function Points
- Defects per 100 Function Points
- Staff Months per Function Point

B. Project Descriptive
- Project Costs
- Actual Costs Compared to Budget Costs
- Progress Against Schedule
- Resources Required
- Training Costs
- Paid Hours per Work Unit
- Personmonths per Project

APPENDIX B: SOME SUGGESTED DIAGNOSTIC MEASURES

Are We Doing Things Right?
- Total Benefits Delivered (user estimate) by IS overall, by project [Cost and Financial]
- Cost per Transaction [Internal Performance, Cost and Financial]
- Average Time-to-Market [Internal Performance]
- Project Progress against Schedule/Budget [Internal Performance]

- Delivery Time for Hardware/Software [Supplier Performance, Internal Performance]
- Number of Calls to Help Desks [Product Performance]
- System Availability Index [Service Performance]
- Number of Abends, Number of Work Requests [Product, Service Performance]
- Customer Satisfaction Index [Customer]

Are We Doing the Right Things?
- Business Revenues per Employee (over time) [Cost and Financial]
- Return on IT Investment versus Return on HR Investment [Cost and Financial]
- Executive Satisfaction Index [Customer]
- Trends in Cost per Transaction, Time-to-Market, Hardware/Software Delivery Time, Calls to Help Desk, System Availability Index, Number of Abends, Number of Work Requests, Customer Satisfaction Index (over time).

Are We Positioned for the Future?
- Competitive Environment [Customer, Product and Service Performance, Supplier Performance]
- Commitment to Research and Development [Customer, Product and Service Performance]
- Portfolio Assessment (function, age, complexity, platforms) [Product and Service, Customer]
- IS Costs, IS Returns, Cost per Transaction compared to Best Practices [Cost and Financial, Internal Performance]

10
Improving System Development Productivity

INTRODUCTION

In the 'old days' of system development, systems analysts hand-crafted systems to meet specific user needs. As a result, it was not unusual for a large portion of a project's total development time and budget to be spent *after* implementation, working bugs out of the system and refining system requirements. The imperfections and uncertainties of this approach led to more rational system development techniques and methodologies. These were designed to control the time and effort involved in system development by ensuring that user needs were properly identified *before* a system was created. Methodologies changed the system development process into a much more predictable and organized activity. Systems could be effectively planned and budgeted and better controls implemented. For the first time, users and IS managers knew clearly what a system was going to do before major time and dollars were spent.

While the system development process became more manageable, methodologies also made it less flexible and considerably more bureaucratic by imposing reporting and documentation requirements and a rigid sequence of steps that all projects—large or small—had to go through. And they did little to decrease the overall time involved. Today, business conditions will no longer accommodate long development cycles and requirements that are 'cast in concrete.' In the 1990s, two key business conditions shape how systems are developed:

Time is a critical factor of differentiation among today's businesses. IS cannot therefore afford the luxury of taking months or years to deliver a completed system.

Change is a constant. Whether companies are redefining themselves, resulting in re-engineering, merging, down-sizing, or taking advantage of global markets, IS is expected to provide the necessary support and services and do so in a cost-effective manner.

To assess the system development process and how it might be improved, given these new organizational imperatives, Forum members examined how their organizations were working to meet new organizational challenges through the system development process.

THE GOAL OF AN IMPROVED
DEVELOPMENT PROCESS

According to Goldratt and Cox (1984), the goal of an organization is to make money. It does this by increasing sales, by reducing operating costs, and by reducing inventories. All other 'objectives' (e.g., increasing market share, producing more products, improving quality, improving customer service, being more cost-effective, keeping pace with technology, and employing good people) are important only to the extent that they further the overall goal. It makes no sense to produce more products if they cannot be sold, or improve quality if operating costs increase and new sales are not generated.

The purpose of any subunit of an organization is to further the organization's goal. While this appears to be self-evident, Goldratt and Cox demonstrate that many subunits make assumptions about how they contribute to the organization's goal. These assumptions, which may even be counter-productive, unfortunately often go unchallenged. The result is the institution of objectives and measures that serve the subunit's goal but not the organization's.

As a subunit, IS must question its built-in assumptions to ensure that every aspect of its work relates to the organization's goal. Clearly, the goal of an improved development process is to help the organization through creating systems that increase sales, reduce operating costs, and reduce inventory. The implications of these objectives are both internal and external to IS:

Externally, IS and its users must ensure that the systems being developed on further the goal of the *organization* and deliver the expected benefits.

Internally, IS must ensure its throughput (i.e., the systems coming out of IS) is optimized, its operational expense is minimized, and that there are no unnecessary delays in creating systems (i.e., inventory the company has invested in but has not seen a return on). Some managers have stated this goal as: reducing the 'time to market' on a system request without increasing IS budgets.

IS organizations naturally have other concerns as part of running a satisfactory IS organization. Quality, testing, training, long-term architecture, security and auditability, to name just a few, are important components of system development. A system developed without testing, for example, would not further the organization's goal. However, these cannot be allowed to become goals in and of themselves. The primary goal of the system development process is still to help the company make money. Actions which further this goal are productive; actions which detract from this goal are counter-productive. This single goal should be the over-riding principle guiding IS managers in their assessment of how the system development process can be improved.

CHALLENGING EMBEDDED ASSUMPTIONS

The need to challenge assumptions about what systems are being developed is well-documented in the re-engineering literature (Hammer, 1990; Davenport and Short, 1990). However, very little has been documented about challenging the assumptions of the systems development process itself. IS managers all know that improving the systems development process is neither easy nor straightforward. If it were, they would have done it by now. However, as with any business, IS managers may be holding on to assumptions about systems development which, if examined, may lead to new and more effective methods of developing systems. The rest of this paper challenges ten of these assumptions and suggests how IS productivity might be improved by addressing them.

Assumption 1: The Development Process Begins at Requirements Definition

Different methodologies may call it by different names, but the beginning of the development process is almost always a phase where the users' requirements are outlined, and costs and benefits are refined. Following requirements definition come phases concerned with system design, development and testing, and implementation. Figure 10.1 illustrates a generic model of this process. People involved in IS will no doubt use some variant of this model in their own organizations and will have little difficultly relating their own methodologies to it. When 'improvements' to system development are considered, it is this process that is referred to.

But a user sees the development process very differently. From the time a request for system development is made until the time the user sees something concrete is what he or she means by the development process. They are most concerned with *elapsed time* which includes any delays due to a wait in a prioritization queue. Elapsed time also includes the time spent performing modifications and reprioritization enhancements at the end of the process to accommodate changes that have occurred since the request went into development (see Figure 10.2).

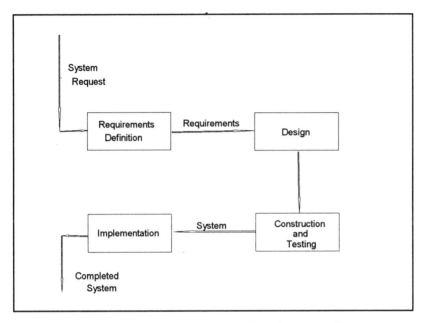

Figure 10.1. *The IS View of the Development Process*

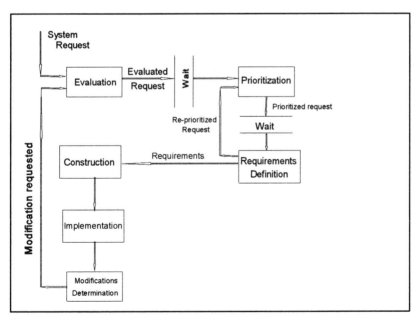

Figure 10.2. *The User View of the Development Process*

When looking for ways to improve the system development process, IS people tend to explore ways to speed up their view of the process. But, from the point of view of the organizational goal, should we not consider the users' view of how systems get developed? If IS' goal is to truly speed up the development process, surely it must consider the total time involved in creating an effective system, including time spent in the front end getting the project started, and time spent at the back end of the traditional development cycle, not simply those activities that IS staff work on. Typically, users understand little about how IS evaluates and prioritizes requests. Often, user requests are poorly researched and documented.

Establishing ways to assist users in preparing system requests may improve their quality and the speed with which they can be evaluated. Similarly, many organizations have prioritization procedures that may not reflect the work that actually gets completed. Aligning prioritization with resource allocation is essential to ensuring that company priorities are paramount in IS' work. At the other end of the process, IS must ensure that valuable function is not cut out of system development in order to meet internal deadlines. All too often IS staff cut function to meet schedules, resulting in ineffective systems and a spate of maintenance requests.

Recommendations for Managers

- To improve the system development process, examine the whole process, not just what IS traditionally calls system development.
- Work with users to clarify and facilitate the evaluation and prioritization processes. By speeding these up, users may feel more satisfied with the overall time to market.
- Identify work that could be done during prioritization and evaluation that would ensure a request's speedy progress through subsequent phases, e.g., better clarification of user needs and organizational impacts so that there are fewer surprises to IS and the organization.
- Evaluate the impact of cutting functions (or moving them to 'Phase 2') on the overall process. This could delay significant system benefits and cause a large number of changes.

Assumption 2: IS Has a Huge Backlog of Work

It is common knowledge in IS that there is a huge backlog of requests for systems. Most IS organizations have queues of many person-years for IS work. Yet if you asked senior IS managers which of the requests in the queue are ready to be worked on if resources were suddenly made available, you would get quite a different answer. In fact, while it is true that many more requests come into IS than staff are able to work on, a significant proportion of these requests will never be worked on because (a) they are not clearly thought out, (b) they are too expensive or would not result in benefits, or (c) other systems already in development will address the problem. Thus, the 'real backlog' in IS is considerably smaller than a simple count of system requests would indicate.

Many organizations have an ineffective or obscure prioritization process. Often, priorities are set annually, but then business changes and unplanned projects occur which affect what is worked on. This creates an environment where the prioritization process has little impact on what actually gets done and where considerable informal lobbying can get projects started even, if they are not on the priority list. This creates confusion over what will get done and when.

Finally, most IS organizations have experienced situations where users simply 'must have' a system but who are unprepared to commit the people and make the decisions necessary to develop the system. Are these systems really ready for development? Will the end product help the company to achieve its goal? Since business expertise is an essential component of effective system development, it would be highly unlikely that it would. Therefore, such systems should not be considered part of IS' backlog.

Recommendations for Managers

- Clarify how the IS 'backlog' is measured and managed to truly evaluate demand for IS services.
- Distinguish between system requests, and evaluated, approved, prioritized system requests. Only the latter should count as backlog.

- Assess the prioritization process and make it truly reflective of the business' priorities. Ideally, the prioritization committee should meet at least quarterly and more frequently if emergencies occur.
- Ensure user commitment to the project is in place before prioritization and that users are aware it is a precondition to IS participation.
- Measure IS productivity and throughput based on the queue of evaluated, prioritized projects (with user commitment) that are completed.

Assumption 3: Users are the Best Judges of What Systems are Most Valuable to the Business

Goldratt and Cox (1984) describe a manufacturing plant where the 'cost per part' measurement increased although the plant's operating costs stayed the same, its inventory reduced, and its throughput increased. The company's productivity manager gave the plant a bad report. This story illustrates how many 'productivity improvements' are actually the result of local optimization which can have a negative impact on a business' bottom line. Such measures do not truly assess a subunit's contribution to the organization. Instead, they assess whether people did their jobs and were fully occupied, and whether they met certain standards of output.

Operational expense cannot be reduced in isolation. For example, trimming a subunit's capacity can have an adverse effect on sales and inventory that is mathematically demonstrable. The objective of productivity is not to optimize an individual subunit, but the organization as a whole.

With systems, many of the same arguments are applicable. A system may reduce costs for a business unit, but may not achieve benefits for the organization as a whole. Systems that perpetuate traditional productivity measures or methods of work may do little to make money for the company. These are the essential arguments behind the work on re-engineering the organization. Therefore, part of evaluating a system must include an assessment of how it will truly contribute to the *overall* goal of the organization, not simply those of a subunit.

Some companies allocate IS resources on the basis of how much money a business unit is willing to spend. This may be an easy way to allocate resources, but it is questionable as to how this strategy will help less profitable business units become profitable. Other organizations do little to encourage joint sponsorship of projects across organizational boundaries. One senior IS manager complains that this promotes short-term thinking and business unit decision-making in isolation. Do these processes truly result in the most effective systems being developed?

Recommendations for Managers

- Ensure that system requests with the maximum value for the organization as a whole get highest priority.
- Challenge system objectives and measures to ensure that true productivity will be improved.
- Promote different methods of resource allocation that reward additional resources to projects with joint sponsors, or discourage resource assignment to divisions with the largest budgets.
- Systems which will reduce operating expenses only should be challenged to prove that they will not affect sales (throughput) or inventory.
- Assess internal IS systems on the same basis as other company systems requests, e.g., what is the business benefit of reusable components?

Assumption 4: IS Throughput Cannot be Improved Once Adequate Resources Have Been Assigned

IS managers have been fond of pointing out that 'nine women cannot make a baby in one month,' by way of highlighting the fact that the process of systems development is a series of dependent activities that cannot be speeded up by adding more people (Brooks, 1975). Thus, in the past IS throughput has been increased by adding resources to enable more projects to be worked on simultaneously (McKeen et al., 1990). But has this assumption obscured some important facets of systems development throughput? Viewing **time** as the critical factor in improving throughput, rather than **cost**, can identify significant opportunities for improving the system development process.

System throughput is dictated by elapsed time, not total effort, as IS managers know. However, what is not always clear is that a significant portion of throughput consists of time waiting, not time working. Time spent waiting—for decisions, for resources, for specialists—could be a significant portion of throughput time on any individual system. Furthermore, if more than one system is waiting for the same valuable resource, that resource could be having a significant impact on IS' total throughput. The mathematical principle of covariance demonstrates that delays caused by such a bottleneck accumulate and result in throughput delays disproportionately greater than the actual delay itself. Identifying and speeding up such bottlenecks could be the most important activity a manager could do to improve IS throughput (Goldratt and Cox, 1984).

Anywhere that work is backlogged in the development process might be an area of improvement:

• Approvals for what to do or what has been done.
• Access to database and other technical specialists.
• Test data production.
• Information about business procedures or technical capabilities.
• Approvals from audit, security, or quality control groups.

Management's objective should be to do all that it can to speed up such bottleneck processes. Perhaps not all projects need to follow the same approval procedures. Perhaps procedures can be streamlined. Are technical specialists bogged down in paperwork? Again, the solutions to these issues are not straightforward or even obvious, but attention to areas where bottlenecks occur can yield some important results in increased throughput—without additional cost.

Recommendations for Managers

- Identify bottlenecks in the development process—anywhere where work must wait for resources.
- Speed up bottleneck processes, e.g., by streamlining, adding resources.
- Maximize throughput, not individual productivity.

Assumption 5: The Traditional SDLC Methodology is the Best Way to Develop Most Systems

Many IS managers feel that systems development life-cycle methodologies (SDLCs) are necessary tools. They argue that as long as an SDLC methodology is applied with common sense, then it is the best way to ensure a quality product. Without it, they contend, business would lose control of the process. But do SDLCs really contribute to the goal of IS? For the last decade, some managers have been questioning this and suggesting two alternative methods of systems development:

Rapid Application Development (RAD or timeboxing). Applications are broken down into small, manageable chunks (of about four months), and developers are given complete control over a project. No formal phases are undertaken, and very little time is spent on management reports or schedules.

Evolutionary Development. An iterative approach to systems development, designed to address the critical problems of clarifying user requirements and throughput. It attempts to deliver usable, albeit incomplete, pieces of systems in a series of short, rapid iterations (of about two to three months).

Both approaches represent a change from the traditional SDLCs still used by many organizations. They break up systems into smaller pieces, gaining additional flexibility and responsiveness to change. Smaller projects are more productive and easily managed, and require fewer management controls or formal processes. Shorter cycles are also more satisfying for users because they feel more involved and in control of the process (Alavi, 1984; Smith, 1986).

Organizations using these approaches caution that they require a change of mindset and new approaches to the user–IS relationship. Developers used to thinking 'big is better,' or who worry that less than optimal solutions will be developed, and users who fear they may never get IS resources if they do not cram all their needs into one request, can sabotage the process. While all managers agree traditional development methodologies work best in some situations, organizations using RAD and evolutionary prototyping have found that these approaches solve many problems with throughput and user satisfaction.

Recommendations for Managers

- Learn about RAD and evolutionary development from organizations using them.
- Establish the architecture as a first step for any projects using these methods.
- Ensure users and developers understand how these processes will affect their work.
- Appoint goal-oriented people who can focus on getting the job done.
- Use only those tools which help the process.
- Manage for results, not the process itself.

Assumption 6: IS Productivity Measures Assess IS Productivity

Typically, IS productivity has been assessed by such measures as: the number of function points delivered, the number of lines of code produced, or the number of projects delivered on time or on budget. Usually, a considerable amount of time and effort is spent preparing and collecting these statistics. While IS managers recognize that these measures are not perfect, they contend that better measures simply are not available and senior management must have a way to control IS expenditures.

Do these measures reflect IS' goal in any way? Consider the measure of number of projects delivered on time and on budget.

As we point out in more detail in Chapter 11, research shows that in organizations where these measures are tracked, project leaders will slash function in order to deliver a project within these parameters, regardless of whether it reduces the benefits of the finished project. Function points too, according to many users, bear little relationship to the benefits of a system request.

IS productivity measures need to reflect two things: how well IT is producing systems, and how beneficial systems are to the organization. There are measures available that do this. Measures of average throughput time for each prioritized request, for example, are straightforward and capture how quickly systems are produced. Benefits achieved, as estimated by the user, can be accumulated or measured against the original project request to determine how the system has contributed to the organizational bottom line. Such a measure can also be computed per IS employee. Other measures, such as revenues per headcount, can be used to compare IS productivity over time (McKeen and Smith, 1993). These types of measures relate closely to what IS is being asked to do for the company and will result in closer attention being paid to facets of development that have direct bearing on company performance.

Recommendations for Managers

- Evaluate all performance measures collected by IS. Determine how they contribute to the overall goal of IS. Consider how they might detract from this goal—either in terms of time spent collecting the data, or in terms of focusing management and staff on the wrong objectives.
- Speak with users regarding how IS performance could better be measured from their perspective.
- Investigate alternative, non-traditional measures that more closely tie to IS' overall goals.

Assumption 7: Productivity Can Best be Improved by Automating Development Activities

Many IS organizations are investing significant amounts of time and money in new system development tools, e.g., CASE tools, fourth generation languages, code generators, in the hopes of dramatically improving system development productivity. In spite of considerable evidence to the contrary, IS managers continue to manage as if technology was the limiting factor in IS productivity (DeMarco and Lister, 1987). Some typical ways IS organizations attempt to improve development productivity include: mechanizing product development, creating standardized procedures, forcing a tradeoff with product quality, and having staff work significant amounts of overtime.

In contrast to this prevailing perspective, DeMarco and Lister believe that the major causes of lost productivity are sociological, not technological. Their book, *Peopleware*, outlines ways to achieve significant performance improvement through more effective ways of handling people, modifying the workplace, and changing the corporate culture. Their 'coding war games' compared programmer productivity across numerous organizations. They found a ten-to-one differential between organizations, not due to language, years of experience, or salary, but as the result of such things as to whether or not the phone could be turned off, how much office space was allocated to an individual, and how many meetings a person had to attend.

DeMarco and Lister recommend 'non-deterministic' approaches to productivity improvement, i.e., instead of managing IS staff to ensure total control, management should enable capable staff to take the actions that make sense for a particular systems project. They criticize methodologies as methods of centralizing thinking that imply staff are not smart enough to do the job. To promote effective working methods, they support such things as training, peer reviews, proven standards, and tools. In short, improved system development comes from looking for factors that allow people to do their best work, not by controlling and limiting how they should work.

Recommendations for Managers

- Identify ways your organization is trying to improve productivity. How many relate to automation of methods? How many are non-technical?
- Examine how much control development staff has over the

development process. Look at the paperwork required, whether a team can adjust its office space, if staff have adequate control over interruptions, and how much control management exerts.

- Identify ways that managers can *help* staff work, rather than *make* staff work.
- Evaluate your methodology. Is it truly flexible? Or are large portions of it compulsory? Consider replacing methodological control with minimum standards and peer reviews.

Assumption 8: Maintenance Should be Minimized to Enable More New System Development

IS managers try to minimize maintenance (i.e., *optional* changes to existing portfolios, *not* error correction or mandated changes) in order to maximize their resources for new systems development. As a result, maintenance is seen as a cost and many IS organizations have rigorously limited this work in the belief that maintenance detracted from the development of larger, more beneficial systems. This has been a major source of frustration to users who often cannot get small, but significant (to them) changes made. Now, some managers are beginning to ask questions about the assumptions on which this principle is based:

- Is maintenance always less beneficial than system development?
- Are current methods of doing maintenance the most effective?
- Can maintenance throughput be improved?

The benefits of maintenance are more immediate and easier to achieve than those of new systems. This makes it harder to make unsubstantiated claims of benefits sometime in the future and means maintenance requests look less glamorous than new systems. However, these benefits are more likely to be achieved, and achieved more quickly and at a lower cost than new system benefits. Maintenance requests may or may not lead to bottom-line improvements. Therefore, like system requests, they must be evaluated on the basis of their contribution to the productivity of the organization overall, and not to local optimums. For requests that pass this test, however, there are good arguments to make maintenance a priority over new systems, notably the likelihood and speed with which the benefits can be achieved relative to the resources invested.

Finally, maintenance throughput needs to be assessed as carefully as other IS throughput. It should not be assumed that the process of evaluating, prioritizing and implementing maintenance requests is unable to be improved. Many of the steps outlined above can be applied to maintenance as well. Particularly important are testing and implementation. Since benefits do not accrue until implemented, the concept of limited system releases should also be challenged. Are releases truly necessary? Could more releases be beneficial? Can testing be improved? A careful look at the process of maintenance may well yield significant results in throughput at no additional cost.

Recommendations for Managers

- Examine your limitations on maintenance. Is beneficial work held up because of limited resources? Are limitations arbitrarily based on industry statistics?
- Consider evaluating maintenance and system requests together, based on the benefits to be achieved versus the cost to develop.
- Assess the maintenance process. Can throughput be improved? Are restrictions on implementation justifiable from a business perspective or for the ease of IS?
- Assess the life-cycle of individual systems to determine an appropriate maintenance strategy. If the system is supporting a growth area, for example, more maintenance may be appropriate.

Assumption 9: Expensive Rebuilding is the Only Way to Upgrade a System Technologically

Most IS organizations must maintain technologically out-of-date systems because redeveloping them merely to upgrade the technology is an extremely expensive proposition. Often, it is only when modifications and the addition of new functions must be limited because a system is technologically unstable, that IS is able to justify redevelopment. While recreating a system's functions and data from scratch may be the ideal, it is the only way to upgrade a system technically. Ricketts (1992) argues that 'information systems renovation' can be equally as effective as rebuilding at a fraction of the cost in time and effort. He defines system renovation as consisting of four steps:

1. **Restructuring**—transforming old source code into new source code, and rationalizing data definitions, using the same technical platform and data access method.
2. **Reverse Engineering**—extracting specifications from existing systems via abstraction and modelling. A system design is extracted from source code and recast as entity-relationship models, data-flow diagrams, structure charts and screen layouts, and stored in CASE repositories.
3. **Transverse Engineering**—transforming derived specifications into specifications designed for a new system via integration of models. This step moves the existing system to another generation of technology.
4. **Forward Engineering**—creating a working system from designed specifications via code generation. The new code can be generated to perform most original functions and new development can begin with a loaded CASE repository instead of an empty one.

In contrast to a traditional system life-cycle project, Ricketts believes that renovation can be accomplished in less than half the time and effort (see Figure 10.3).[1] He also notes that while the steps must be completed in sequence, they do not all have to be completed in order for benefits to be gained. Restructuring results in greatly improved technical quality and is also quick and well supported. Reverse engineering is longer and more costly, but results in modest technical and functional gains. Transverse engineering greatly improves both functional

---

[1] Both Ricketts and some IS managers have pointed out that the tools for use in system renovation still leave much to be desired.

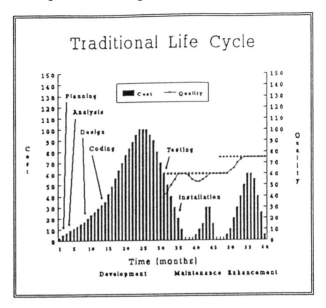

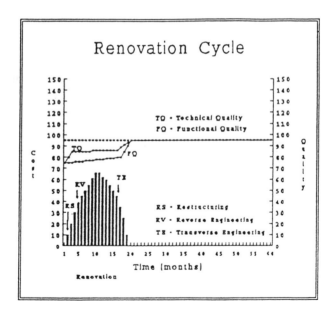

Figure 10.3. *The Traditional and Renovation Life Cycles*
(After Ricketts (1990), reproduced by permission of Irwin at MHLG Inc Co)

and technical quality. Taken together, these three steps form a ladder that enable systems to be developed using forward engineering principles.

Recommendations for Managers

- Investigate the system renovation process as a substitute for expensive redevelopment.
- Use inexpensive restructuring to gain technological improvements and enable new function, to be added without putting an existing system in jeopardy.

Assumption 10: Systems Consist of Inputs, Processes, and Outputs

A final assumption that needs to be explored in order to improve the system development process is the nature of systems themselves. Traditional systems theory states that systems consist of inputs, processes, and outputs. But newer theories suggest that we may be better off to do away with the concept of a 'system' altogether, because it encourages tying data and processes together. Why not conceive of 'data management' as one form of IS work and transaction processing as another?

Looked at from this perspective, IS work becomes an exercise in assembling the appropriate components to fulfil a user need. IS' responsibilities would include establishing certain components of the infrastructure (e.g., security) and ensuring consistency of presentation. IS' technical objective would be to achieve interchangeability of access across platforms. Its business objective would be to empower users with tools to extract, process, and manipulate the data needed to do their job. The ultimate goal would be to simplify system assembly through such things as object-oriented techniques until many user needs can be addressed in a matter of minutes rather than months.

How can this perspective be used to improve the system development process today? Changing the way 'systems' are viewed will encourage IS staff to develop data and transactions for the organization, not for individual business units. From a technical point of view, adopting interchangeability of access and consistency of presentation as standards now will further this goal, with minimal impact on throughput. Finally, viewing process building as the least significant element of IS work will discourage the hand-crafting of transaction processes where-ever these can be assembled with pre-built pieces.

Recommendations for Managers

• Separate data management from processes as much as possible.
• Encourage users to jointly sponsor data files.
• Adopt standards for accessing data from multiple platforms and to ensure consistency of presentation.
• Encourage IS staff to look for less expensive ways to process data than programming transactions themselves.
• Provide consulting and technical support for users to enable them to manipulate data for individual business units.
• Encourage system renovation (see above) as first steps towards a 'systemless' organization.

CONCLUSION

This chapter has examined ten common assumptions about system development with an eye to improving how the system development process delivers to the organization. It was designed to challenge the thinking of IS managers, rather than to be a blueprint for change. Not every idea outlined here will be useful in every organization, nor will every idea bear fruit if implemented. Most will not be easy to implement. (It is hoped by now that IS managers will have learned that there are no 'silver bullets' in system development.) Nevertheless, these ideas are worth your serious consideration as opportunities to develop an IS organization that is much more closely aligned with and supportive of business than it is today and has been in the past.

Some common themes have been developed throughout this chapter. First, focus on activities that bring IS closer to the basic goals of the organization. Never forget that businesses are in business to make money. Other goals can only be realized if this main goal is being achieved. IS is responsible for helping business realize this goal. Second, IS must continue to question assumptions about what it does and what is important. Often, IS managers 'go with the flow' in the industry rather than questioning if something is good for their organization. Third, IS must work to develop and use meaningful measures to evaluate the work it is asked to do. These need not and should not be complex. Beware of measuring something that does not contribute to the goals of the organization. Finally, IS must use tools where appropriate but only where they make sense. New technology should not be adopted for its own sake but because it can improve on what IS can deliver to the organization.

11
System Development Tools: Do They Make a Difference?

INTRODUCTION

Over the last 20 years, a wide variety of information systems tools have been introduced into organizations with the promise of vastly improving system development and maintenance. These products have been touted to Information Systems management as having the ability to (a) improve system flexibility and maintainability, (b) improve systems development productivity, (c) develop more effective or strategic systems, or (d) all of the above. Yet, 20 years later, observing the numerous circulars and sales pitches still arriving from consulting firms—each promising a tool or a technique that will solve system development's problems—one cannot help asking: Do these tools really work? Have they really delivered on their promises? What about the 'magic answers' being sold today? Are they worth the money and the effort?

To help put the issue of system development tools and their impact on systems development into perspective, Forum members discussed the tools, techniques and strategies that their organizations had pursued and were pursuing in the attempt to develop better systems. It was clear that each organization, although different in many ways, used remarkably similar tools and techniques in system development. Also, each had similar hopes for the system development tools of the future: productivity was going to improve dramatically, maintenance was going to be sub-stantially reduced, and systems were going to be more in-keeping with the needs of the business.

What was notably *absent* in the discussion, however, was the bottom-line impact each of these tools has had and is having. Is IS delivering better quality systems as a result of these tools? Are they providing a better service to the users? Are systems cheaper to maintain and more bug free? Do they result in greater dollar savings to the organization? While no one suggested that the tools currently used in system development have not contributed in some fashion to such an 'IS Bottom Line,' it is also clear that system development, as currently practised, is still experiencing significant problems in achieving recognizable results in these areas.

PROMISES, PROMISES . . . AND DELIVERABLES

A variety of tools and techniques have been widely adopted by IS organizations. Each, in turn, has been promoted as having a significant impact on system development. While these tools, in varying degrees have delivered benefits to IS, their 'bottom-line' impact has been nowhere near what their purveyors promised. The list below assesses what they promised and what they have delivered.

Structured Tools (including structured programming, structured design, structured analysis, structured walk-throughs). These tools were among the first adopted by IS to improve system development. Essentially, they involve organizing the development activities using a series of diagrams and following certain 'top-down' principles to ensure that pieces of systems fit together.

- **What they promised:** ease of maintenance, self-documenting systems, more bug-free systems, and systems that addressed user requirements more effectively.

- **What they delivered:** these tools imposed order on the then chaotic processes of requirements definition, system design and programming, thus eliminating the horrors of 'spaghetti code' and enabling the development and testing of significantly more complex systems. Maintenance too, is easier using structured techniques. However, in spite of these benefits, structured techniques did not lead to the dramatic improvements in maintenance, documentation or user satisfaction that were promised.

System Development Methodologies. When the limitations of structured techniques became apparent, organizations began to structure the system development process itself. Methodologies are step-by-step guides on developing systems from beginning to end. The life-cycle methodology has been most popular and consists of a series of phases with activities, documentation, responsibilities and sign-offs for each phase.

- **What they promised:** better requirements definition, fewer system changes, more effective system development, greater user participation, and better documented systems.

- **What they delivered:** the use of methodologies has resulted in a better understanding of the system development process and the need to define requirements before beginning programming. Methodologies also introduced checkpoints in the development process when a system could be evaluated and cancelled or redirected.

Unfortunately, most methodologies also require large amounts of paperwork and formal bureaucratic procedures which tend to bog the development process down and rigidify thought processes. One IS manager has described formal methodologies as 'a licence to stop thinking.' The degree of user participation and the effectiveness of the systems developed still tends to be a function of the people involved and their skills, rather than the use of a methodology *per se.* While methodologies result in large amounts of documentation being produced, this is mostly useless as soon as a phase is completed and does not result in a better documented system for maintenance purposes.

The net result of methodology use has been more carefully controlled systems that take considerably longer to deliver. While most companies would not want to be without some form of methodology, few would agree that methodologies are the panacea for system development ills that was promised.

Data-oriented Tools (including data modelling, data dictionaries). These tools focus on the data used by the system development process. Data modelling is a way of identifying the individual data elements and groups of elements used by business processes. A data dictionary is a repository for this information.

- **What they promised:** simplification of the system development process by removing the analysis of data from the analysis of a system, simplification of maintenance, the ability to specify requirements more easily, and uniformity among systems to facilitate integration.

- **What they delivered:** data-driven techniques enable a different perspective on user needs and help to identify duplicate pieces of data. Separation of data from requirements analysis has indeed simplified the requirements analysis process, but has added an additional layer of complexity and documentation through the data analysis process. While systems managers feel that data-driven techniques have improved the individual system development process, albeit at a cost, there have been no discernible benefits from using data analysis techniques at the corporate level. Overall, it is unclear whether the payback from data-driven techniques has been worth the investment of time and effort required.

User-oriented Tools (business modelling, joint application development (JAD), end-user computing). These tools emphasize the user's role in system development and encourage the user to understand his or her business requirements better, participate more effectively in the development process, and/or develop systems themselves with end-user tools.

- **What they promised:** a closer fit between business needs and the systems designed to serve them, more effective systems, fewer system changes, reduced maintenance.

- **What they delivered:** while some users have 'found a niche' in end-user computing, resulting in some very effective user-developed systems, in general, user-oriented tools have had some mixed results. In some IS communities, JAD sessions have lost favour since they often resulted in impractical solutions and huge user wish lists. Other IS organizations find them useful as a means of making users prioritize their requirements. Business modelling, after an initial flurry of enthusiasm, has rapidly come to be viewed as yet another layer of IS bureaucracy. Users quickly become frustrated when their models cannot be turned immediately into systems. Models themselves become out of date rapidly and often require additional staff to document and maintain. While some user-driven approaches appear to be working well in some organizations, user-oriented tools such as business modelling and JAD require substantial management support and overheads from both users and IS. As a result, many organizations feel the benefits obtained from these tools have not been worth the costs.

CASE Tools (e.g., code generators, design aids, documentation aids, reusable code) have been on the market for several years and are designed to make system developers more productive. CASE tools assist the developer to trace system and data flows, to create programs from 'structured' language, and to enable certain generic programs (e.g., 'READ' modules) to be used by a variety of programs.

- **What they promise:** enhanced developer productivity, a substantial reduction in development time, and improved system documentation.

- **What they deliver:** at present, CASE tools appear to be most effective in generating certain forms of system documentation (e.g., data flow diagrams)—usually the documentation required by other system development tools!

Some organizations also use their code generating features, particularly to assist prototyping, if this is done. However, although they were designed to eliminate overhead, CASE tools require a substantial investment of developer time to learn, thus creating significant overheads to their own use. CASE tools have enormous potential, but there is general agreement that they are not being fully exploited in system development today. If they can be used to eliminate hand-offs and prevent duplication of effort, CASE tools may yet live up to the promises being made for them. However, in many organizations, CASE tools add complexity and eliminate very few developer activities, thus resulting in limited productivity gains at present.

Object-oriented Tools (object-oriented analysis, design and programming) These tools attempt to combine the best attributes of both structured and data-oriented tools. The basic unit is the 'object' which encapsulates both the data descriptions (or attributes) and the operations that apply to it. Object-oriented tools are just becoming available to IS departments.

- **What they promise:** better analysis of requirements, substantially enhanced developer productivity, elimination or reduction of the systems design phase, improved system documentation, reusable code.

- **What they deliver:** while there are great hopes for object-oriented technologies, they are not widely used in IS departments at present. Chapter 12 takes a more in-depth look at OO technology and what organizations can realistically expect from its implementation.

To suggest that system development tools such as structured techniques or methodologies have made no difference to the systems being developed would be untrue. Certainly, systems are better organized and documented than they were in the past. It is equally true, however, that the tools have not fulfilled their promises of vast improvements in productivity and the quality of systems. With each of these tools have come a set of overheads, costs, and hand-offs that also contribute to many of the problems that plague IS departments everywhere: bureaucracy, poor communication, high development costs, schedule and budget overruns, etc. This fact appears to be poorly understood by many IS managers when the tools are adopted. As a result, disappointment with existing system development tools is widespread (Wang, 1991) and business continues to boom for purveyors of new 'magic answers' to the problems of system development.

IMPROVING THE 'INFORMATION SYSTEMS BOTTOM LINE'

If there were an 'IS bottom line,' it would be based on how well and how quickly IS can deliver effective, high quality systems. Most managers agree that IS could and should be working to improve its bottom line; hence, the ongoing search for better system development tools. Improving bottom-line results means doing a better job of selecting the 'right' systems to develop, increasing system development productivity, and doing every aspect of the job better (from identifying requirements to design and programming through to implementation).

Today, it is recognized that system development is a very complex process combining a large number of technical and organizational components to create a computerized process that supports and assists the people working in an organization. There is also an increasing understanding among business and IS professionals that information systems cannot be deployed effectively unless supporting changes occur within the organization. Michael Hammer (1991) notes that information systems are just one component of effective organizational change. Without the business processes, management processes, organization, and beliefs and norms, and without support from the corporate culture, information systems will not be accepted in the organization or have the desired impact (see Figure 11.1). In fact, it is unlikely that the most appropriate systems will even be selected. To be truly effective, systems development cannot be viewed in isolation.

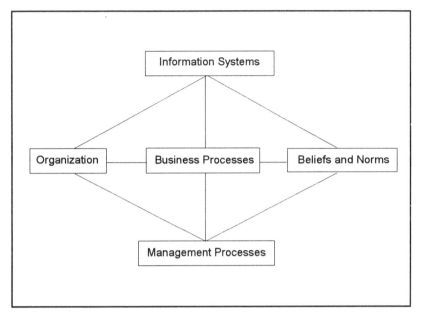

Figure 11.1. *The Components of Effective*
Organizational Change
(After *Hammer Forum* (1991),
reproduced by permission of Dr. Michael Hammer (Harper Business))

Just as IS cannot be effective in isolation in the organization, so technical practices (such as identifying data, determining functional requirements, or designing and programming systems) cannot have a significant impact on the IS bottom line in and of themselves. These technical practices are *only one* component of effective system development (see Figure 11.2). Yet the system development tools currently in use attempt to gain their 'leverage' by addressing only this component of system development. Because of this, it is not surprising that their impact on the IS bottom line has been limited. Until practices and tools are developed that address the total system development process, it will be unlikely that we will see the kind of quantum leap in systems productivity or effectiveness that we have been told are possible.

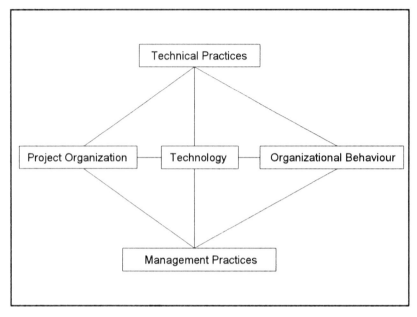

Figure 11.2. *The Components of Effective System Development*
(Adapted from *Hammer Forum* (1991),
reproduced by permission of Dr. Michael Hammer (Harper Business))

SYSTEM DEVELOPMENT THAT WORKS

While there is uncertainty about the impact of most current system development tools on the IS bottom line, members of the focus group agreed that certain things really *did* work to improve system development, sometimes substantially. Not surprisingly, many of these affect components of system development other than technical practices, as explained below.

Project Organization

- **Team Size:** The system development teams that work most productively are generally small—no more than two to six people—and wellmatched to ensure they can work together and have a complementary balance of skills. One manager noted that a project estimated as taking 500 personmonths was completed in 90 personmonths by such a team. It was suggested that the effectiveness of such teams may be due to improved communication and to the reduced number of 'hand-offs' between team members. The startling success of small teams compared with large teams highlights the fact that much of the important information required for system development may not be the kind that is documented by our currently available tools.

- **Project Size:** System development projects that work are generally small as well. IBM studies have shown that there is a 10–20 fold productivity difference between small projects (of about ten function points) and large projects (around 200 function points) (Agrawal, 1991). Managers have known for years that small systems are more easily 'visualized' by developers and users, that the risks involved are smaller, and that these projects are simply easier to manage. Unfortunately, current system development practices tend to push IS to 'redevelop the world,' leading to large, high-risk projects that are often ineffective when finally complete.

Management Practices

- **Authority:** Productive and effective system development teams are those that have the authority to make the business and technical decisions required to develop and implement the job. Today, many productive hours are wasted by the laborious decision-making processes that are currently imposed on system development teams. Naturally, it is substantially easier to grant such authority on smaller projects where there is less risk, than on bigger ones.

- **Support:** Effective teams are those that are fully supported by their management. All too often, projects are confronted by roadblocks of a technical, organizational or political nature that can cause them to lose momentum and direction. Management practices that ensure that roadblocks do not appear or are quickly removed enable greater productivity.

Furthermore, the most productive teams have the fewest distractions in terms of day-to-day 'administrivia.' Effective management support minimizes any activity that takes attention away from the task at hand.

Organizational Behaviour

• **Vision:** Michael Hammer (1991) notes that all of the tools and techniques we use are no substitute for an effective vision of how things *should* happen. Business modelling and 'top-down' procedures designed to help IS to understand business processes and data can act as a 'strait-jacket' that locks in an existing view of the business preventing useful but revolutionary ideas from emerging. Effective systems solutions arise, not from process models, but from clear visions, that are carefully articulated and followed through.

• **Visualizing:** It remains a common truth that if users and developers can clearly visualize a system and its impact before it is developed, then fewer changes will occur, users will be better prepared for implementation, and roadblocks can be identified and addressed earlier. The best means currently available for visualizing is prototyping (sometimes called evolutionary system development) which has been consistently proven to lead to more effective systems, more satisfied users, and fewer system errors (Cerveny, 1986). Yet very few organizations have adopted prototyping in any significant way, possibly because these techniques fit so poorly with other system development practices, such as methodologies and structured techniques and because they require more proactive user involvement in the development process.

Technical Practices

• **Documentation:** The system development tools available today largely address technical practices involved in determining system requirements, identifying data, designing, programming and testing system solutions, and documenting them. As more and more tools have been introduced into technical practice, the overhead work required for documentation and to communicate the work that has been done has become a major drawback to system development productivity. Current tools rely heavily on text documentation, which is ambiguous communication at best, and are so poorly integrated that documentation produced with one tool does not 'talk' with documentation produced by another. Because of these considerable documentation headaches, development productivity is reduced and maintenance has become an increasingly expensive task in IS.

Some organizations are beginning to see a significant productivity increase in system maintenance through the use of 'application repositories,' which are essentially data bases that describe the programs and data used in systems. These repositories enable a comprehensive impact analysis of a proposed change to be completed that specifies the programs and data that would be affected. Not only do such repositories save considerable analysis time, they also ensure system quality while reducing the need for integration testing.

- **Reduced Hand-offs:** Many companies believe that the current large number of 'hand-offs' of work between IS staff on a typical system development project seriously impairs communication between team members and thus, substantially reduces productivity. They are investigating ways that technology can be used to reduce hand-offs so that large development teams can experience the productivity gains of smaller projects. One way to do this is to integrate the technical tools currently available for modelling, design, and development. Documentation could then be entered into an application data base thus resulting in a substantial reduction of hand-offs and improved communication.

RECOMMENDATIONS FOR MANAGERS

Managers who wish to improve the performance of their information systems organizations should undertake to do the following:

1. Stop looking for a single 'magic answer' to dramatically improve system development productivity.

2. Evaluate how your organization addresses each component of the system development process including, project organization, management practice, organizational behaviour, and technical practice.

3. Consider ways to implement techniques that have been shown to work well in each component (see above). This *may* include the implementation of new tools, but more likely will involve changing the way things are currently done.

4. Investigate tools that will **support and facilitate** effectiveness in each component of system development.

5. Build a repository of applications and the data they use.

6. Look for tools that will **integrate and synchronize** documentation from the various phases of system development rather than adding another layer of documentation to the development process.

7. Look for ways to eliminate hand-offs and to improve communication in all aspects of information systems management.

CONCLUSION

Over the last 20 years, IS managers have continually searched for tools that would have a dramatic impact on the 'IS bottom line' in the form of improved productivity, more effective systems, and better quality systems. While a wide variety of such tools have been acquired by IS departments, most have delivered significantly less than was advertised and the search for better tools is ongoing. While many IS managers remain confident that the panacea to system development problems is just around the corner, some are beginning to question whether *any* change in technical practice will have the desired impact.

This is because technical practice is just one component of the complex process of systems development.

Current management thinking suggests that effective systems development results from a concatenation of management practices, project organization, and organizational behaviour with technical practices. Although there is evidence that certain types of organization, management, and behaviour can yield substantial results, relatively little attention has been paid to these components of system development. Instead, companies continue to spend time and money in a desperate search for tools to improve technical practice in the hope they will yield the desired bottom-line impact. While we do not suggest that the use of current system development tools in technical practice has been a failure, we believe that their impact in IS will be limited as long as the other components of system development remain under-addressed.

12

Object-Oriented Technology: Getting Beyond the Hype

INTRODUCTION

These days, everyone in the Information Systems world is talking about object-oriented technology—known as 'OO' to its afficionados. The enthusiasm about OO has even reached the mainstream press and executives are hearing success stories about dramatic productivity gains and 'programming with lego blocks' (Hammonds, 1991). Within IS, some people are talking about an OO 'revolution' that will dramatically change how IS does its work and which has the potential to eliminate or significantly reduce IS staff.

All this hype is putting IS managers under pressure to get on the OO bandwagon. Once again, managers are being asked to make critical decisions about an unproven technology. On one hand, IS is actively looking for new ways of improving its quality and productivity. On the other, managers know from bitter experience the problems and costs of introducing a new technology. This chapter attempts to look critically at the current state of OO technology, beyond the hype, to identify the issues managers must face in making decisions about using it in their organizations.

In order to explore and assess what IS organizations are doing with OO technology, Forum members discussed their current encounters with OO, the benefits and problems they had experienced, and other issues surrounding the introduction of OO technology in their organizations. The chapter first gives a brief overview of OO technology and its relationship to other IS technologies. It then evaluates the key benefits and problems organizations can expect in introducing and using OO. Finally, it attempts to answer some key questions about how and when to introduce OO in an organization.

WHAT IS OO TECHNOLOGY?

'Object-oriented technology' is actually a fairly broad term encompassing several different tools and techniques that all share a common perspective (Kay, 1993; Sprague and McNurlin, 1993). This common perspective focuses on an 'object'—which is another name for a person, place or thing—such as a customer, a store, or a sales transaction. Objects consist of information about themselves plus all of the processing associated with that object (e.g., all the information about a customer and how to update it). Objects communicate with other objects by sending messages back and forth to each other (e.g., a 'sales transaction' can ask a 'customer' to check its credit status).

Unlike traditional data processing, where 'data' (in files) are separate from 'processing' (in programs), in OO technology, information about an object and how that information is to be processed are kept strictly together and separated from everything else (i.e., other objects). For example, a customer object would contain all information about a customer and all the processing necessary to check or change that information.

At present, OO technology consists largely of OO programming languages for creating systems using objects. Anyone who has ever used their mouse to take a 'letter' and dump it in the 'trash' on their PC is actually doing simple OO programming. In contrast, procedural programming, used by most IS professionals, requires the programmer to request the computer to do something to a file, e.g., DELETE C:\JONES.LET. OO programming is already the primary method of programming for the PC, while procedural programming remains the dominant method for developing mainframe systems.

Other components of OO technology will eventually include OO design and OO analysis. These are techniques to enable more complex applications using objects to be developed in a consistent and coordinated fashion. CASE (computer-assisted software engineering) tools for objects and object storage bases are also under development. None of these tools and techniques are fully developed as yet. However, when available, each will involve new ways of thinking and working that are considerably different from the procedural tools now in use. Unlike other new technologies of the past, OO technology will affect not only how IS professionals work, but also how managers do their jobs.

Thus, OO technology is a deceptively simple change of focus that has enormous implications for how IS work is done:

- OO technology will focus IS attention on real things that exist in business, rather than on records and programs that have been artificially created to reflect a partial view of the organization. For example, a customer is a customer to all applications, rather than a credit rating, a name and address, and a purchasing record to different programs.

- It means that building new applications will become considerably easier. New programs will simply reuse existing objects with minor modifications. For example, the programming required to introduce a new financial product could use existing customer and sales transaction objects, creating only a new object for the product. This new object may be very similar to a group of financial product objects already in use, and may require only minor modifications to create.

- The ability to reuse objects will improve productivity and quality dramatically since systems do not have to be built from scratch each time. Using objects as the building blocks of a system will mean less coding and therefore less testing.

- Modifications will also become considerably easier since a change to an object will be known immediately by all the systems that use that object. For example, when a new way of calculating sales tax is added to the sales transaction object, all systems using sales transactions are automatically modified. Using current data processing techniques, sales tax could be calculated in many different programs, all of which would have to be changed and tested.

But OO technology is more than a new method of developing systems. It is also a powerful agent of change within IS and, potentially, in the business itself. One CIO described OO technology as 'a Trojan horse that lets you make organizational and cultural changes and impose discipline under the guise of adopting a new development approach.' (Deyo and Gillach, 1993.) A Forum member noted that 'OO is really a code word for the re-engineering of IS.'

OO technology introduces new roles, methods and deliverables for IS management and staff. Organizations that have implemented OO technology have found that they can reduce IS staff by at least 30% because programming and maintenance time is reduced. Within the IS industry, technology gurus are predicting that OO technology will do for software what the microchip did for hardware, i.e., change the economics of the business by factors of ten. All of these changes, while poorly defined at present, mean that OO technology has the potential to be more than a mere technical improvement.

OO TECHNOLOGY IN PERSPECTIVE

The impact of OO technology on IS and on the larger organization will be determined by how and when OO technology is introduced and the decisions that are made about it. In order to make effective OO decisions, managers need to clearly understand how OO relates to other technologies they may be using in their organizations.

Personal Computers/Client Server. PC and client server technology is often seen as being inextricably mixed with OO technology because, as noted above, OO programming *is* the dominant form of programming for the PC. The GUI (graphical user interface) screens business people love to use are developed using OO technology. PC–C/S technology can be implemented without moving to OO technology through using pre-programmed, off-the-shelf software (e.g., spreadsheets) and links to mainframe applications (e.g., E-mail). However, if an organization wishes to develop graphical interfaces for their own systems or to create applications for a PC network, it will need to develop expertise in OO techniques. Thus, PCs are often the 'front door' through which OO technology is introduced to the organization.

Mainframe Systems. By contrast, it is often believed that it is not possible or practical to implement OO technology on a mainframe. This is largely because current OO programming languages are designed for workstation applications rather than mainframe applications. Actually, it is possible to program using objects without a special language, but this is not practical for most organizations because the majority of programmers need the discipline of OO tools and techniques. However, once OO COBOL is widely available, it will become considerably easier to use OO technology for mainframe applications.

Reuse. One of the benefits of OO technology is that it facilitates reuse and therefore enhances productivity. But it is possible to obtain the benefits of reuse without implementing OO technology. Tools based on Bassett Frames (e.g., Netron/CAP) (Bassett, 1990), for example, introduce many of the benefits and disciplines of reuse without the use of objects. Such tools can be used with existing mainframe languages and require considerably less training for programmers to use effectively than OO technology. Managers looking for the benefits of reuse do not, therefore, have to move to OO technology to get them.

Development Techniques. Current development techniques, which include: structured analysis, design and programming, CASE tools, and data design, make many assumptions about system development which have their basis in procedural thinking, rather than object thinking. For example, they assume that data and processing will be separate and that processing will take place in a step-by-step fashion (e.g., first the order number must be entered, then the colour, and then the price). System design techniques must be developed for objects that eliminate these assumptions while retaining the benefits that formal techniques bring to development. At present, with the exception of enterprise data-modelling, most current development techniques are inconsistent with OO technology and new techniques for OO are not highly developed or widely available (Yourdon, 1993).

The incompatibility of current development techniques and OO technology has two major implications. First, it means that such OO projects as an organization does undertake will probably be designed and developed outside current standards and practices. Second, it illustrates the difficulties of training IS staff in OO technology. With OO, not only does the programming language change, but so do almost all of the methods of working that the IS industry has so diligently developed over the past 20 years.

Prototyping/Rapid Development. Most OO applications are developed using prototyping and OO technology facilitates this kind of system development because of its focus on business objects and reuse. However, prototyping is supported by a wide variety of other development technologies including frames, CASE, and relational data bases, as well as specific prototyping tools, such as screen painters. While prototyping in OO technology is relatively simple and straightforward, it actually masks a much larger amount of work that must be done before prototyping can take place, i.e., defining a library of objects.

THE BOTTOM LINE ON OO TECHNOLOGY

The reality of OO technology is something considerably less than vendors and the media have led managers to expect. It is not a 'silver bullet' that will make all IS problems magically disappear. However, it is not a mirage either. OO technology has the potential to deliver much benefit to an organization, if managers understand what they are getting into and can address the weaknesses and problems that come with it. This section addresses the key strengths and problems of this technology.

Strengths of OO Technology

- **A sound academic basis.** OO technology comes with a solid scientific pedigree. Unlike fourth-generation languages and other IS innovations that have never quite taken off, OO technology is based on sound theoretical principles. The practical benefit of this is that academic research provides the necessary support to develop and improve the technology. In contrast, fourth-generation languages were developed by the commercial sector and were largely ignored by the academic community.

- **Flexibility and ease of modification.** The traits of OO technology make system development and maintenance considerably easier than with traditional procedural programs. For example, being able to change an object only once and have that change reflected in all applications where that object is used means that fewer hours must be spent poring over old program listings and testing to make sure changes did not disrupt something else. Similarly, once object libraries have been created, much new development consists of moving objects around in different configurations. For example, many Nintendo games are developed in this way. It is relatively simple to change the 'bad guy' from a dragon to a space invader simply by changing the image on the screen and not the underlying code. Finally, the ability of objects to pass messages back and forth means that different objects can respond in different ways to the same message. Thus, a 'bomb' dropped on one kind of bad guy might do something different than a bomb dropped on another kind of bad guy. Once these objects are created it is relatively straightforward to vary the scenarios and the results.

  All of these traits mean that OO systems are more flexible than procedural systems. Traditional systems managers are often amazed and users delighted at how quickly a change can be made to a system. These features of OO technology make it highly attractive to both users and IS professionals.

- **Supports complexity.** The ability to reuse many components of systems enables software developers to create increasingly complex systems with greater and greater assurance that it will work. Paul Bassett notes: 'a civil engineer would start the design process with a choice of models . . . and adapt these to the specifics of a given bridge. And he would take for granted most of the thousands of details that have already been worked out in the past which he can trust will enable his bridge not to fall down . . .' (Bassett, 1990). This is what software engineers are aiming for with reuse strategies and OO technology is a key way to promote reuse. Complexity is facilitated because objects are predesigned and pretested and need not be reinvented from scratch each time. As experience with objects and their reuse grows, it is expected that this technology will prove to be much more able to reflect increasingly complex and highly interactive applications (Deyo and Gillach, 1993).

- **Supports GUI.** The ability to use graphics in user applications is more than just a technological nicety. Graphical interfaces enable humans to perform increasingly complex tasks with computers because they make it easier for users to do a wider variety of transactions. Typically, humans can only remember a limited number of procedural commands, e.g., 'Delete,' 'Move,' 'Copy.' This number is further reduced when different computer applications use different methods to accomplish the same thing, e.g., 'Del,' '/D,' 'F7' etc. Graphics mean that the user does not have to remember these codes since icons guide them to the appropriate actions.

  GUI also means that every possible transaction does not have to be preprogrammed by an IS professional. For example, rather than predetermining all the different sorts of deletions a user might wish to do, OO technology can enable a user to combine graphical transactions in a wide variety of ways, e.g., a 'trash can' can be used for all sorts of deletions. A user using graphical objects can therefore actually accomplish a variety of functions that were not specifically designed by an IS professional, thus encouraging much wider uses of technology than are enabled using procedural technology.

- **Improves productivity.** Early experiences with OO techno-logy suggest that applications can be created faster and with higher quality using objects. EDS believes that it can develop systems in two-thirds of the time and cost of traditionally developed systems, even factoring in the costs of training staff in the new techniques (Cappello). Other companies have experienced similar productivity improve-ments (Hammonds, 1991). However, it should be noted that productivity improvements are a long-term benefit of this technology. In the short term, productivity actually falls as staff learn new skills (see below).

- **Supports change.** Because OO technology requires IS pro-fessionals to think and work in such different ways, its implementation can be the catalyst for senior IS managers to take stock and re-engineer their organizations. New skill re-quirements and job descriptions can lead to new methods of evaluation and remuneration for example. They can also help IS management to introduce standards and disciplines, and new team philosophies. The changes involved may mean that many existing staff cannot adapt and will leave, resulting in opportunities to reduce or reconfigure IS staffing. While such changes are disruptive, most IS managers believe that the next decade will see many of these things come to pass whether they like it or not. The introduction of OO techno-logy makes it more imperative to change and therefore easier to implement.

Drawbacks of OO Technology

- **Lack of tools and techniques.** One of the key drawbacks of OO technology at present is the limited number of tools available to support it. While OO programming languages have been developed (notably, Smalltalk and C++), OO design and analysis techniques are simply not available. The same is true of CASE for objects, for object bases and object libraries, as well as mainframe programming languages and development methodologies. While the lack of such tools and techniques has not stopped the introduction of OO technology or its use by determined advocates, it does make it difficult for OO technology to expand to become the dominant form of the technology. For organizations considering investing in OO technology, the risks of OO not becoming the dominant technology are substantial (Fichman and Kemerer, 1993). Thus, a significant weakness of OO technology at present is the lack of complementary products and techniques available.

This lack also means that companies choosing OO technology must invent their own standards, tools and practices. For example, Kash and Karry Supermarkets (Cappello) had to create their own language, technical architecture, and data bases. Not only does this represent a substantial overhead cost to the organization, it may also put the organization at risk when new industry standards are developed which the organization does not meet.

Finally, the lack of tools and techniques puts the development process at risk. Current procedural tools have evolved out of 20 or more years of experience with computer technology and they provide good support to the professionals using them. By moving into a world where such tools and techniques do not exist, the organization is again putting itself in the control of a few specialists of varying talents and abilities. This is a risk that many organizations may not wish to take at present.

- **High learning curve.** OO technology represents a major change in IS work. In order to achieve the benefits associated with this change, IS organizations must train their staff in the use of this technology. But training is just the beginning. As Page-Jones notes (Yourdon, 1993), attending a course does not make someone an expert in a new technology. After training, people need considerable experience in using it to become journeymen and ultimately experts. King Walling of EDS estimates that it takes about two months of 1:2 mentoring for a trained person to become useful on a project and about six more months until he/she becomes competent

(Cappello). Other business people have found it difficult or impossible to turn procedural IS professionals into OO specialists. The cost of initial training (which can run from between $15,000 to $35,000 per person), 50% overhead in project staff (due to mentoring), and the risk that for some, training may not 'take' all add up to a significant downside to OO technology at present which any organization would be well advised to consider in its technology planning.

- **High costs.** The transition to OO technology is expensive. One organization estimated that its MIS budgets increased by 35% (Cappello). There were six components of these costs:

    1. **Ongoing costs.** These included the costs of maintaining existing systems.
    2. **Cost of new technology.** There were new tools to support the new development environment, the design and modelling of enterprise information, costs associated with ensuring applications were portable between different hardware, costs of developing vendor-independent applications, and the cost of fixing bugs that were distributed throughout systems because of the new technology.
    3. **Productivity of IS.** While productivity should eventually increase with OO technology, initially it goes down. At first, much time is spent creating and testing objects. One estimate is that for every hour spent developing an object, an additional two hours are spent making it reusable. Until enough objects are created to support reusability, productivity may actually be lower than with procedural technology.
    4. **Steep learning curve.** As noted above, even with substantial training, many procedural programmers will take a long time to become proficient in OO techniques.
    5. **Hidden costs.** The transition to OO technologies will involve user departments as well. Often there are major IS costs hidden in the budgets of these departments—either in technology or expert users.
    6. **Salvage costs.** These are the costs involved with eliminating PCs and replacing them with the higher cost work stations required by OO applications.

- **Lack of objects.** When a company decides to move to OO technology, it must first develop a library of objects to use. Creating and building objects requires an intensive effort to develop an information architecture at the enterprise level, from which objects can be created. Objects must then be developed and tested extensively to ensure their reusability. Finally, formal libraries must be established and maintained to ensure easy access to existing objects. None of these is a trivial task. Taken together, they can represent a formidable barrier to the adoption of this technology. While some prepackaged objects are available for purchase, most of these are technical in nature (e.g., Print objects) and do not relate to specific business needs.

- **Lack of metrics.** Not only IS staff, but IS managers too, have a great deal to learn when it comes to OO technology. One experienced manager complained that he lacked a 'gut feel' with OO projects and had no idea what to expect with them. For instance, changes he thought would be serious setbacks to the project, were fairly simple to make. On the other hand, most OO experts stress that OO projects take considerably more 'front end' time than traditional projects—often making traditional managers extremely anxious because it takes so long before coding begins. Currently, the metrics associated with procedural projects, while by no means perfect, have some relationship with what they purport to measure. For example, 'lines of code' is a very gross measure of a programmer's productivity. Such metrics, however, often have no meaning in OO. How does one assess productivity when most of the code in a system is reused? New metrics also need to be created to measure reuse and reusability, to give just one example.

  Other forms of project evaluation and assessment must be reconsidered as well. Organizations have found that, because of their high initial overheads, new OO projects are not cost-justifiable using traditional ROI techniques. How, then, should project prioritization take place? Also, because much time will be devoted to the creation of objects, there needs to be a means to measure the quality and performance of these objects. In short, IS must develop a new range of metrics and management techniques that will more accurately reflect the quantity, quality, and performance of IS projects. Without these, the organization will have no effective control over the development process and IS costs.

• **An organizational 'trojan horse.'** OO technology will bring change to IS. Unfortunately, this change may not always be welcome or predictable. In many organizations, managers will bungle through it all without putting the plans, procedures, controls and communications in place to manage it effectively. This will have a devastating effect on people who, at the very least, will become confused and thoroughly stressed. Under such conditions, morale and productivity will suffer and mistakes will be made. One of the key dangers of OO technology is to regard it as simply a technology, rather than a much broader force for change within IS. Failing to address these issues will not only lead to organizational disruption but could result in expensive blunders.

MAKING DECISIONS ABOUT OO TECHNOLOGY

It should be clear from the above discussion that the decision to move to OO technology is by no means simple. Managers must weigh the risks and benefits for their organization of such a move very carefully. While the benefits of OO technology look impressive, most managers have been badly burnt by similarly impressive (and expensive) technologies in the past. IS managers should ask two important questions about OO technology before making any decisions about it:

• Is OO technology likely to become the dominant form of technology and if so, when?

• What advantages will be gained by becoming an early user of OO technology?

Will OO Technology Become Dominant?

In IS, it is important to select a dominant technology because committing to a technology that does not become dominant can be extremely expensive. Fichman and Kemerer (1993) note some of the problems of choosing a non-dominant technology which include: difficulties in hiring experienced staff, limited enhancements to the core technology available, few complementary products available, fewer training opportunities, lack of wisdom about how to improve the technology's performance, and possible loss of vendor support. To address the question of whether OO technology will become dominant, they examined two perspectives on how new technologies are adopted, and then evaluated OO technology against these criteria.

- **Perspective #1. Diffusion of innovations.** Research has shown that organizations are more willing and able to adopt innovations that offer clear advantages, that do not drastically interfere with existing practices, and that are easier to understand. They are also likely to be more favourable towards a technology they can implement for a trial period and whose benefits are easy to see and describe. Fichman and Kemerer have concluded that while OO technology has had much favourable press, the fact that it is disruptive to existing practices, is highly complex, difficult to try out, and has long term, rather than immediate benefits all weigh against rapid adoption of this technology.

- **Perspective #2. Economics of technology standards.** In this research, a new technology is assessed on the basis of how well it is sponsored and the expectations about it, as well as the 'drag' that existing technologies exert over switching (because of the trouble and the cost) and the irreversibility of investments made in the new technology. By these measures as well, OO technology comes up short. While it has a sponsor (the Object Management Group (Bozman, 1993)) and it is well supported in the academic community, they also note that 'OO faces a more sophisticated and sceptical adoption community as the passing years have provided a larger array of proposed . . . technologies that failed to live up to early expectations.' In addition, because OO technology represents an entirely new procedural paradigm for IS work, there is considerable prior technology drag and investments in OO technology are largely irreversible.

Are There Advantages to Becoming an Early User of OO Technology?

If the promotion about OO technology were to be believed, more and more organizations are adopting OO as their main development paradigm and gaining strategic advantages from its myriad benefits. In fact, OO technology is still highly immature, and those who making the switch could be classified as 'early adopters' (Yourdon, 1993). Are there any advantages to getting there first? And are there risks associated with not moving to OO technology? Fichman and Kemerer remark that:

'publicly available technologies rarely provide a *sustainable* competitive advantage in and of themselves: they require mating with some other relatively unique organizational competence . . . In fact, in the case of OO, first movers will be in the ironic position of having to hope they are quickly followed so that critical mass will be reached and the technology will become dominant' (Fichman and Kemerer, 1993).

They conclude that it is unlikely that there will be many advantages for corporate IS departments in being the first movers into OO technology. These conclusions are echoed by internal IS assessments which suggest that moving to OO technology at present is a 'leap of faith.' In short, there are few advantages to be gained by adopting OO technology on a large scale at present, unless an organization wishes to undertake substantial PC development.

Despite these considerations, most Forum members felt that OO technology will eventually become the dominant development technology. It simply seems 'right' to them and has too many potential benefits to ignore. However, they also believed that this was going to be a long, slow process because companies with a significant investment in larger-scale systems will most likely take their time about the decision to move to OO. In the short run, they felt that many companies will dabble with this technology in small-scale PC applications and to give applications an attractive GUI front end, rather than making a full commitment to OO technology. This will come, but only when the tools are available and the technology itself is better understood (about three to five years from now).

PREPARING FOR THE SWITCH
TO OO TECHNOLOGY

While the prevailing wisdom appears to be that the industry is not ready to switch to OO technology, there are many things that IS organizations can do to ready themselves for it when it comes. These will make the switch less traumatic and enable organizations to try out potential strategies for coping with change.

1. **Establish Reuse.** As noted above, it is possible to establish a culture of reuse without adopting OO technology. Making reuse a priority will help to establish the attitudes, disciplines, and standards necessary to make a switch to OO. It will also deliver some of the benefits of OO such as improved productivity and quality. Finally, establishing reuse will help the organization create and experiment with much of the infrastructure (e.g., libraries) needed for OO technology.

2. **Develop Graphical Interfaces.** These are the most well-understood components of OO technology and deliver many benefits to users and IS through establishing standard graphical objects and introducing ease of use. Graphical interfaces are a way for organizations to 'get their feet wet' in OO technology and to develop some expertise in the area.

3. **Work on Metrics.** Develop metrics that are not paradigm-specific but instead focus on value delivered to the organization. These might include contributions to reducing

costs and improving financial performance, internal performance measures, measures of customer satisfaction and service performance. (For more details on these types of metrics, see Chapter 9.)

4. **Develop transition strategies.** Such strategies include plans for training and mentoring employees in OO technology new roles and job descriptions, enforcing standards and disciplines, and such disciplines as prototyping and reuse libraries. These can be implemented in existing non-OO development projects and in small-scale OO projects. Evaluation and modification of transition plans based on this experience is essential and will minimize the impact of changes to come.

5. **Work on enterprise data models.** These are an essential first step to the creation of objects and will give an organization a faster start when moving to OO technology. At this level, the entities and entity relationships produced by data models can assist in object identification and so work done will not be wasted and should give IS managers some insights into the challenges ahead.

6. **Look at everything with OO 'eyes.'** IS managers contemplating new hardware and software purchases should evaluate them in light of the support they provide for OO technologies. One senior manager told us that he would not consider any vendor that did not have a commitment to OO and to supporting it. In this way he is making sure he is well-positioned for the switch to OO without actually making the transition at present.

CONCLUSION

The interest in OO technology is growing, and managers will be seeing many OO 'success stories' in the short term (The, 1993). Managers are cautioned to take these stories with a large grain of salt. They should attempt to evaluate a number of things when reading them—the degree to which the system was truly object-oriented; who did the development; the kind of system that was developed; and has the company truly made the transition to OO technology? (Fichman and Kemerer, 1993). Although increasing in popularity, OO projects are decreasing in success and Ed Yourdon notes 'object orientation has become such a phenomenon that I believe we'll see the beginning of a backlash soon' (Yourdon, 1994). In short, OO technology still has to demonstrate that it can deliver. At present, it is still long on hype and short on results, so managers can stay off the bandwagon for a little while at least, with assurance that they will not get left behind.

13
Improving Testing

INTRODUCTION

Testing is never noticed until it's not done.

This statement sums up how most IS managers feel about testing. Although in the last decade testing has become increasingly complex, very little about testing has changed since the earliest days of systems development. Recently, however, some managers have begun to realize that testing deserves more management attention. Different kinds of hardware, software, and applications have proliferated, and testing new applications and changes to existing systems have begun to take up increasing amounts of development time. There is also growing pressure from users and senior management to finish quickly so that staff can be moved on to other critical projects. Furthermore, the risks of implementing poorly-tested systems are growing. Whereas previously, systems were in the back office and downtime only affected internal company operations, today, a bug in a system is more than likely going to have serious repercussions throughout a whole network of applications and inhibit a company's business for hours. As system interfaces have become more intricate, it is not unusual that obscure system components get overlooked in testing, leading to expensive system downtime. These are the kinds of mistakes no CIO wants to land on the President's desk.

There are enormous benefits to be gained from improving the process of testing and major business risks associated with it being done poorly. Testing now accounts for between 30 to 50% of all system development time. If testing could somehow be shortened, systems would cost less to develop and would be delivered to the business faster. If testing could be made more accurate (i.e., if more defects could be identified), systems would be more effective in organizations. In short, testing is both a productivity issue and a quality issue that can have a major impact on the benefits IS delivers to the organization.

To address how testing might be improved, Forum members discussed what their organization was doing to address the challenge of improving testing. This chapter looks first at what systems designers can learn from other complex design processes. It then outlines the traditional process of testing in systems development and how this might be re-engineered by changing our thinking about testing. Finally, it identifies some strategies for improving both testing quality and testing productivity.

WHAT OTHER COMPLEX DESIGN PROCESSES CAN TEACH IS?

Testing in IS has two objectives: to ensure that the computer system is built right, i.e., that it works correctly without errors; and to ensure that the right system is built, i.e., that it is what the users need to conduct business. Before examining testing in detail, it is worth looking at other complex design processes to see what systems development can learn from them about defect prevention, detection, and their relationship to overall productivity. What principles have they established that systems designers could learn from?

1. **Reuse wherever possible.** Engineers make extensive use both of pre-tested components and of pre-tested designs. Paul Basset (1990) writes:

   'Would you cross a bridge that had been designed from scratch? . . . A civil engineer [starts] the design process with a choice of models . . . and adapts these to the specifics of a given bridge. And he would take for granted most of the thousands of details that have already been worked out in the past which he can trust will enable his bridge not to fall down. **We don't do that in software.**'

Similar forms of reuse can also be found in car manufacturing where different models appear different but look the same under the hood.

2. **Create general-specialists.** In the 1980s, Japanese car manufacturers stunned the industry with their ability to speed up new car design by almost 50% and thus take advantage of changing customer demand much more quickly than American or European manufacturers. How did they do it? Womack et al. (1991) suggest that the Japanese approach to human resources was the key to this productivity improvement. First, unlike other manufacturers who trained people in one particular area of specialty (e.g., car lock design), the Japanese trained their staff in all aspects of the car business—manufacture, sales, new product development—before training them to become specialists in one particular area. By ensuring that their specialists retained the big picture, there was a much greater likelihood that all of the pieces in development would fit smoothly together and work in harmony. In IS, specialists have frequently been created to serve specialized needs with the result that, all too often, the needs of the overall system are lost or become secondary.

3. **Eliminate hand-offs.** A second reason for the improved productivity in the Japanese process was that there were no hand-offs to different groups of specialists where things could fall between the cracks. Instead, the specialists are made a true part of the team, participating in the decisions that were made for the car as a whole. This not only facilitates communication because all the relevant specialties are present *from the outset*, it also forces the group to confront all the difficult trade-offs they will have to

make to get the project going. As a result, the number of people needed on the team is highest at the outset and drops as the project goes on. By contrast, in more traditional mass-production organizations, the number of people involved is very small at the outset but grows to a peak near the time of the launch. Womack et al. (1991) note:

> 'The mass-producer keeps the line moving at all costs but ends up doing massive amounts of rework at the end, while the lean-producer spends more effort up front correcting problems before they multiply and ends up with much less total effort and higher quality in the end.'

In spite of much evidence that problem prevention can save time and effort (e.g., Boehm, 1981), testing in IS still bears greatest resemblance to the mass producer.

4. **Elevate the team.** A third difference in the Japanese approach elevates the development team to a central position in the organization. The team leader is given the authority to make and enforce decisions about the product under development, and all members of the team report to this leader for as long as they are on the team. In contrast, in typical Western teams, the leader is more of a coordinator with limited authority, and individual career paths are typically up functional ladders (e.g., from junior piston engineer to senior piston engineer). In IS, project teams typically resemble Western teams. They consist of loosely associated individuals whose strongest allegiances (particularly regarding career development and progression) are beyond the team. As a result, they are less focused on team activities and less empowered to accomplish them compared with Japanese teams.

5. **Eliminate bottlenecks.** Goldratt and Cox (1984) note that the greatest improvement in productivity comes from the elimination of wait times at key stages in a manufacturing process. While managers have spent a great deal of effort trying to optimize the productivity of every machine in a

factory, Goldratt and Cox demonstrate mathematically that the productivity of a whole process is governed by the throughput of a few, key bottleneck machines. As a result, bottlenecks have a much larger impact on overall production than it would first appear. The amount of time spent waiting for them does not simply add to the time required to produce a single item; instead, there is a multiplicative effect resulting in bottlenecks that *drive* the productivity of the whole factory. Similarly in IS testing, bottlenecks (such as inadequate testing resources or unavailable IS staff or users) slow down the development process and significantly impact overall productivity.

6. **Develop in parallel.** In car manufacturing, one of the main reasons for the long design-to-production cycle has been the time that it takes to retool the factory for a new design. The traditional mass-production approach has been to wait until precise specifications are ready for each part before cutting the dies. Then there is a big rush with many hold-ups waiting for specialized machines. The best lean-producers managed to cut the time from design to implementation by 50% by improving communication between the different groups involved, enabling simultaneous car and die design. For example, die designers begin to rough cut their die blocks as soon as they know the approximate size of the car, working closely with the car designers to refine their dies. While some mistakes are made, in most cases this approach optimizes the use of scarce resources. The traditional approach has many similarities to the life-cycle style of development. Prototyping or rapid development more closely approximates the model of simultaneous development, but more work needs to be done in systems to incorporate this principle of simultaneity into all forms of system development.

7. **Non-technical participation.** A feature of the best manu-facturers is a well-trained sales staff who knows the product it is selling. This staff is also systematically trained to solve owners' problems as they arise. Furthermore, the entire sales team meets regularly to compare notes on problems

and to determine their root causes. This is valued information to the company that is acted on. When new products are being developed, members of the sales staff are part of the development team.

While users are certainly part of most development teams these days, how well trained are they? Many organizations do not use true end users but staff users who may be more knowledgeable in systems development techniques than in what the customers want. In addition, very few IS organizations spend any significant amount of time addressing and correcting problems at their root. Most often, problem-solving is on an emergency basis only, with other problems relegated to the dreaded maintenance queue from which they may never emerge.

These principles of engineering have worked to reduce defects significantly in a number of complex design processes that have important parallels with systems development. While IS organizations will certainly be familiar with many of these principles, they are worth restating for two reasons. First, often IS organizations have not truly thought through the implications of these principles for their work. American car manufacturers in the early 1980s had to face a crisis before they learned from others' experience. IS should not wait for a similar crisis before applying new approaches to the systems development process. Second, the application of these principles has led to dramatic increases in both productivity *and* quality in complex design processes that can be considered the equal of systems development in many ways. And, each of these principles contains important aspects of problem prevention and resolution—both from a technical perspective and from a business perspective—that can be integrated into systems testing.

WHAT IS UNIQUE ABOUT TESTING IN SYSTEMS DEVELOPMENT?

While defect prevention and detection in systems development shares many things in common with other complex design processes, it is also unique in some aspects. These need to be understood before improvements in systems testing can be addressed. Three aspects of systems work are particularly challenging:

• **Multiple Platforms.** In the past decade, systems design work has shifted from being predominantly mainframe-based to a wide variety of hardware and software platforms. The lack of standards prevailing in the industry means that interoperability is often very poor. For example, applications that work on one PC may not work on another kind of PC, or worse, may bring the system down. In organizations with diverse equipment and software, testing applications on each platform can multiply the testing effort several times over. Multiple platforms mean that even a simple change to a stable system may take an inordinately long time to test and install. Furthermore, trying to distribute changes to different locations can become a major headache since problems can arise when different locations use different versions of the same system.

• **Rapid Technical Change.** While new advances are occurring in virtually every field, changes in information technology are among the most rapid. Not only is it difficult to keep up with new hardware and software, but changes in the technology mean that there is often little time for it to stabilize and for systems designers to learn about its idiosyncrasies. This means that technical staff often must test both applications *and* the platforms they run on. Designers' inexperience with new technology can lead to errors over and above those that occur in system development.

• **Unstable Business Environment.** Increasingly, business needs to continually reinvent itself to meet the demands of consumers and the economy. While this is causing change in almost every organizational subunit, with business' increasing dependence on IT, it means that most changes end up in IS. Furthermore, these rapid changes lead to a difficulty in maintaining an accurate test environment.

Testing in systems development, as in other design work, means operating the system under the most rigorous conditions to see how it performs. The ability to standardize and replicate tests for a particular application would enable testing of changes (regression testing) to be performed both effectively and efficiently. However, this requires stable business data. With business needs changing so rapidly, many IS organizations find that they must recreate test data each time the system is worked on and cannot maintain a standard test bed.

The climate of instability surrounding systems development leads to enormous uncertainties about applications testing, *within IS,* as well as within business. In this climate, it is difficult to make effective judgements about what should or should not be tested. As a result, many IS staff opt to test everything they can, even with small modifications to a stable system. Most IS professionals have seen small, unlikely changes cause important systems to crash. As a result, testing has grown enormously in both complexity and effort in recent years.

THE CURRENT TESTING PROCESS

Testing, as it is performed in many organizations, typically consists of four steps: **Unit testing** is the responsibility of the individual programmer. It ensures that each module of code is defect-free and meets specifications. **Integration testing** is designed to ensure that system components work together. It tests both subsystems and the interfaces between them and is usually carried out by the project team. The final test done by IS developers is the **system test**. This test ensures that the entire system is production ready and meets the business' requirements. **Acceptance testing** is usually done by the users and is supposed to test that the system meets the end users' requirements. Ideally, this test is performed by end users. Other forms of testing that are sometimes done before acceptance testing include: **stress testing**, designed to test the limits of large production systems shared by many users; **useability testing**, designed to address users' ease of use and ease of understanding requirements; and **model office testing**, which is designed to simulate everyday use and to ensure that the user procedures surrounding the system work well.

Testing is typically a phase in a system's development cycle beginning after coding is complete and occupying the majority of the team's effort until installation. In maintenance work, testing often represents the majority of work involved in making a system change. To test the system, test data are usually created, often by users, which attempt to replicate all the possible scenarios that might occur in the business. At later stages of testing, live operational data are often used to simulate operational conditions. In addition, IS staff often create special test situations that will attempt to break the system. Particular attention is usually paid to interfaces with other systems to ensure that the data received and the data passed on are as expected.

To date, efforts to improve testing quality and productivity have had little impact on the process. In fact, the effort involved in testing has grown in the past decade. To improve testing therefore, the testing process needs to be thoroughly re-examined and re-engineered, if possible.

RE-ENGINEERING TESTING

Re-engineering a process involves challenging the assumptions on which it is based (Hammer, 1990). Applying the principles of other complex design processes can assist managers to reorient their thinking about how to achieve a system that correctly meets users' needs and which is error-free. Some of the innovative ways Forum participants are thinking about testing include:

1. **Eliminate testing.** Clearly, other complex design processes do not wait until the end of their development cycle to ensure that their product is going to work. Instead, testing is incorporated into every step of the development process. Some IS organizations are trying this approach, known as full life-cycle testing (FLT) (Hetzel, 1988) (see Figure 13.1).

The main objective of FLT is to discover and eliminate defects as early as possible in the development life cycle. It includes both static and dynamic testing.

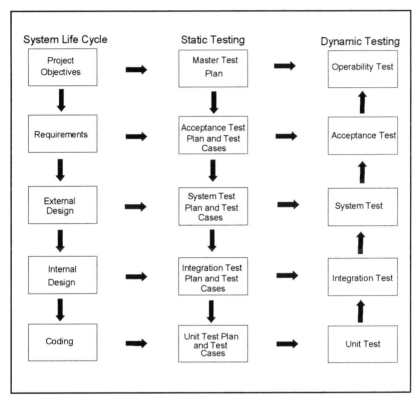

Figure 13.1. *Full Life-Cycle Testing*
(After Jones (1990), reproduced by permission of Capers Jones)

Static testing focuses on planning what is to be tested and how it is to be tested. In the process, user requirements and expectations are reviewed and checked for completeness and correctness. By carefully thinking through testing requirements, many errors and omissions can be identified at very early stages. When users and others are also involved in static testing, FLT closely approximates the design principle of 'no hand-offs' outlined above, where all the relevant specialties are involved with a product's design from the outset. *Dynamic testing* follows the traditional testing steps of unit, integration, system, and acceptance testing but uses the guidelines and plans developed during the static test. As a result, testing proceeds more smoothly and with fewer surprises.

Because FLT incorporates testing throughout the development process, the system is actually tested both iteratively and incrementally. The goal of this kind of testing is to reduce the expensive redevelopment effort that often occurs during traditional testing (similar to traditional mass production where products with defects are reworked after manufacture to correct mistakes). Instead, the objective is a process designed to find and eliminate defects *before* testing; hence, the goal of eliminating the testing phase.

2. **Defects are Good.** In addition to eliminating testing as we now know it, Forum participants suggested that IS needs to change its way of looking at errors or other defects. At present, there seems to be a hopelessly optimistic outlook among IS staff that believes that, in spite of a demonstrated industry average of 60 defects per 1000 lines of code, they *should* be able to design and develop a system without defects. Thus, every defect that is found is perceived negatively.

It is clear that finding errors earlier in development is much more desirable than finding them during testing. Therefore, Forum participants suggested reorienting management's thinking to reward defect detection early in the process. Furthermore, since industry statistics (Jones, 1990) show how defects are distributed over the development process (see Table 13.1), some managers have suggested that developers *be required* to find a certain number of defects at each development phase before moving on to the next one. In this way, teams become more positively oriented towards defect discovery and are less likely to ignore or not look for problems in early phases of development.

Table 13.1. *Origin of Software Defects*
(After Jones (1990), reproduced by permission of Caper Jones)

Company 1.		**Company 2.**	
Design	45%	Requirements	20%
Coding	25%	Design	30%
Testing	20%	Coding	35%
Documentation	5%	Testing	10%
Other	5%	Documentation	5%
Company 3.		**Company 4.**	
Design	60%	Design	64%
Coding	40%	Coding	36%

3. Test in Parallel. When testing comes at the end of the development cycle, it can add significantly to the elapsed time involved, or worse, it can get squeezed out by schedule and budget pressures. While static testing introduces some parallelism to testing, a shift in thinking about the way the actual dynamic testing is performed can also save time. Traditionally, testing starts with unit testing and is done in a *bottom-up* fashion. That is, integration testing starts with lower-level modules joining them in larger and larger components until the whole system has been tested. Thus, system testing cannot begin until all the lowest-level details have been finalized.

With *top-down* testing, user interface modules are developed and tested first with lower-level programs being replaced by program stubs that simply return a message. As additional modules are developed and unit tested, they are added to the whole system until all the modules have been added and the system is complete. The advantage of this approach is that it clearly enables substantial system testing to be undertaken *in parallel* with lower-level system development and unit testing. Adherence to this principle should enable developers to reduce the amount of time testing takes beyond the end of development.

The principle of parallelism must be carefully applied however. One organization tried to conduct system testing and user testing in parallel with disastrous results. System developers were changing the system to correct technical problems at the same time as users were trying to see if the system met their requirements. Both ended up getting in each other's way, the system was very unstable, and no one was happy. For more about how parallelism can be effectively applied, see below.

4. **Discover and eliminate bottlenecks.** Testing bottlenecks, such as limited response time or the time spent developing test data, will drive the speed of the whole process. Strange as it may seem to some managers, it is better to have some staff sitting idle than to optimize their productivity. The only productivity that should be optimized is that of the bottleneck staff and processes. When these have been addressed rigorously, management will find that new bottlenecks appear that need optimization and so on throughout the process. The objective here is to identify and speed up the key sub-processes that are holding up the whole process rather than forcing everyone to work faster. The process of uncovering and speeding up bottlenecks is not easy in systems work. However, with some sleuthing and improved measurement, it can be done and the rewards involved can be substantial. Because of their importance to productivity, all IS managers should make it their mandate to seek out and address bottlenecks in the testing process immediately.

5. **Involve users in unit and integration testing.** Typically, unit and integration testing has been a wholly IS responsibility. Users, especially end-users, are not usually involved in testing until system and acceptance testing. However, some organizations are experimenting with involving users in all aspects of testing and having extremely positive results. One organization combined user involvement with the programmer at unit testing with more detailed test planning. Unit testing then enabled the user to sign off each module as it was constructed. The project manager noted:

'although programmer testing had improved [in the past], there were still some sloppy defects and the users were more diligent and caught the vast majority of unit process type defects in their testing . . . We removed far more defects in this manner because the programmer was right there to dialogue with and take note of the defects . . . plus the programmer was able to use the animator to pinpoint the problem, rather than have to try and reconstruct the error later had the user done the testing in isolation.' (Forum member's internal company document.)

The principle of non-technical involvement in development is supported here, but in an unusual way. While users have been involved with development before, their activities have usually been separate from developer activities. Having developers and end-users working together to test a system is an approach that may yield more defects earlier in the process than waiting until the end of the IS portion of testing.

Rethinking the assumptions of the testing process means challenging the sacred cows of testing—those things that *everybody knows* are fundamental to the testing activity. Only when IS managers truly incorporate new ways of approaching testing will they achieve significant productivity and quality gains in this area.

ENHANCING TESTING

While re-engineering is central to improving testing, there are immediate strategies that will result in incremental improvements in the overall quality of testing. Ideally, these should complement the re-engineered testing process. However, the strategies suggested below can also be used to enhance the existing testing process.

- **Professionalize Testing.** Testing is a skill that must be learned. In the past, programmers and analysts were assumed to know how to test their work. Forum participants agreed that while for some, testing may be a natural talent, most IS professionals need to learn more about how to do it. Because of the complex number of skills needed, some managers have suggested that a separate testing group be established within IS consisting of professional testers. Unfortunately, they have also noted that IS staff perceive a full-time testing job as being 'worse than maintenance.' In addition, such a group creates hand-offs, which should be avoided. This is not to say, however, that personnel skilled in testing should not be part of a development team from the beginning, nor that IS personnel should not be taught and expected to practise testing skills as part of their career development. A more effective use of testing as a professional skill, therefore, would be as part of a career development plan for every programmer, first as an apprentice to learn the skill, then as a journeyman, and finally as master— interspersed with positions in coding, design, and maintenance. This approach supports the principle of general-specialists, encouraging all-round development of staff before specialization.

- **Manage Testing.** It is a management truism that if managers want their staff to pay attention to something, all they have to do is ask about it. Similarly, staff tend to ignore matters in which managers appear to have little or no interest. Forum members agreed that formal test plans and professional approaches to testing yield improved testing results. One industry study (Jones, 1990) showed that with the addition of test plans and other components of static testing, the number of person hours and costs involved in defect removal were reduced by 51%, and elapsed time by 15%, compared with traditional testing methods. The best way to get IS staff to produce test plans is to ask to review them. By focusing on testing, management can make it important to IS staff and improve the attention they pay to this issue.

- **Follow proven design principles.** Incorporating proven principles for increasing quality and reducing defects into system design can lead to considerable improvements in the testing process itself. For example, the introduction of reuse can lead to a reduced number of defects. One Forum manager found that the defects were reduced by 50% with reusable code. Indeed, a major benefit of object-oriented development is the ability to reuse fully tested objects. Other proven defect prevention techniques include use of prototypes, JADs, structured methods, code reviews and inspections, and focusing on error-prone modules in testing (Jones, 1990).

• **Control the test environment.** As noted above, instability in the test environment leads to a lack of confidence in systems by both users and IS staff. A stable test environment is therefore highly desirable. This is easier to achieve on a mainframe than with PCs and, thus, the PC test environment should be a source of particular management attention. IS staff must be able to easily test systems on all PC platforms (e.g., laptops, desktops, 486s, 286s, etc.). Developers also need to have a separate test system where programs can be tested without fear of having changes made to them in mid-test by other developers. Similarly, some form of change control is required during the testing process so that changes are not continually disrupting tests. (While necessary, change control should not be too stringent. Forum members told of test environments which approximated production environments which slowed testing to a snail's pace.) In short, a stable, well-managed test environment is essential to effective testing.

• **Create a Defect Model.** Good measurement is important to effective management of testing. It need not be complex. A simple count of the number of defects found in a system at each phase of development and after implementation is a good start. These can be standardized per 1000 lines of code. A good starting number is 60 defects per 1000 lines of code—approximately 60% in design and 40% in coding. Use of a defect model illustrates clearly that management knows and expects that errors will occur and underscores to IS staff that it is better to find defects before implementation rather than after. Once a basic defect model has been established, other systems developers can use it as a guide to determine how many errors they *should* be finding at each phase of development and encourage them to find them. The basic model can be then enhanced with further information about the type of system (e.g., type of hardware, software, numbers of transactions) which can further assist management and developers in error detection. Following the principles outlined above, defect monitoring should continue after installation and should include users in detection, correction and problem-solving. Ideally, defect identification should be an 'egoless' exercise with positive rewards going to those who identify errors.

- **Provide extra support in problem areas.** If management's goal is to produce a defect-free system in as short a time as possible, it must pay extra attention to those areas which are particularly problematic in testing. These include:

  Incompatible platforms. Managers must support adherence to international standards in hardware and software wherever possible. Contracts with vendors should specify this, as should any underlying system architectures approved by IS. As standards improve and are more closely followed by vendors, the problems of testing on multiple platforms will decline.

  Version control. Migration of systems to PCs and LANs currently causes numerous problems for IS: different versions of one system can end up being operational at different locations at any one time; installing systems on different platforms can cause different versions to be operating on different platforms at once; the actual work of installing new versions of a system across an organization can be extremely time-consuming; and, IS has even found that personal programs on PCs can disrupt operational systems. Organizations need strong controls over how systems should be tested, installed, and upgraded across a network of locations to ensure that problems do not arise as a result. Again, planning and management attention is key to reducing these problems, in the absence of automated tools to assist this process. Some organizations also forbid the use of any non-standard software on PCs.

Test data creation and maintenance. Test data creation is a time-consuming job. Forum participants agreed that there is no 'silver bullet' in this area. Some IS organizations 'solve' this problem by making it a user responsibility. Other organizations recognize that users have fewer skills in testing systems than do systems developers—particularly when it comes to designing scenarios that test the boundaries of a system. Some organizations work with test data generator tools; others feel that these tools are so complex, they are more trouble than they are worth. The creation and maintenance of a test bed that can be used for regression testing is one solution that some organizations have tried. Unfortunately, developers often feel that the effort involved in maintaining such test beds equals that of creating it from scratch each time. This may be the case, but the creation of test beds has the advantage of being able to be done in parallel with development work and thus speed up the elapsed time of testing. Therefore, until the creation of test data becomes substantially easier, managers should ensure that test data generation does not add to the elapsed time of the project by creating it in parallel with other activities.

GUI Testing. Testing Graphical User Interface (GUI) applications can be particularly challenging because of the many scenarios that users can create with GUI. Due to their complexity, these applications take more time than normal to test in the traditional manner (if they can be tested in this way at all) and the testing of modifications can be a major testing headache. As a result, many organizations are investigating Computer Aided Software Test (CAST) tools to assist them with GUI testing. Managers in organizations where GUI is becoming a significant part of their systems would be well advised to investigate tools for testing GUI system components. Such tools will not however: replace analysis in creating test cases; assist the testing process where regression testing is not applicable; or act as debuggers. GUI testing is a new aspect of testing about which the whole industry is learning. Managers should work closely with their technical advisors in this area.

- **Use tools appropriately.** Tools are an important part of a developer's tool kit. Key types of testing tools include:

  Interactive debugging tools which help programmers find errors in logic by stopping execution at certain points, displaying values and stepping through source code statements one at a time. Developers feel they are invaluable if they are easy to set up and easy on resources.

  Capture/Playback tools to assist regression testing capture users' keystrokes for subsequent playback after program modification. To date, many organizations have had limited success with these tools because they are cumbersome to set up and use.

Other types of tools are: GUI test tools and test data generators (both discussed above), path analysers, abend analysers, and virtual terminal emulators.

At present, testing tools appear to be at a fairly rudimentary stage of development—limited in scope and somewhat complex to learn and use. Managers should monitor the market in this area to learn what is available and to determine when and how testing tools can most benefit their organizations. Caution should be used, however, and tools should not be considered substitutes for other forms of management attention to the testing process. As one Forum manager noted:

'Test tools help, but they do not replace THINKING about: what you want to test; specific test scenarios; expected results; the structure of the test environment; who participates; and other facets of the process.'

CONCLUSION

Testing is a part of the system development process which has grown increasingly complex in the past decade. However, the way testing is done has changed very little during the same time. As a result, testing has become one of the largest single components of systems development. Improving testing will take more than simply throwing technology at the problem. IS managers who seriously wish to simultaneously speed up testing and improve the quality of the systems they develop, must rethink the entire process. Such a re-engineering of testing means borrowing from other successful complex design processes as well as focusing their attention on the areas which make system testing truly unique. Until IS challenges the 1960s thinking on which system testing is built, improvements in testing will be limited. There is significant leverage to be gained by improving testing, but achieving it will take a profound commitment to doing so.

Executive Interview:

Robert Rubin
Vice President, IS
Elf Atochem North America

Could you tell us a little about your background?

I started out as a physicist who found computers useful and gradually moved into helping others with them. Over the years, I have held almost every responsibility within IS—development, hardware/software configuration, tele-communications. I have even run a small business unit selling IS services.

Have you found your scientific training helpful now that you are working in IT?

Absolutely! I have found my scientific training has served me very well. In physics, you must understand *why*; you cannot have any preconceived notions. Measurement is also important. To paraphrase Lord Kelvin, 'If you can't measure it, you can't understand it.' For example, in IS we do not do a very good job of measuring what we do. Sometimes, we end up measuring the wrong things. The trick is to find out which are the relevant statistics *for the organization*. In our company, if you come into IS and walk around, you will see all our metrics up on the wall. We look at the goals of the organization and try to build metrics around them. Then, we look at how the metrics make a difference and whether they make sense in the context of our organization.

There is a big gap between these kinds of metrics and those that IS departments usually collect.

We do not measure things like function points here. They are just not meaningful. We want to measure those things that mean something and that we can control. If management cannot understand it, it is not meaningful. This is what you say in your benchmarking chapter.

Let me give you an example of what I mean. A few years ago we decided that response time was critical to our business. We spent quite a bit of time arguing about how to measure it—whether to measure it at the computer, where we could control it; at the end of a network (which included public telephone lines); or when transactions were entered. Once we got focused, we realized that the question we were *really* trying to get at was whether or not the order entry person was satisfied. So I suggested we just *ask* them. It is not high tech. And it is not a survey—we ask them every time they sign off 'Were you satisfied with the response time in this session?' This gives us a great diagnostic tool. When there is a problem, we really go into monitoring the details; otherwise, this measure gives us a good idea of how we are doing, where it counts.

With this type of metric, if your order entry staff are satisfied, but your competitor's responding faster, would you not miss a market change?

No, because we also ask what it is you need to sell to customers. If we find out that in a certain business, personal contact is important, we would build into the system a place for keeping notes about the customer. In other words, we need to know from the marketplace about what is important to measure. How did we know that response time is important? That is what the sales people told us.

So, is general user satisfaction the best way to measure IS' impact on the organization?

IS' impact on the organization is very important but often the measurements are done improperly. I would ask how frequently do we ask about the contribution of Human Resources or Finance to the bottom line? We tend not to because we believe they are integral to an organization's success. What we *should* say is that IS is an enabler, not a stand alone function. We should ask: *What projects were a success and what was the IS component?* That is how you measure value. IS alone rarely saves anything in and of itself. You have to change a business process.

Is IS valuable to your organization?

There is a difference between being invaluable and being efficient. The fact is we could not run modern businesses without information technology—they would shut down. But that does not mean IS is effective or efficient.

The way we measure value is we say, *forget IT—what projects worked? Was IS involved? What was the IS component?* We get at value by talking to the business people. Once you get the emotion out of it, if they are proud of what they have accomplished, they will tell you. Chances are, if you have a good working relationship, they will give you the appropriate credit. It does not always work, but viewing our projects holistically and in context of the business gives us a good idea of the value of IS.

I should say that in our company, IS is totally centralized. However, I would not present a project without a business partner. In fact, I have stopped projects because they did not have a strong business component. Here, business *always* leads the projects.

IS must have some intrinsic value to the company, otherwise it would be outsourced. If you look at companies where IS has been outsourced, chances are you will find that IS was viewed as a commodity and did not provide a good service to the company. If IS is perceived as a specialized function, it will have value in the eyes of the beholder.

Well, that takes care of effectiveness. What about efficiency?

Efficiency only makes sense when compared to others. What we do is compare ourselves to others in the same types of business. We have had consultants in here who tell us that we are providing service at or above the industry average at one-half the average cost in the chemical industry. Therefore, we feel we are efficient.

As well, we benchmark some of our functions with other similar functions. For example, we do our own payroll in-house. We know that we are in the top quintile of all companies for payroll. We have never had any other company offer us payroll services for anywhere close to what we can do it ourselves. If anyone can provide the service cheaper, I will be happy to give it to them.

Would you say that you benchmark both within your industry and by function?

Yes, we would like to do more benchmarking but we do not have the resources or the time to do it. We do it to the point of 'envisioned diagnostic benchmarks.' We focus on the critical pressure points in the organization.

Then, if we are doing well in an area, we talk to the team and try to cross-fertilize some of their ideas into other teams. We encourage them to come up with more ideas and they are spurred on and keep making things better. Sometimes, we will ask these people to help on projects that are not doing very well.

What happens when you do not perform so well?

Then we sit down with the people involved and develop a plan to make it better. If that does not work, we tighten up on management. If we still have a problem, we will rethink the organizational design and question whether the task that is being given is impossible and whether the goals are poor. If nothing else works, you have to replace the people.

Are you often surprised with benchmark results?

Not on the big things. We do little formal benchmarking but lots of talking to people and sharing information. With big formal studies, we often have trouble relating what the results mean to us. As you say in your chapter on benchmarking, *Is it good or bad if you have a large number of IS staff?* I would say we are not frequently surprised because we spend time talking to people and trying to understand their problems and successes.

So, your first source of how well you are doing is talking?

In order to know what is important, you have to communicate, communicate, communicate. We do this in two ways:

First, we have to understand the business, so once a month I hold business awareness breakfasts. We invite a leader from one of our business divisions to attend and describe what they do, their problems, and their perspectives on the business. All the IS staff are invited to attend, although attendance is optional. The only rule I have for the business people is that they *do not* talk about computers. It is amazing how much people enjoy talking about what they do. And the IS people love it. We get over 80% IS attendance. We even have people from other business departments wanting to come. My objective with these breakfasts is to make IS a part of the company. The more they understand about it, the better service they will provide.

Our second tool of communication is our IS plan. Now, your typical IS plan is several inches thick and written in highly technical terms. My rule for our IS plan is that it must be readable and it must fit easily into an overcrowded briefcase. It is a small book filled with interesting graphs and charts and it is very conversational in tone. We also include the hard figures such as headcounts and progress against budgets, but if the plan is not readable, I will make my staff rewrite it!

Your plan sounds like it is a real working document.

It is. It is designed to be read and worked from. We rewrite it annually and update it once in between. Our plan is important in helping us meet our objectives. For example, in the last few years we have reduced our IS headcount significantly, and we have accomplished this without layoffs. The reason is that we had a good plan and were able to manage the reductions through attrition. We have never yet screwed up in planning so that we have had to lay people off without cause.

Layoffs are really unfortunate. They will come back to haunt you too. People need to trust you and to trust that you will always be honest and open with then about what is going to happen. That is why I consider planning to be so important.

Before we go, we would like to hear your reaction to the chapter on benchmarking.

I liked it! I actually enjoyed reading it. I would disagree with you about some points. For example, I feel that organizational learning and change are the *result* of the rapid change in markets and products rather than being hallmarks of the organization in and of themselves. And when you talk about accurate and adequate information, I would emphasize appropriate information too. In general, however, you have really captured the concepts of measurement well. I especially liked your emphasis on collecting both qualitative and quantitative information.

I also think you should emphasize the importance of industry organizations and the benchmarking they do. The Society for Information Management (SIM), for example, does a lot of benchmarking. It has a working group that has produced a handbook on benchmarking. You can learn a lot by participating in organizations such as these.

Any last words?

I would just like to say that our mission in IS at Elf Atochem is *not* to build systems—it is to simplify complex processes. This is so important, I have had it printed on the back of all our business cards.

ELF ATOCHEM NORTH AMERICA, INC.

Elf Atochem North America, Inc. is a customer-focused, innovative supplier segmented into the following business groups: Industrial Chemicals; Fine Chemicals; Specialty Chemicals; and Agrichemicals.

Elf Atochem North America was formed in late 1989 through the merger of Atochem Inc., M&T Chemicals Inc., and Pennwalt Corporation and has annual sales in excess of $1.6 billion, employing more than 4000 people in North America and a total of 5000 worldwide. It has more than 30 manufacturing facilities in the United States—with 20 other sites located around the world—and is headquartered in Philadelphia, Pennsylvania.

Elf Atochem is an affiliate of Elf Atochem S.A., a $10 billion chemicals manufacturer, which is part of the Elf Group headquartered in Paris, France. The Elf Group ranks among the world's top 30 industrial companies and is a top producer of oil and gas, chemicals and minerals, pharmaceuticals and other health care products. It has annual sales of approximately $36 billion and employs more than 89,000 people in 80 countries.

PART 4

Managing the Information
Resource

14
Managing IS Complexity

INTRODUCTION

There is little doubt that the world is becoming more complex. With the published volume of information doubling every few years, with technological innovation moving at breakneck speed, with the upheaval associated with the transition from an industrial society to an information society, with the realizations of a resource-constrained shared planet, and with the dizzying rate of change, people must cope with a level of complexity in their daily lives unsurpassed in history. According to Senge (1990), 'humankind has the capacity to create far more information than anyone can absorb, to foster far greater interdependency than anyone can manage, and to accelerate change far faster than anyone's ability to keep pace. Certainly the scale of complexity is without precedent.'

Since the engine behind much of this change is information technology, the information systems function in most organizations has assumed the front line position in coping with this accelerating complexity. IS is a gatekeeper. It falls to IS to decide what technology will be introduced, at what rate it will be introduced, and how it will be interwoven within the organizational fabric. It also falls to IS to manage the attendant complexity. Its ability to do this often dictates the well-being of organizations. There are two outcomes faced by IS—either you manage complexity or it manages you.

Forum members were asked to examine the sources of complexity in their organizations, to explore alternate methods for managing IS complexity, and to debate their ideas with the other members. This chapter is derived largely from the insights that emerged from that discussion.

UNDERSTANDING COMPLEXITY

We know very little about complexity. Generally, if we say something is 'complex,' it usually means that it is difficult to understand—it is complicated, or intricate, or involved. The 'something' could be an object, an idea or concept, or a relationship between objects or ideas. It is our inability to grasp all aspects of a subject that leads us to suggest that it is complex. There are three key causes of complexity.

- **Uncertainty.** Complexity is a relative term. Something may be complex to me but not to you. This raises an important point in understanding complexity and IS complexity in particular. Some subjects are innately more complex than others. One way to deal effectively with complexity therefore is to increase one's level of understanding of that subject. Daft, Lengel and Trevino (1987) suggest that the absence of skills or information is one of the major causes of complexity in organizations. In this case, uncertainty is defined as 'the difference between the amount of information required to perform the task and the amount of information already possessed by the organization' (Galbraith, 1973). However, while much uncertainty can be reduced or eliminated by the acquisition of the appropriate skills or knowledge, uncertainty still creates complexity in other arenas simply because we do not know enough about a subject yet.

- **Ambiguity.** In the absence of true knowledge, ambiguity often arises. Multiple and conflicting interpretations about an organizational situation can lead to confusion, disagreement, and lack of understanding. Managers are not certain what questions to ask and, if questions are posed, there is no store of objective data to provide an answer. Unlike uncertainty which can be reduced by information, ambiguity requires the exchange of subjective views among managers to define the problem and resolve disagreements (Daft et al., 1987).

- **Interactions.** A new field of investigation, called complexity theory, suggests there is a third source of complexity. This work, which is still in its infancy, proposes that complexity stems from numerous relatively simple processes and systems. These interact in different ways and at many levels causing complexity. While some form of organization emerges spontaneously from the rich and varied interactions among the parts, it may be highly tenuous hovering constantly on the brink of collapse or disarray. In other words, complexity arises from simplicity and is a natural process inherent in many natural and biological systems—from colonies of bacteria, to human economies. Looked at in this light, complexity is highly desirable because it reflects a 'deep, inner creativity that is woven into the very fabric of nature' (Ross-Flanigan, 1993).

Taking a somewhat different tack, Senge (1990) differentiates two additional variants of complexity:

- **Detail complexity** is involved in those situations where there are many variables that need to be taken into consideration before a situation can be effectively managed. Conventional forecasting, planning, and analysis methods are examples of techniques designed to handle detail complexity. Detail complexity is closely related to uncertainty, because high levels of knowledge are required. However, Senge identifies an important additional feature of complexity and that is sheer *logistics*. We may know everything we need to about a problem but managing the details involved can still be a complex process. It should be noted, however, that once we know all the details that are involved in a process, it becomes considerable easier to manage because we have mechanisms, i.e., computer systems, to help us handle them.

- **Dynamic complexity** results from situations where cause and effect are subtle and where the effects of interventions over time are problematic. Improving quality, lowering total costs, and satisfying customers in a sustainable manner is a dynamic problem. Again, there is a close affiliation with ambiguity, but Senge distinguishes the *relationships* between the elements of a system as being a critical feature in understanding complexity. He points out that understanding dynamic complexity requires a holistic perspective based on the 'big picture.' That is, an ability to see the major interrelationships underlying a problem is necessary to gain new insights about how to solve it.

Complexity and its causes are only just being understood as a critical factor in both nature and human organizations. As a result, it is still difficult to link theory and practice together in understanding complexity, as tightly as we might wish. Nevertheless, these strands of perception of the subject can be applied to a greater understanding of complexity in IS and to more effective management in this area.

UNDERSTANDING IS COMPLEXITY

IS operates in a very complex environment astride two opposing forces. On the one hand, IS must keep abreast of technological innovation which is currently moving at an alarming pace. On the other hand, IS must introduce technology into organizations which are not capable of changing at an equivalent rate. Organizations which are too slow to change often suffer in the marketplace. Organizations which attempt to change too rapidly suffer the pangs of instability—a situation which drives up the level of complexity within organizations and particularly within IS. IS resembles a circus performer riding two galloping horses—a task which is manageable only as long as the horses remain in step.

In order to understand IS' position, IS can be viewed as a gatekeeper (see Figure 14.1). Positioned in the middle, it is IS' job to assess new technologies and introduce the most promising of these to the organization. As a result, complexity for IS can develop within each of three areas: emerging technology, IS itself, and the organization.

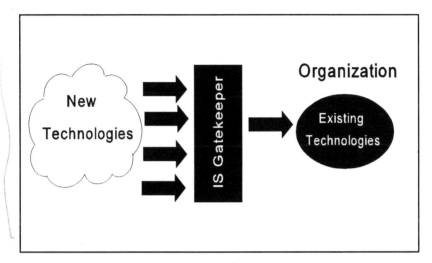

Figure 14.1. *Role of IS as Gatekeeper*

1. *New Technologies*

New developments in communications, hardware, software, and new applications of these technologies such as imaging, EDI, and networking all offer potential opportunities for organizations. As a gatekeeper, IS must stay abreast of these developments lest it fall behind and miss a significant opportunity to take advantage of a new technology. The following factors highlight how emerging technology affects the level of IS complexity:

• **Technological Uncertainty.** Unless the IS function is willing to ignore emerging technologies, then the degree of IS complexity is directly related to the rate of new technological development. In a world of only one type of computer and only one computing language, the IS function would be much less complex. That world, unfortunately, does not exist. The world that does exist is one in which the rate of technological change is ever increasing. The complexity which arises from these new technologies has more to do with the number of technologies than the nature of the technologies. Emerging technologies, in fact, are not always complex by themselves.

Sometimes emerging technologies simplify older technologies tremendously. However, it is the task of keeping informed with regard to emerging technologies that presents the challenge. All organizations have limited 'bandwidth'—that is, capacity to keep on top of all emerging technologies, and so must select only the most promising new technologies for evaluation. Under these circumstances, choosing the 'right' technology for business is never easy. Thus, the ability to stay abreast of technology while marrying that technology with legitimate business activity is a key IS problem.

- **Technological Interrelationships.** The explosion of new technologies has created a high degree of uncertainty due to the existence of so many alternative ways of accomplishing given tasks. Many operations can now be run on a variety of computing platforms. Software choices impact design options directly. While individual technologies may be straightforward, in combination with other technologies and continual change, a highly complex and potentially unstable environment can easily develop.

- **Provider Dynamics.** The number of technology and service providers has also increased over time. This means that IS must manage a larger base of service providers as the number and form of technology solutions grows. Previously, an organization could deal with a single computer manufacturer who would provide the hardware and software and a single communications company who would provide telephone service and data transmission. Organizations today must deal with many providers causing a proliferation of licensing agreements, warranties, service contracts, leasing arrangements, etc. Management in a multi-provider environment raises the overall level of IS complexity proportionately.

2. The IS Function

How IS chooses to organize itself, how it makes decisions regarding make versus buy, the number and variety of development tools it chooses to use, and the legacy of past decisions embedded within hardware platforms and software systems all combine to affect the level of IS complexity. In its role of gatekeeper, IS manages much of the complexity as experienced by the organization as well as that within the IS function. Key sources of complexity within IS are the following.

- **Organizational Ambiguity.** In the course of its work, IS must in many cases, take responsibility for introducing change into the organization—breaking down barriers, building commitment and reinforcing new patterns of work—as well as implementing new technology effectively. The role of the technology and the role of IS and business people in promoting and implementing it are often unclear. Levine and Rossmoore (1993) cite problems at all levels in answering the following questions:

  - What should the new technology/system do exactly?
  - Is there general agreement in the organization about what goals the technology/system will support?
  - Who is accountable for its success/failure?
  - How well does the technology support corporate strategy?
  - Who controls project decisions?

  This organizational ambiguity creates complexity for IS in accomplishing its work. In other words, if IS were preparing to give a concert, it not only has to learn to play new instruments, but it has to lead a band whose members have not agreed on the musical score!

- **Interacting Objectives.** IS has many objectives to accomplish. Achieving any one or two might be relatively easy, but taken together, they can lead to enormous complexity. For example, IS has a mandate to develop systems quickly and cheaply. IS also has a mission to introduce new tools into the development process and new technologies into the organization. Even though, ultimately, the new tools may prove superior, staff members may take much longer developing systems with them than with existing tools because of the time it takes to become proficient with these. Similarly, IS must develop secure, auditable systems. But improving security and auditability may directly impact the time and cost of development. They may also affect user satisfaction with systems—another of IS' main objectives. In short, because of its position in the organization, IS must constantly balance multiple and often conflicting objectives. It is the interactions among these objectives, each individually straight forward, that drive up IS complexity.

- **Technology Mass.** The IS technology mass consists of the entire collection of operating systems, application systems, hardware, development tools, data bases, languages, data files, and documentation. This mass tends to grow over time as new systems and tools are added to the mass but seldom removed. It behaves like the 'comet's tail' in that the tail of debris left behind by the comet's passage through space becomes so massive that it creates a gravitational pull on the comet which limits its direction and speed. In similar fashion, the technology mass in an organization can severely limit the organization's flexibility. New developments must be integrated into the current portfolio of systems. New systems must link with old. Expertise must be maintained to deal with systems written in older languages. This adds to the complexity of IS and impacts future technology decisions. If this technology mass is left unmanaged, it can gridlock an organization thus rendering it unable to change with any degree of confidence.

- **Logistics.** Finally, in addition to stickhandling through the ambiguous roles, conflicting objectives, and extensive technology mass, IS must actually deliver effective technology to the organization. The sheer number of tasks to be accomplished in system development and implementation can create a logistical nightmare that is highly complex. At a departmental level, managers must juggle staff and service levels for numerous systems. Limited budgets often increase logistical complexity further. At a project level, coordinating the sheer number of tasks that need to be completed and their interrelationships is a daunting task for many project managers.

3. *The Organization*

Organizations themselves can be very complex due to the nature of their business or due to the way in which they are organized. The following factors are sources of IS complexity arising within the organization:

- **Organizational Detail.** Organizational complexity seems to be directly related to the size of the organization. Because the IS function serves the organization, the law of requisite variety[1] would dictate that the IS function must be as complicated as the organization. In one insurance organization, the automated premium billing system was unable to handle any policies with attached riders causing these to be dealt with on an exception basis. Roughly 50% of all premiums fell into this category. Obviously, the billing system was not sufficiently complex. This example shows how IS complexity derives from the overall business complexity. IS complexity is also affected by the ongoing change processes within organizations as they reorganize periodically. Decisions to flatten organizational structure, empower employees, matrix business processes, or strengthen customer–supplier links typically have a bearing on IS complexity.

- **Organizational Insulation.** There is a trend to insulate business managers from the complexity of information technology. Most people including managers, if given the option, prefer to deal with menu-driven, graphical interfaces with point and click selection operation. This effectively insulates them from the complexity that occurs behind the interface. The governing principle appears to be to minimize the technology that managers must master to a level of a

---

[1] According to Davis and Olson (1985), the law of requisite variety (one of the basic notions of system control theory) suggests that there must be at least as many variations of control to be applied as there are ways for the system to get out of control. In organizational terms, a manager who wishes to control an inventory of 10,000 stockkeeping units needs to have available detailed information on each stockkeeping unit and to generate a control response for each possible variation in the state of each stockkeeping unit.

'need to know' basis. For example, a manager may need to know what data to ask for but may not need to know on which platform it is physically stored. The importance of this trend is that slick interfaces which hide a lot of complexity leave managers with the impression that systems are less complex than they really are. With this impression, they sometimes see systems work as simple and fail to fully appreciate the complexity behind the scenes.

- **Complexity Tradeoffs.** Similarly, in organizations there is also a trend to decrease the level of business complexity as seen by the customer. In many businesses, this has taken the form of the 'one-stop' shop. In a bank, for instance, a customer representative is now able to do all of the normal banking operations plus handle many other types of transactions having to do with payments, investments, credit cards, loans, etc. The customer sees a simple uncomplicated way to enact different transactions. What is not seen are the detailed and complicated support systems that enable this to occur, such as integrated computer systems capable of extracting and updating information from many different sources all seamlessly and instantaneously. Thus, simplicity for the customer is most often achieved at the expense of increased complexity for IS.

  The difference between complexity tradeoffs for customers and the insulation of business managers is one of degree. Where business is concerned, customer satisfaction is usually paramount, so there is continual pressure on IS to provide the systems that will support company plans. In many cases, business people do not realize the extent of the complexity that is imposed by these plans. However, while IS has more control over how much complexity it takes on *vis-à-vis* the business, in the case of customers, such tradeoffs are much less likely to be negotiable. Management believes that as the technical experts in the organization, IS should be able to deal with the additional complexity if it makes good business sense.

These nine factors are presented in Table 14.1. Each factor individually and collectively has a role to play in creating and sustaining IS complexity. With an understanding of their role as a source of complexity, we can work towards effectively managing IS complexity by attacking its source. The next section presents strategies for the effective management of IS complexity.

EFFECTIVE MANAGEMENT OF IS COMPLEXITY

The effective management of IS complexity involves striking a balance—that is, IS must limit unnecessary growth in complexity while at the same time ensuring sufficient flexibility within IS to enable it to react to change. The challenge is in knowing where to set this balance. There are easy methods for reducing complexity (e.g., allow only one type of computer and only one language) but, if rigidly adopted, these methods can severely constrain the organization. These methods are not suggested. Instead, members felt that the following strategies provide a more balanced approach to managing IS complexity:

1. *Manage Your Technology Mass*

A proactive approach must be taken when managing the technology mass for the simple reason that it is much easier to add to this mass than it is to subtract from it. Past decisions, as manifested in this mass, can create an unusually complex environment (e.g., one that is expensive to maintain, difficult to manage because it is unstable, and difficult to change because it is inflexible). In one organization, investigation uncovered the fact that 27 different programmer tools existed necessitating some level of expertise in each! It seems a state of nature that IS is too inclined to adopt new technologies.

To counter this, organizations should adopt a renewal strategy. With this strategy, all applications and tools should be examined annually to determine when they should be retired. 'Legacy' systems (i.e., systems which are old and frail and are often left untouched because IS is afraid that any modification will cause them not to work) should be evaluated

Table 14.1. An Overview of IS Complexity

Origin	Source	Cause
Emerging Technology	Technological Uncertainty	Uncertainty
	Technological Interrelationships	Interactions
	Provider Dynamics	Detail
IS Function	Organizational Ambiguity	Ambiguity
	Interacting Objectives	Interactions
	Technology Mass	Dynamics
	Logistics	Detail
Parent Organization	Organizational Detail	Detail
	Organizational Insulation	Dynamics
	Complexity Tradeoffs	Dynamics

under this strategy. New functionality can often be used to justify the need to update/replace old systems. Alternatively, renewing old systems can be justified by proving that new functionality can be produced faster with newer technology. A third strategy for renewal is to upgrade systems on a piecemeal basis. While not as 'neat' as other solutions, it may be easier to cost-justify where budgets are tight.

Ideally, no area of the application portfolio should remain dormant. One organization devotes 15% of total IS resources to the refurbishment of old applications. Under this renewal strategy, life-cycle management techniques are used for the entire application portfolio—all applications and tools are continually reviewed, updated, enhanced, and eventually retired. This reduces the mass of technology as well as the age of technology, reduces the need for expertise in older technologies, and produces a much less complex environment for IS to manage.

2. Manage Your Technology Migration

Each addition of new technology starts your IS organization up another learning curve. For example, suppose an IS organization decides to adopt a different development tool. Considerable time is spent researching potential tools in order to choose the best tool. Once chosen, it can take an organization several years to become truly productive with the new tool. This involves training, support, and experience using the tool in the particular organization in order that it can be effectively tailored to fit within the organizational culture. Once online, the new tool will require regular maintenance and updating to accommodate new releases. When the full costs are tallied, the decision to adopt this new tool has resulted in a substantial investment for the organization with the associated risks. The decision to migrate to new technology must be managed carefully. How should this be done?

First, minimize the IS tool set. IS complexity can be reduced substantially by allowing only one 'screen painter,' for example. Look to see how many different tools are used to accomplish the same or similar function. Where there is substantial overlap, eliminate all but one. Everyone always has their favourite system and will argue for why Excel is preferable to Lotus. End the debate and make a choice—for better or worse.

Second, migrate to new technology only when necessary. Realizing the productivity downfall while climbing new learning curves, limit the number of learning curves. Sometimes it is possible to skip versions (if not generations) of new technology. Many organizations adopt major versions of software and skip the intermediate steps (i.e., V1.0, V2.0, . . . instead of V1.0, V1.1, V1.2, V1.22, . . .). This strategy of taking bigger steps less frequently means that startup costs are reduced.

Third, use integrated tools. If these can be purchased, they should be. If this is not a possibility, then integrated tools can be developed. The advantage of integrated tools is the provision of common interfaces and the ability to move from one tool to another easily thereby reducing the learning curve climb.

3. *Manage Your Vendors*

IS complexity varies directly with the number of vendors. There is a tradeoff between locking in with a single vendor (which limits options and ties your technology strategy with the vendor's) and dealing with many vendors (which drives up the complexity significantly). Single vendors often offer a degree of integration that is difficult to achieve across vendors. This is becoming more important as organizations develop applications to operate on more than one hardware platform. The most popular strategy seems to be to limit the number of vendors to the smallest set possible, i.e., enough to ensure competition, but not too many to cause integration problems). Another strategy is to prepare an architecture document outlining your organization's requirements (i.e., If you want to do business with us, this is what you have to do . . .). Vendors then take on the responsibility for many of the integration issues caused by multiple vendors. Both strategies try to minimize integration problems while keeping various technology options open and controlling the level of IS complexity arising from vendor relations.

Managing suppliers effectively can ensure service level delivery. One organization keeps detailed performance appraisal records on all vendor supplied items. Operating statistics track hardware, software, parts, response, service, and even invoicing. For each of these items, acceptable limits (agreed to by the vendor) are set and points awarded for attainment of goals. Any item falling below limits is noted and discussed with the vendor. Vendor performance becomes much more focused as contracts are tied directly to this performance appraisal.

Even with software vendors, it is also possible to push some of the burden of integration back on to the vendors. By demanding software portability across hardware platforms, development tools which integrate with current tool sets, and migratability of existing systems, IS organizations can force vendors to build in a level of integration at source. This relieves the degree of IS complexity enormously.

Finally, many strategic partnerships with a variety of vendors are possible. Recently, companies have entered into such partnerships to develop specialized software for various industries. Examples include banking machines, point of sale equipment, and investment brokerage software. These partnerships share the development costs, shorten the development times, bring together the necessary talent base and spread the risk thus making them attractive to many organizations and in particular many smaller organizations.

4. *Manage Your Architecture*

Managing architecture starts with a clearly articulated set of principles for an IT framework. This set of principles must be defined and maintained by skilled IT professionals and must be based on business strategies, current investment portfolios and industry directions. It must include the design and delivery targets for computing platforms (hardware and software), communications and networks, systems software, information access, and systems delivery. Finally, it must acknowledge existing platforms and technology constraints and a migration path to move from the old to the new at the right time.

A key element of this architectural framework is a policy of adherence to standards. They must be based on industry accepted practices and accompanied by a strategy to ensure usage. They must be clearly defined, readily accessible and regularly reviewed. Standards apply to development as well. Organizations should develop to as many widely-recognized standards as possible. As a part of vendor management, organizations should push for standards and their adoption. If no standards are available, applications should be developed in layers so that layers can be replaced later when sufficiently well-accepted standards appear. Applications should be as independent of the platform as is possible.

With such an architectural framework in place, IS organizations can make informed decisions with assurance that they will form a cohesive whole. This approach works to reduce IS complexity by eliminating decisions which do not conform to the established framework.

5. *Manage Your Research*

Research is critical for IS in order that they can fulfil their role as technology gatekeeper for their organizations. The danger lies in creating yet more infrastructure in the form of 'research for the sake of research' or the creation of the 'department of innovation.' How then should organizations conduct this type of research?

First, the research must be focused on business practices and/or opportunities. This is best accomplished by researchers with a knowledge of the business combined with a knowledge of the technology. One organization uses advanced technology groups (ATGs) to carry out the following duties:

- Set formal policies and procedures for investigating and implementing new technologies.
- Work with business units in developing overall IT architecture principles.
- Act as the enabler of technological change.
- Provide technological advice and assistance to business units.
- Act as information broker between various business units.

- Act as filter for project proposals (to ensure adherence to architectural principles, assist with coordination of vendor relationships, and assess match of technology to business activity).

These ATGs are best formed as 'virtual' groups around a promising technology and business opportunity. They should not be permanent organizational fixtures. Their formation should always include a sunset clause.

The same duties as those listed above can be accomplished in an alternate manner by simply assigning these responsibilities to all senior members of the IS function. That is, the search for new technologies and innovative uses of these technologies is embedded in IS job descriptions. These individuals are charged with the responsibility to act as change agents. In this role, they are evaluated on the basis of how successful they are in introducing new technology to the workplace.

There are advantages and disadvantages to both approaches. Both, however, need senior management vision and direction. Researchers need to know what latitude they have. Are they encouraged to be leading edge? or Are they encouraged to adopt only proven technology? Not every technology needs to be investigated in-depth. With senior management vision and direction, certain technologies can be bypassed while others are highlighted. Attempting to keep current in all technologies at a detailed level will soon bankrupt your IS resources. Direction and vision allow the research to be focused. Research carries risk. Those conducting research must have direction as to the risk level they are empowered to expose their organizations. This also must be a senior management directive.

6. *Manage Your Parent Organization*

We are not being so audacious here as to suggest that IS could and should actually manage their parent organizations. The point is that part of IS complexity derives from the parent organization because of the need for requisite variety, complexity insulation, and/or the complexity seesaw factor. Thus, it is to be expected that any organizational change would have a direct impact on the level of IS complexity. Therefore, IS should have some input into decisions regarding organizational change.

In Chapter 2, we outlined the role of IS in re-engineering the organization. Within this role, IS has the capability to suggest how technology can be marshalled to support different organizational forms. During this exercise, IS should be aware of the resultant effects that these changes will have on its own complexity. Specifically, each alternative organizational structure should be considered in light of its effects on each of the nine factors which lead to IS complexity. We are not suggesting that organizational re-engineering decisions should be entirely based on these factors—we are suggesting that these factors are important and should therefore be explicit elements in the decision process. The consequence of not doing this is to risk driving IS complexity to unmanageable levels.

CONCLUSION

IS complexity stems from several sources—ever-increasing technical detail, logistics, an uncertain and ambiguous direction for IS due to technology and organizational issues, and the significant interrelationships required of effective IS work. Management strategies must deal with complexity either by reducing the absolute level of complexity (e.g., by limiting choices) or by implementing strategies for increasing our ability to cope with increased complexity (e.g., training, technology research groups). These strategies, if followed, should enable IS organizations to deal much more effectively with the complex environment in which they exist.

15
Mining for Corporate Information

INTRODUCTION

Almost all large businesses today produce mountains of data from the vast array of operational computer systems they have put in place over the last 25 years. Flowing out of functional systems designed to parallel the traditional functionally-organized business, these operational data typically come in a wide variety of shapes and sizes, using different timeframes and reporting formats. As a result, it is next to impossible for senior managers to compare and collate data from different systems or to integrate it with outside data to get the *information* they need to do their jobs effectively. At a time when many organizations are trying to re-engineer and reposition themselves in the marketplace, such confusing and disorganized data are beginning to represent formidable obstacles to organizational change and growth. In a survey of CEOs, 80% named inadequate information as their number one IT problem. It was also the problem that drew a high level of dissatisfaction with systems, with a rating of -.83 (on a scale of -1.00 to +1.00) (Moynihan, 1990).

Recently, some organizations have been successful in 'mining' operational data for the information executives' need (Bessen, 1993; Southerst, 1993). The success of these ventures, whether in improving control (e.g., Mrs. Field's Cookies), or reducing costs (e.g., Wal-Mart), or micro-marketing (e.g., R.R. Donnelley), or simply in knowing one's customers better (e.g., Journey's End Corp) have prompted many senior managers to push IS to look for ways to extract information from operational data.

On one hand, this high level attention to corporate information is music to the ears of IS executives, who have spent many years trying to get senior business managers to buy into the benefits of data modelling and corporate data bases. On the other, extracting information from the data available is not a trivial task. Determining what information executives need, finding it in the organization, and delivering it in a useful fashion is a monumental activity (Giordano, 1993). It can also be an expensive one requiring new hardware and software (i.e., data 'warehouses' and access tools) as well as the staff to develop and maintain them. Furthermore, there are significant organizational risks involved. More 'information' may not always yield the benefits expected. So, while most IS managers are committed to the *concept* of corporate information, they are still struggling with how best to *implement* it in their own organizations.

Will mining corporate information yield diamonds or coal? To address the issues surrounding how corporate information should best be created, accessed, and managed, Forum members discussed their strategies for delivering information to the corporation, how they determine the benefits of this information, the costs involved, selection of the most effective tools and technologies to manage the data, and the significant organizational and people issues associated with implementing their plans.

This chapter first examines the 'need' for ever-increasing amounts of information from a historical and social perspective. Second, it looks at the expectations surrounding corporate information that are fuelling its demand. Then, it addresses how information is used effectively in organizations and some of the problems associated with corporate information. Finally, four strategies for creating and controlling corporate information are then discussed.

HOW MUCH INFORMATION DO WE *REALLY* NEED?

Business' increasing 'need' for more and more information is not a particularly new concept. In fact, social historians see it as part of a much larger trend that has gradually discounted the judgement of the individual and inflated the importance of quantitative data (Postman, 1992). The need for information is based on certain assumptions that underlie our thinking about the 'correct' way to approach work, including:

- technical calculation is superior to human judgment;
- subjectivity is an obstacle to clear thinking;
- our affairs are best guided by experts;
- technique can do our thinking for us.

All of these assumptions lead to greater and greater reliance in 'information' rather than human discretion.

Technology critic, Neil Postman suggests that really, very few of our problems arise because of insufficient information; a much bigger problem is 'information glut,' which can lead to information chaos and a loss of the ethical, moral, aesthetic, and spiritual underpinnings of our enterprises, be they personal, political or commercial:

'Attend any conference on . . . computer technology and you will be attending a celebration of innovative machinery that generates, stores, and distributes even more information, more conveniently, at greater speeds than ever before . . . We are driven . . . [by] the quest to 'access' information. For what purpose or with what limitations, it is not for us to ask.'

Henry Mintzberg echoes these concerns in his book *The Rise and Fall of Strategic Planning* (1994). Here, he documents why formal planning processes have been a dismal failure.

'The failure of strategic planning is the failure of systems to do better than, or even nearly as well as, human beings . . . Formal systems have offered no improved means of dealing with the information overload of human brains; indeed, they have often made matters worse.'

By isolating top management from its own grassroots organization and from the outside world, strategic decision-making based on quantitative data, inhibits intuition and saps the entrepreneurial instinct.

Systems and information technology provide us with numbers that can be seen and worked with, and which make us feel comfortable. The problem is that all too often, these numbers direct our attention in the wrong direction. Postman notes:

> 'It is apparently sufficient that the computer has pronounced. Who has put the data in, for what purpose, for whose convenience, based on what assumptions are questions left unasked.'

In spite of such warnings, many organizations continue to believe that more and better information will solve their problems. The next section looks at the key rationales for this belief.

THE CASE FOR CORPORATE INFORMATION

Many CEOs are convinced that corporate information will dramatically increase the profitability of their businesses by improving the quality of decisions made by their managers. According to many of our Forum members, the development of corporate information has been made one of their top three IS priorities. By eliminating inconsistencies, allowing different views of operational data to be reflected (e.g., all products purchased by a single customer), providing appropriate summaries, and being accessible across the corporation, corporate information should *theoretically* provide more accurate support for decision-making, leading to four key benefits:

1. **Better Cost Management.** Improved corporate information should enable managers to track the profitability of products or customers over time. This, in turn, should give them a better ability to manage profitable or unprofitable ones differently.

2. **Improved Productivity.** Access to corporate information should provide managers with the ability to identify best practices, improve productivity, and streamline processes.

3. **Improved Risk Management.** Better information should enable companies to identify patterns of behaviour and activity that are associated with increased risk to the business which, in turn, will allow them to manage the risk more effectively.

4. **Better Customer Management.** Since most data tends to be functionally organized, it is easy for a business to lose track of who its customers are. Better corporate information should be able to give a business a picture of its customers, facilitate more focused marketing initiatives, and enable cross-selling and specialized selling.

Very few organizations have much experience with corporate information and so, to date, there is no proof that these benefits are being realized by businesses that have made an investment in creating corporate information. Although it has become the prevailing wisdom that the benefits of corporate information will be significant, those that are actually demonstrable are considerably more modest.

THE DEMONSTRABLE BENEFITS OF INFORMATION

In spite of their concerns about the exalted stature of information in modern society, even Mintzberg and Postman recognize that information can have many benefits. What are the known benefits of information to the organization? Mintzberg (1994) suggests that the proper role of information is **operational support**. Information can be extremely useful helping the organization take its day-to-day pulse. By organizing and making sense out of myriad pieces of data produced each day, organizations can improve customer service, determine which products or promotions are working, and identify their penetration of markets. Wal-Mart's inventory management systems are classic examples of the effective use of information for operational support. Wal-Mart shares data and a data model with its suppliers that enable specific quantities of merchandise in specific sizes and colours to be sent to specific stores. The result is simpler logistics, lower inventory costs, and fewer stock outs (Haeckel and Nolan, 1993). Similarly, Mrs. Field's Cookies uses information from its many outlets to advise them each day about what to order and how many cookies to bake (Haeckel and Nolan, 1993). With the proper use of operational models, organizations can make extensive use of this kind of information to make the day-to-day operations of their companies as seamless as possible.

A second known benefit of information is in supporting **tactical** activities. For example, some organizations have had success using information to micro-market to their customers. Bessen (1993) cites the example of publisher, R.R. Donnelley which has an extensive customer database which enables it to provide as many as 8000 tailored editions of its *Farm Journal* each month. Fingerhut target-markets successfully to low-income households by monitoring their purchases and carefully extending increasing amounts of credit. Both organizations have had healthy increases in sales, despite the recession, and both attribute their success to their detailed knowledge of their customers.

A less well-supported benefit of information is the **identification of historical trends**. While some Forum members argued that a knowledge of history does not help in predicting the future, others felt that the ability to track certain key variables over time (e.g., performance) helps management to uncover its strengths and weaknesses. The value of historical information, however, comes from the quality of the analysis applied to it. As Goldratt and Cox (1984) point out in *The Goal*, if the wrong measures are being tracked, the organization can end up becoming less profitable because efforts are focused on the wrong things. Historical information therefore can support effective analysis and decision-making, but is not a substitute for it.

Information can also **support new strategic ideas**. Postman (1992) suggests that rather than quantitative data being viewed as 'scientific proof' of a strategy, which he clearly demonstrates they are not, information should be viewed as a form of 'storytelling.' Once a strategy has been identified, corporate information can be tapped to determine whether or not it might work. To paraphrase Postman, a strategy cannot be proved or disproved, but draws its appeal from the depth of explanations, the relevance of the examples, and the credibility of the themes given to support it. Information provides one method of support (but not the only one) for new strategies by providing depth and credibility to a new direction. This is how many 'trend watchers' do their work. They talk with people until they identify a trend that might be starting. Then they use data to examine and refine their hunches and to support their overall case when presenting new trends to their clients.

The underlying theme of each of these benefits is that they *support* human management and decision-making, they do not replace it. Poor managers at all levels will continue to make poor decisions, with or without corporate information. In fact, it is very likely that corporate information will help poor decision-makers to become worse because it can imbue the manager with an aura of correctness since he/she is supported by the 'facts.' However, if viewed as an additional source of input by the manager who knows what he/she is doing and looking for, corporate information can indeed deliver benefits to the organization. The challenge for the organization is to distinguish between these two types of use.

THE PITFALLS OF CORPORATE INFORMATION

Although corporate information can be valuable, it also has significant costs to the organization, over and above the obvious costs of creating it. Forum members identified nine pitfalls managers often fail to see when deciding to create corporate information.

1. **Playing.** One manager who has implemented an extensive data warehouse over the last ten years, noted that use of corporate information has grown 'exponentially' each year since implementation. Even when the company reduced staff by 25%, usage of the data warehouse actually went up! 'The more information you give end-users, the more they want' he

remarked. However, in spite of much searching, this company has been unable to find significant benefits accruing as the result of widespread access to company information. Where benefits are being achieved, they are obtained by a 'handful' of staff who have a very tight focus on how they want to use the data. The question remains, therefore, whether the remainder of the staff are really using corporate information effectively or just playing with it?

2. **Price.** The costs of physically creating and maintaining corporate information should not be underestimated. A typical strategy involves the purchase of specialized data storage devices to create a 'data warehouse.' These are necessary because of the large quantities of data involved (usually gigabytes or terabytes). To access these devices, companies need data warehouse management tools, data access and reporting tools, and software to connect the data warehouse to the other technologies installed (Inmon, 1990, Hewlett-Packard, 1994). In addition, staff are needed to manage the physical equipment and to administer and maintain the contents. As well as the actual costs of these items, there are also hidden costs associated with introducing another layer of technology and new specialists to the organization. Less complex technologies are cheaper, but all implementations of corporate information will come with costs in each of these areas which companies would do well to assess fully.

3. **People.** A real risk of corporate information is the loss of 'instinctive' business skills amongst decision-making staff. As noted above, corporate information can actually get in the way of doing effective business by becoming a substitute for entrepreneurial skills. Once a skill falls into disuse, there is a danger it may end up being lost. Postman (1992) notes how doctors have lost judgement and diagnostic skills as they have come more and more to rely on medical technology and less on the patient's subjective feelings. Unfortunately, it is all too common today that a patient is told that an illness is 'all in his head' if technical tests do not reveal what is wrong.

In business, if senior managers become insulated from their customers and frontline operations behind walls of data, it is also likely that they will fail to diagnose opportunities for growth and improvement. Several Forum members wondered whether simply spending a few hours with customers would yield more benefits to managers than complicated and expensive corporate information-building projects.

4. **Data Mapping.** A central activity in the creation of corporate information is the extraction of data from operational files and its mapping on to corporate data models. This involves a number of complex steps. First, a model of the data required must be developed. Next, the data to be extracted must be identified. Then, rules for its transformation must be determined and coded. The 'hype' in the industry is that this is simply a matter of figuring out what goes where and 'translating' different versions of the same data into one standard version (e.g., MM/DD/YY into DD MMM YYYY).

Giordano (1993) points out that most data mapping is not this simple. Given that most organizations' data are inconsistent, poorly defined, and functionally-oriented, the process of creating corporate information promises to be a long and arduous one. He gives a typical example of what many companies are up against. He describes a field in a system which was originally designed to record an employee's IQ—data which subsequently fell into disuse. A few years later, when a new government regulation requires that all employees be issued hard hats, the field is 'recycled' to contain hat-size. However, to simplify programming, it is not renamed. Thus, it becomes an information minefield that only existing programs know how to use properly.

This is only one of a large number of problems with data that are lurking in existing operational systems ready to destroy corporate information. One Forum manager noted that his systems have 27 different ways of identifying 'sex'! Giordano cautions managers that overselling the idea of corporate information can raise unrealistic expectations that will be impossible to provide, especially in the short term, given the state of most companies' data.

5. **Path-Finding.** Access to corporate information is generally based on the creation of libraries and directories which users search to find where the data they need is located. Not only must these be created and maintained, they must be usable by a diverse number of users. Forum members who have implemented corporate information in their own organizations have pointed out that, all too frequently, users lack the skills or the time to find out what information is available. In other words, getting corporate information into an accessible format is only half the battle. The other half involves helping users to get at it.

6. **Politics.** Introducing corporate information means that individual functional areas must be able to agree on what should be selected as corporate information and what it should look like. This requires a level of agreement between users that is rarely simple to obtain, given the territoriality of most functional managers. Other political problems relate to funding. Where does the money come from to implement corporate information? Many organizations are still functionally structured and funding for IS is structured in the same way. Getting individual functions to fund or partially fund corporate information may not be easy as a result. One manager noted:

> 'One of the biggest political barriers seems to be people trusting other people's data as a source and being prepared to fix the source if it is broken . . . The bulk of the work is reconciling different people's views of the data and confirming it really is the same stuff.'

Politics is one aspect of information systems work that is rarely addressed by industry experts. Yet, in the 'real world,' it is responsible for many less than ideal solutions. Corporate information is not only not immune to these politics, it is probably more vulnerable to them because it is unlikely to have a single, powerful corporate sponsor. A manager remarked that politics has forced her to abandon establishing a corporate information strategy. 'Implementing corporate information is never anyone's top priority.'

Instead, she is proceeding slowly and taking advantage of opportunities as they arise and enforcing standardized 'points of consolidation' i.e., common terminology, that present 'the biggest problems when we try to draw the data together across systems and departments.'

7. **Security.** IT managers must consider two facets of security. First, they must ensure that production systems are not compromised by users accessing corporate information. Often, this is interpreted as not allowing users to work with operational data. However, in addition, managers need to ensure that production resources are not affected by use of corporate data. One manager noted that he has had 'enquiries from hell' that can bring a whole production system 'to its knees' by churning up valuable production time and preventing operational systems from doing their jobs. Effective security means screening out such enquiries before disaster occurs.

A second facet of security concerns determining who has access to which data. While corporations are generally more open about data access these days, the fact remains that there are many types of data which remain sensitive, either because they concern individuals (e.g., personnel or performance information) or the company as a whole (e.g., information which should not be shared with competitors). Along with the commitment to corporate information comes an increasing responsibility to monitor and control access to this information.

8. **Privacy.** Many organizations have yet to recognize privacy as a problem, but as companies collect more and more information about individuals, it is a potentially explosive one. Bessen (1993) notes that in 1991, 30,000 people phoned Lotus Development to complain about invasion of privacy when it introduced Lotus MarketPlace, a product that provided household information on CD-ROM. Bessen considers it likely that companies will be regulated in the future in three areas: collection of personal data; its use; and the transfer and sharing of data. These regulations will not stop the use of corporate information, but could make it

more costly to collect and administer (e.g., there will have to be facilities to remove people from marketing lists if they request it).

9. **Paradigms.** Finally, one of the most difficult perils of corporate information to address is the problem of existing organizational paradigms. When extracting and organizing corporate information, data and mental models are used in which these paradigms are implicit. Thus, these views of the organization colour how information is organized, summarized, and presented. Executives wishing to break free of existing ways of thinking can find themselves thrust back into them because of the way information is presented. For example, if current thinking suggests that all families making less than $25,000 are poor candidates for credit, then corporate information may eliminate these families or lump them together. Or, perhaps home-based businesses are aggregated with other small businesses. Both are potential sources of growth and profit that companies may not discover until the business has gone elsewhere. In these ways, decision support systems, based on corporate information, can actually be detrimental to a business, because they reinforce existing perceptions and do not challenge the *status quo*.

CREATING CORPORATE INFORMATION

Companies that decide to 'mine' their operational data for corporate information can follow four strategies. Some members of the Forum were variously pursuing each, or several at once, depending on their assessment of their needs and their organization's objectives. Other members pointed out that these strategies could be considered evolutionary steps towards increasingly more complex corporate information.

Strategy #1. *Create Corporate Information as needed*

In this strategy, organizations move slowly and cautiously towards corporate information by adapting and linking operational data to meet specific informational needs. IS works closely with its users to define the information they would like to see, and determines an approach for obtaining it from the data and the systems available. Wherever regular information needs can be identified, these are built into the reports produced for management. Users must cost-justify their needs, and pay for them, in the same way as other system requests are justified.

One of the managers following this approach explained his company's choice as follows:

> 'We don't question the idea of a data warehouse. Ideally, it's very appealing. Our question is how to get there . . . We feel that once a data warehouse is produced, it is used, regardless of the costs and benefits. Our strategy is that, with 80% of our users having access to LAN terminals and tools, where benefits can be justified, we can easily provide derivative files for them . . . However, if you turn people into hackers, the costs will kill you.'

This is a very focused, practical approach that is driven, first and foremost by cost. This strategy recognizes that users need information and gives it to them in two ways. First, users have access to some operational level data through end-user computing (EUC) tools. Second, if users have specific informational needs that can be cost justified, the information will be provided for them. As information is derived, and as operational systems are redeveloped, organizations following this option will make the necessary modifications and decisions to ensure that the data can be effectively transferred to a data warehouse. However, these organizations feel that the move to corporate information should be an evolutionary one, rather than a major one-time investment.

Choose this approach if:

- senior management insists on rigorous cost-justification;
- users need assistance in analysing and thinking through their information needs, and what they would do with the information if they had it;
- maintenance of data accuracy is a problem.

Strategy #2. *Enhanced Query Management*

Most organizations provide some *ad hoc* query functions, so that users can access operational data for their informational needs. Whether it is through an Information Centre or through copies of operational files on local area networks, query functions have been available for many years. Some companies have decided to expand their query facilities, rather than to build a formal data warehouse.

This option works well when a large percentage of data is divisional or departmental in nature. Specific files can then be extracted and downloaded to each department. Many businesses have been surprised by how much data is department-specific, rather than corporate. One manager noted: 'Here, there are relatively few useful sources of corporate data.' Another estimated that only about 10% of their data was 'corporate.' He felt that by imposing a more generalized data warehouse between the operational data and the users (i.e., by standardizing the terminology and the frames of reference), data which has a great deal of meaning at the departmental level will be lost.

An enhanced query option is also a strategy to extend the life of a legacy system without major revisions. Online queries against a derivative file may satisfy user needs for information in the short term while IS is coming to grips with their larger information needs. Finally, extended query management is useful if information is needed by a small group of users who have very specific needs. A disadvantage of this approach is that because the data are designed for use by operational systems, queries against these data tend to be awkward and inefficient.

Choose this approach if:

- it will extend the life of a legacy system;
- most of your data is divisional or departmental in nature;
- a small group of users can justify the need for some tightly-focused data;
- cost justification is an important consideration.

Strategy #3. *A Customer Information File*

Another approach to solving the problem of corporate information is to create a customer information file which integrates operational data from a variety of sources by customer. This option is more expensive than the previous two because it involves the creation of a corporate database specifically for the purpose of providing information about a corporation's customers. However, because it is more specific in intention than a data warehouse, it is easier to create, manage, and control. Its advantage is that it pulls together information about customers that are hidden in a variety of functional files, enabling companies to learn more about their customers, and facilitating target marketing of specific groups.

A customer information file is a focused implementation of the data warehouse concept and one which many companies have used effectively. Bessen (1993) notes how Fingerhut increased its sales in recent years, in spite of selling to households with less than $25,000 in income, by studying what they bought, marketing to their needs, and personalizing their approaches to each customer. Southerst (1993) describes how examining previous guest registrations at Journey's End Hotels exploded several corporate 'myths' about who their customers were and what they wanted. Customer information files facilitate target marketing, one of the key benefits of corporate information. Also, because they promote a 'customer view' of the business, rather than a 'product view,' they are very much in keeping with current management perspectives.

On the negative side, customer information files do have a limited scope, which can frustrate some users, especially those who do not know exactly what they want and wish to explore various avenues of information. Also, they can be difficult to maintain accurately. One manager noted that his company had a customer data base which had not been maintained, resulting in data that was only 32% accurate. 'If it hasn't been maintained, it's not really needed' he believes. Nevertheless, customer information files are a good way to introduce the concepts of corporate information to the organization, in a controlled manner.

Choose this approach if:

* your systems are organized by product or function and you want to become more customer-focused;
* target-marketing is a primary information objective;
* some financial justification is required.

Strategy #4. *A Data Warehouse*

A data warehouse is a data base or a collection of data bases that a company uses to support its decision-making activities. A data warehouse contains data that is copied and extracted from operational data, rather than the operational data itself. In one sense, many companies have been using the data warehouse concept for years in that they may already be extracting operational data and providing users with derivative files for their use. There are two key differences about data warehouses as they are being promoted today.

First, the scope of data involved is considerably larger than most companies have previously undertaken. Although, it is recommended that companies start with a manageable project to implement the data warehouse concept, rather than an 'intergalactic data model,' the volumes of data involved and the fact that data warehouses generally contain several years' worth of historical data as well, mean that the data warehouse must be designed to store and retrieve data on a much larger scale than previously envisioned.

A second new feature is the technology. Current mainframe and PC technology is designed for fast processing, not data management. The new 'data boxes' on the market (i.e., units designed specifically for data storage and retrieval) address this need. The data warehouse is an additional layer of hardware and software on top of an organization's operational system. A complete data warehouse system consists of the hardware (i.e., data boxes), data warehouse management software (to extract and manage the data), data access and reporting tools (for users to use), and connectivity software to enable the data warehouse to connect to the organization's mainframe and PC hardware and software.

The jury is still out on whether data warehouses will deliver the perceived benefits of corporate information. Managers considering implementing a data warehouse should ask the following questions:

- Will my company receive real value from a data warehouse (as opposed to other forms of obtaining corporate information)?
- Are our users able to use the data provided in a disciplined way, or will they just play?
- Are our executives aware of the limitations of corporate information in the formulation of company strategy?
- If the answer to the first three questions is yes, will the benefits we get outweigh the costs of the additional hardware and software, and the additional staff time?

If a data warehouse becomes part of a company's overall IS strategy, the most effective way to implement it is, *carefully*. Even vendors recommend building a data warehouse in small pieces. One manager doing this is working with a specific area of the business to determine the key pieces of data necessary for most information needs and to build a set of 'pre-canned' enquiries for users who want access to corporate information but who will find it difficult to learn access tools. By proceeding slowly with small sets of data, and by focusing on the areas of the business where information needs are highest, he hopes to avoid many of the pitfalls of corporate information and generate significant benefits to the business.

Choose this approach if:

- you have a senior management mandate;
- you have the support of a disciplined group of users;
- you are prepared to undertake a data modelling effort (at least for the area of interest);
- you are prepared to invest time and money in new technology and its administration;
- you believe the benefits will come, if the data are provided;
- your corporate strategies are clear and the data will be used to implement them.

CONCLUSION

Mining for corporate information can be a hazardous business! Information does not just lie around in chunks waiting to be picked up in today's organizations. Most of the time, it requires skill and fortitude to delve into a mountain of data, and there is little guarantee of what you might find. Like the old-fashioned prospector, today's information prospector needs to venture into the unknown and take significant risks. Sometimes, gold will be found; more often, not. For companies not willing to bear the risks and the costs involved, some smaller sorties are recommended where both the costs and the rewards are more certain.

16

Managing Legacy Systems

INTRODUCTION

'Legacy' was written in the late 1960s to handle the core activities of the business. The system consisted of over 4000 programs and approximately 1.5 million lines of COBOL and Assembler. The code was rambling and unstructured, followed few programming conventions (as we know them today), and had been patched many times in an attempt to meet the changing needs of business. It was littered with creative 'work-around' solutions making it an exceedingly complex system. Furthermore, it seemed that every system in the company was linked to Legacy—no one was exactly sure because the documentation was sketchy. As a result, even minor changes to Legacy frequently 'blew other systems out of the water' unsuspectedly. To complicate matters, when the original programmers left the company a few years ago, there was no one who really knew Legacy in its entirety. And given that it would take months if not years to master Legacy, no programmers wanted to stay in 'maintenance' long enough to justify the training investment. Management acknowledged the 'problem' but always put it off for another year. Besides, Legacy 'worked' so why spend money to replace it? The matter

> *finally came to a head when a request to increase the*
> *length of a single field was submitted to IS who estimated*
> *that it would require between 2500 and 3000 hours of*
> *effort! Suddenly the company had a PROBLEM!*

This situation, while fictitious, is typical. Most organizations have hundreds or even thousands of legacy programs and data files that need revitalization. It is not uncommon to find over half of IS development personnel working on legacy systems. The difficulties are legend—unrelated product files when the business needs customer files, old fragile code difficult to change and highly prone to failure if it is changed, and expertise that disappears with each resignation. But with the business' continual drive for new IS functionality, there is little enthusiasm for replacing these systems. Unfortunately, these legacy systems get one year older every year and instead of going away, the problem compounds. For many organizations, the time has finally come to face up to their legacy systems.

To address the issues surrounding legacy systems, Forum members were asked to describe their legacy systems, the strategies they use to manage these systems, the organizational and people issues that surround these systems, and finally, what can be done to ensure that these systems continue to provide realizable benefits to their organizations. This chapter first examines the nature of legacy systems from a number of perspectives. A number of proven strategies for managing legacy systems are then presented, including a contingency model for assessing the status of an organization's legacy systems. Finally, it looks at ways of preventing legacy systems in the future.

WHAT IS A LEGACY SYSTEM?

A 'legacy' is something handed down by a predecessor—usually implying the inheritance of something old. The term is not value-laden and implies neither good nor bad. However, when applied to systems, 'legacy' is usually used in the pejorative sense. Dietrich (1989) suggests that legacy systems are . . .

'systems that have evolved over many years and are considered irreplaceable, either because reimplementing their function is considered to be too expensive, or because they are trusted by users. Because of their age, such systems are likely to have been implemented in a conventional procedural language with limited use of data abstraction or encapsulation. The lack of abstraction complicates adding new applications to such a system and the lack of encapsulation impedes modifying the system itself because applications come to depend on system internals.'

This definition covers a number of different aspects of legacy systems that need to be explored, if not challenged:

- **Legacy systems are old.** While it is true that the majority of legacy systems are old, a system's age does not, in and of itself, make a system a legacy system. Indeed, many organizations already have legacy PC systems! Inflexibility, not age, is perhaps the key feature of legacy systems. Businesses change constantly in order to meet the demands of the marketplace and this necessitates the need for information systems to evolve accordingly. Were it not for change, we would have no legacy systems—those first implemented would still be meeting the organization's needs perfectly well.

  In his definition, Dietrich identifies the limited use of data abstraction or encapsulation as the culprit in making systems difficult to modify, i.e., inflexible. Again, because older conventional languages lacked the ability to use these techniques, there is a relationship between age and inflexibility. This relationship, however, is spurious. Inflexible systems, whether young or old, are difficult and expensive to change. When it requires many hours of effort to make a simple change, a system is surely a legacy system.

- **Legacy systems are irreplaceable.** According to Dietrich, legacy systems are irreplaceable either because 're-implementing their function is considered to be too expensive, or because they are trusted by users.' However, this is inaccurate. Arguing that redeveloping a system is too expensive simply means that management considers the costs of reimplementing a system to outweigh the benefits and it does not necessarily mean that a system has become a legacy system. Also, the fact that systems are irreplaceable simply because users trust them probably says more about the inability of the company as a whole to replicate the functionality within these systems than it does about whether or not the system is a legacy system. Using a reverse argument, if users did *not* trust the system, would it cease to be a legacy system? Probably not.

The fact is that legacy systems, due to their mere existence, have not been replaced. This, however, does not imply that they are irreplaceable. It simply reflects the fact that management has sought to invest in other systems based on their belief that those other systems would return greater value to their organizations. Contrary to Dietrich, the issue of irreplaceability adds little to our understanding of legacy systems.

- **Legacy systems are a problem.** IS managers tend to see legacy systems as a *problem*, not simply because they are difficult to change, but also because they present a host of management issues. Primary among these is that work done on legacy systems is called *maintenance* and despite efforts to enhance the image of maintenance, it is not a high profile IS activity. Maintenance by any other name (e.g., 'marketing support.' 'enhancement') is difficult to camouflage. Maintenance is still maintenance and IS personnel see it as a less attractive career option than new development. The fact that many organizations break in new IS recruits on maintenance continues to feed this mentality. As a result, it is difficult to get experienced personnel to work on legacy systems and this compounds the IS manager's problems, leading to longer timeframes to make changes, more errors, and increased pressure from users.

- **Legacy systems are expensive.** Because legacy systems generally handle core functions, they are vital to the successful daily operation of their organizations. What they were designed to do, they continue to do well. However, when it comes to supporting and enhancing these systems, they have two serious limitations which usually result in substantial costs. First, changes to legacy systems take longer to make. Even simple modifications can be expensive because of the way data and code are liberally distributed in a legacy system. Thus, a field pertaining to 'sales tax' may appear in hundreds of programs, as can sales tax calculation procedures. Poor documentation means that tracking down each and every instance that must be changed takes days of reading program listings. Furthermore, because of the many systems that interface with it, testing a legacy system becomes a long and arduous process. All too often, forgetting the interface to an obscure program that no one thought about can cause major system problems resulting in serious detrimental effects on the business.

A second reason legacy systems are expensive is that they are often based on obsolete technologies. There is more to this than just an IS desire to have the latest and the best of everything. It is difficult to find staff who want to (and are able to) work on older technology. Hardware and software companies will only support a few previous generations of their products. Any systems based on older technology are therefore highly vulnerable to having their basic technical support removed. This vulnerability is compounded when new technologies no longer interface with older ones. As a result, IS organizations are regularly faced with having the rug pulled out from under their systems when a language or operating system is eliminated from a supplier's catalogue. Thus, often organizations have no choice but to upgrade older systems to newer technology whether they like it or not.

• **Legacy systems are a one-time phenomenon.** Legacy systems are often thought to be those systems that were implemented 25 years ago. Taking this approach encourages a mindset of a one-time solution; that is, 'let's spend a lot of money and fix this legacy problem once and for all.' Unfortunately, many of the systems we are implementing today (as elegant and structured as they are) will undoubtedly be the legacy systems of tomorrow. Therefore, legacy systems are not a one-time phenomenon but rather a continuous one. That is, legacy systems will not likely be 'fixed' once and for all.

So what is a legacy system? First and foremost, a legacy system embodies software and processes that constitute valuable intellectual capital of an organization. Thus, it can be seen that legacy systems are an extremely important asset to a business and should be viewed as such. Legacy systems present problems as well. They can generally be identified by their inflexibility and the difficulties they present when changes are needed. However, legacy systems are unlikely to go away in the foreseeable future; it is more likely we are creating more of them each year. Therefore, instead of viewing them as an increasing problem they wish would just go away, IS managers must begin to recognize legacy systems as a challenge and an opportunity to be seized in order to effectively manage their information technology resources and to conserve their company's intellectual property.

MANAGING YOUR LEGACY SYSTEMS

The significant corporate assets which legacy systems represent deserve more IS attention than they typically receive in an organization. Forum participants agreed that new approaches are needed. While there was no general consensus about what these were, the following five strategies represent some newer ideas that companies are trying in an attempt to manage their legacy systems more effectively.

1. *Organize for Maintenance as well as Development*

Maintenance is a fact of life for IS. Despite this, however, goals are rarely established for maintenance leaving organizations unclear about what exactly they hope to accomplish with their maintenance effort. Organizations are continually surprised by how many of their resources are devoted to maintenance, rather than new development. Without a goal-setting exercise akin to that used for new development, the majority of maintenance activity will remain reactive. Quite simply, we need to organize for maintenance as well as development. But what does this mean? Information systems never wear out. Maintenance arises from the need for change—either business-driven or technology-driven. Since change is a constant in both business and technology, demands for maintenance are unceasing; and since existing systems are the ones operating the business, maintenance work can easily overwhelm new development. Hence the IS manager's dilemma: How many resources to devote to maintenance—which supports the existing operations of the company? versus, How many resources to devote to new development—which will support the future operations of the company? In combination with the negative reputation maintenance has amongst IS personnel, structuring IS to provide both effective development and maintenance has become a formidable management challenge.

Two basic approaches are currently used by IS managers to organize for maintenance:

• **Combine Maintenance and Development.** In a combined maintenance-development group, IS personnel rotates through both activities. This avoids the 'maintenance ghetto.' In some situations, maintenance and development have been blended with everyone doing both. This approach has its advantages. First, it tends to lessen the segregation of IS personnel into skill camps, with older COBOL programmers in maintenance and younger C++ programmers in development. Merging maintenance with development works toward a more class-free IS society. Second, new development is seldom of the 'green fields' variety. Development usually needs to be closely integrated with existing systems. Thus, the knowledge of existing systems gained by performing maintenance is invaluable in development.

The disadvantage of this approach is that the natural tension between maintenance and development for IS resources tends to be won by maintenance and this leads to developmental delays. Unless measures are taken to guard against the erosion of development activity, maintenance can grow to consume all the IS resources very quickly. Because of the business' need for immediate function, development, with its longer delivery cycle, gets shoved down in the priority queue.

• **Separate Maintenance and Development.** One of the primary reasons for separating maintenance is the fact that maintenance is actually a different kind of work than development. Separating maintenance allows specialization. The maintenance group can develop its own processes, methods and tools to allow it to do a better job of maintaining systems. With separated maintenance groups, it is less likely that maintenance will erode development because this requires the secondment of IS personnel from one group to the other. While possible, the secondment is noticeable and requires the physical reassignment of personnel which mitigates against this happening. This organization structure therefore enables managers to minimize maintenance time by assigning maintenance groups only enough resources to do a limited amount of work.

The major disadvantage of this method of organization is that it creates two classes of IS staff—development and maintenance. Maintenance requires a different set of skills than development. Certainly there is no replacement for experience with the existing systems in doing maintenance effectively. As has been noted above, this results in fewer people wanting to do maintenance because they know their skills will rapidly become out of date and their value in the marketplace will decline accordingly.

Organizing for maintenance means recognizing maintenance as an integral and important part of IS. Rather than treating maintenance as an irritation, managers should approach it as an opportunity to develop staff and their skills while providing a valuable service to the business. While there is nothing wrong with either of the above approaches, assuming IS managers manage to address the disadvantages of each structure, Forum members suggested some different ways IS could organize for maintenance which might minimize the perceived disadvantages of maintenance:

- **Rotate maintenance staff to the business.** IS support staff could move to the various business areas for a fixed period of time to do maintenance. After serving in the business, staff would be rotated back into IS to work on new development. The main advantage of this approach is that IS staff obtain a broader view of the organization. This is particularly helpful for 'growing' systems analysts from programmers. Another benefit of this strategy is that users react extremely favourably to the chance to build long-term relationships with IS personnel assigned to their area of the business. They learn too that maintenance resources are finite and changes must be properly prioritized. Co-location can therefore be an extremely effective means for users and IS to learn more about each other.

  The disadvantage of this approach is that it tends to isolate IS staff even more than separate maintenance and IS groups with the resulting 'class problems' identified above. Because there is so much integration between systems, putting programmers in business units where they cannot get in touch with each other quickly could potentially create a problem with responsiveness. Thus, like most managerial decisions, this is a double-edged sword where the benefits of building ties with users and gaining business knowledge must be weighed against the possible loss of integration.

  IS managers implementing this approach must ensure that staff benefit in many ways from this rotation (e.g., using it as a training ground for promotion) and that they are not forgotten when it comes to technical training. The tendency will be for users to want to hold on to good staff rather than rotate them through and this will lead to problems keeping staff current. Thus, rotations must be for fixed periods of time and should be relatively inflexible.

- **Use Maintenance as Training.** Many IS staff recognize what can be learned from maintaining a group of systems (e.g., better appreciation of the business, broader understanding of operational problems, clearer knowledge of systems and systems concepts, improved appreciation for methods and disciplines). They also recognize the value of maintenance to an organization and therefore the contribution they can make in maintenance. The problem has been with others'—especially management's —perception that maintenance is a backwater. This is enhanced by the lower value IS managers often put on maintenance staff (e.g., lower salaries, less experienced staff) and by the fact that, once in maintenance, staff often get 'stuck' for a long period of time.

One approach to maintenance is to use it as a training ground between various organizational levels. A programmer trainee might start in maintenance for a year to 'get his or her feet wet.' This would be followed by two years in development as a full-fledged programmer. A second rotation into maintenance would allow the programmer to develop valuable business knowledge and simple analytical skills in preparation for more challenging programmer-analyst jobs. Finally, aspiring lead programmer-analysts and project leaders, would learn these skills first in maintenance before tackling the bigger, more complex development jobs. The key to using this approach effectively is to *move* people regularly so that no one gets stuck and everyone benefits from the learning in both development and maintenance. Making maintenance an integral part of a career path at several points eliminates the stigma of the work as well. Enabling people to use their time in maintenance to take courses in newer technologies (in preparation for their time in development) would also encourage staff to see maintenance as a necessary period of training and development.

• **Outsource maintenance.** One way to eliminate the staff problems caused by maintenance is to get rid of maintenance altogether. There are many organizations and contract staff willing to do this work. Outsourcing enables IS to manage their maintenance 'problem' at arm's length, thus making maintenance simply an issue of how much money the company is willing to pay. Managers can also pick and choose which activities to retain in-house and which to delegate.

The disadvantage of outsourcing this activity is that the organization loses valuable expertise and becomes dependent on an outside source for this knowledge. Whether or not outsourcing is a practical alternative depends on the centrality of systems and systems work to the organization. If IS is a mere 'support group,' outsourcing may be an effective solution to an important organizational problem. However, if systems are integral to the 'core competencies' of the organization, it would be wise to keep maintenance in-house.

2. *Assess Installed Systems Regularly*

The general consensus of the Forum managers was that neglecting legacy systems, or doing the barest minimum work on them, carries extreme consequences not the least of which is the inability of information systems to deliver the products and services necessary for organizations to respond to the marketplace. Because of this danger, the group felt that organizations needed to take stock of their application systems on a regular basis.

One company is using a system referred to as the Application System Asset Management (ASAM) review process. This process, based on an article by Glenn Mangurian (1985), consists of four steps carried out on an annual basis for each installed system:

1. summarize the current state of the system;
2. obtain input from the business users;
3. evaluate and assess the application's technical condition;
4. make appropriate recommendations.

Upon completion of steps 1 to 3, each application can be rated on the basis of its business importance, its functional support, and its technical support. Step 4 then recommends specific actions to be taken for each application based on the decision chart shown in Table 16.1.

The ASAM approach is based on a management philosophy that explicitly recognizes application systems as valuable assets of the company to be carefully managed. This philosophy and an attendant commitment from senior management are necessary for the ASAM approach to be fully beneficial. Regular periodic reviews form a vital part of the overall management of each system. Without them, the ASAM approach cannot do what it is designed to—prevent obsolescence, improve effectiveness, increase usage, and address new opportunities, all of which result in a well-managed application portfolio.

As a company's application portfolio is very dynamic, ratings of systems will change continually. Over time therefore, application systems will move from cell to cell in the ASAM decision chart. *Technical support*, for instance, will degrade over time as systems become less and less efficient relative to newer technologies. The *functional support* an application system provides to the business will also degrade in direct proportion to the rate of change of the business. Finally, the *business importance* of application systems can also be expected to change as the business changes focus. For example, recently many businesses have seen their customer profile database system jump overnight from the 'nice to have' category to the 'need it yesterday' category.

There is only one exit from the ASAM chart and that is the 'eliminate' cell. It can be expected that the number of systems in this category at any time will be relatively small. The bulk of an organization's application systems most likely reside in the remaining cells. Of these, the three cells 'renovate,' 'replace,' and 'augment' will entail more extensive IS activity than the maintain cell. Those applications residing in the 'maintain' cells are primarily 'wait and see' situations which typically go relatively unattended with minor functional or technical upgrades until such time as they move to other cells. That is, either they move towards elimination as their perceived business importance lessens or they move towards refurbishment.

Examination of the decision chart reveals the relationship between usage of the ASAM approach and legacy systems. Most of the IS activity involves those systems that have poor functional support and/or poor technical support. While the ASAM methodology is designed to manage the entire application portfolio, it is apparent that it is most effective in highlighting those systems which are in the greatest need of attention before they become serious problems.

Table 16.1. Application System Asset Management (ASAM) Decision Chart

(Adapted from Mangurian (1985), reproduced by permission of Glenn E. Mangurian)

Business Importance[1]

Functional Support[2]	Low	High	Technical Support[3]
Good	Maintain	Renovate	Poor
Poor	Eliminate	Replace	Poor
Good	Maintain	Maintain	Good
Poor	Maintain, augment or replace	Augment	Good

Condition Assessment

[1] 'Business importance' indicates the application's overall value to the business.
[2] 'Functional support' indicates how well the system meets the business requirements.
[3] 'Technical support' indicates the system's efficiency and effectiveness.

Recommendations

- 'Maintain' existing capabilities in their current state.
- 'Renovate' the existing system (i.e., correct technical deficiencies)
- 'Augment' the existing system (i.e., add new capabilities)
- 'Replace' the existing system (i.e., redevelop)
- 'Eliminate' the existing system (i.e., discontinue use)

3. *Tune-up Your Systems*

In many ways, systems are like cars. Both benefit from regular tune-ups. Often, such tune-ups are minor adjustments. However, as the years go by, more and more major maintenance needs to be done, until finally a complete overhaul is necessary. Forum members agreed emphatically that regular tune-ups of systems can go a long way in preventing more serious system problems. These regular maintenance needs can be identified during the system assessment process and can include:

* upgrading to current generations of software or hardware;
* improving input methods or reports;
* updating documentation and data dictionaries;
* simplifying processes and interfaces—both human and technical.

Obviously, legacy systems will need more maintenance than newer systems. However, even the oldest systems will benefit from regular assessments and tune-ups, rather than waiting for disasters to happen.

4. *Overhaul Systems*

If your legacy system needs to be renovated or augmented, they can be substantially overhauled, rather than replaced. Sprague and McNurlin (1993) outline two ways of doing this:

* **Restructure your system.** If your system is basically doing its job, but doing it inefficiently or is 'fragile' (i.e., difficult to change without something else going wrong), it can be restructured. This basically means turning 'spaghetti code' into structured code. Once structured, the system is much more maintainable and easier to change. Numerous software products are now available which will evaluate the amount of structure in the current system—for example, the number of layers of nesting and the degree of complexity—and provide a trace of the program's control logic. Once this

evaluation is complete, a structure engine will simply replace poor coding conventions with structured coding conventions and optimize the code to make it run faster.

The group's experience here raises an important point. The restructuring of your code has good news and bad news. The good news is that you now have code that is more maintainable and easier to change; the bad news is that you have just 'deskilled' all of your maintenance programmers who had mastered the old spaghetti code. In one organization, productivity levels actually dropped since the restructured code resulted in the maintenance programmers having to 'relearn' once familiar programs. In this case, management must weigh the short-term costs against the long-term benefits. In addition, anyone attempting to restructure their code should expect some opposition by IS personnel directly affected by this decision.

- **Re-engineer your system.** A step beyond restructuring is re-engineering, which means extracting the data elements from an existing file and the business logic in order to move them on to new platforms. Sprague and McNurlin (1993) cite Bachman who points out that there should be two phases to re-engineering systems—reverse engineering and forward engineering. Reverse engineering takes existing systems, along with their file and database descriptions, and converts them from their implementation-level description (records, databases, and code) into their equivalent design level components (entities, attributes, processes, and messages). Forward engineering goes in the opposite direction—from requirements-level components to operational systems. Design items created by reverse engineering are used to create new applications via forward engineering.

  Recently, products have appeared on the market to aid in systems re-engineering. These fully automated systems promise to convert and migrate data, databases (eg., IDMS/R to DB2), languages (eg., COBOL OS/VS to COBOL II/370) and technology platforms, taking these structures from an outdated environment to a more modern, advanced environment. Migration can be performed across dissimilar technology platforms and operating systems. To date, the group felt that the current products available do a good job on *data* but are less effective on *logic*.

Note that both of these options focus on upgrading the system technically before its functionality can be improved. This reflects the major costs of adding functionality to a system that is technically out of shape. If the system is basically technically sound, major enhancements or supplemental functionality can and should be added to augment the system without such major technical changes.

• **Layer your legacy systems.** While restructuring and re-engineering systems involve maintaining the basic integrity of a system, another way to overhaul a system is to break it up into layers. This strategy attempts to exploit legacy systems rather than replace them. Systems can be divided into three distinct layers—data, processing/function, and presentation/delivery. When most legacy systems were created, these three layers were tightly coupled. That is, systems were written to access files with specific fields and records, to process the data in specific ways, and to produce specific output files and reports. Changes to data, to the processing performed, or to a report meant changing the whole system. By stripping the layers out of systems, each layer can be treated as an entity in and of itself. Changes, therefore, can be minimized or eliminated in the other two layers of the system.

For example, a legacy batch system that updates customer accounts can be replaced by a new presentation front-end and relational data which interact with the legacy processes. While the core of the legacy system remains, it is much reduced in size and insulated by modern presentation and data management techniques. One company has implemented this strategy through client/server desktop technology. On the desktop, a number of 'applets' appear to the user. These applets are icons representing different applications. This approach brings a high degree of multi-functionality to the desktop. That is, a salesperson can perform a number of functions simply by 'pointing and clicking' without having to log on to various different systems. Each applet is implemented on a client/server system and invokes applications residing on other LAN servers which, in turn, invoke database systems on other servers—all invisible to the salesperson. This layering preserves the 'guts' of the legacy system (i.e., its processing) and prolongs its value to the organization while optimizing newer presentation (front-end) and data (back-end) technologies.

Layering facilitates the introduction of newer technology into legacy systems. The data and delivery layers are both particularly amenable to newer technologies. Thus, a legacy system can be accessed with a client/server front-end complete with GUIs, IVR, and image processing and back-ended with a database machine perhaps running DB2. 'Cocooning' your system in this way within new technology means that a sizeable portion of a legacy system is no longer legacy. This approach has the added benefit of enabling maintenance personnel to work with current technology which they are likely to find more exciting and rewarding.

5. *Replace Legacy Systems*

Extending the car analogy presented earlier, it is evident that even the most fastidiously maintained car will eventually require replacement as it ceases to meet the needs of a continually changing environment. Systems are no exception. Eventually they will need to be replaced. IS managers naturally dread replacing their legacy systems largely because of the perceived risks involved within the change process and the costs involved. This is why organizations tend to stick with awkward, out-of-date systems, year after year. Fortunately, there are options that can, in some cases, make replacement more manageable and can even affect replacement costs.[1] Sprague and McNurlin (1993) offer two:

• **Package substitution.** There are an increasing number of

---

[1] Some degree of caution must be exercised here. The Forum members advocated that package substitution and downsizing are options that they felt should be investigated at systems replacement time. They did not, however, feel that it is always cheaper to downsize or to acquire a package product.

commercially available packages which may perform many of the functions of a legacy system. Many offer selectable features which allow purchasers to tailor the package to their particular environment and these features can be turned on or off using control files, so no programming is necessary. Even end-users can specify some of the operating instructions. Those packages written using an application generator usually provide the generator with the package allowing the resident IS personnel to tailor and extend the package. Legacy systems in the accounting, billing, and human resources areas may easily be replaced with packages, since the functions of these systems tend to be more standardized than in other areas. Order entry and inventory management may also be good candidates for a package. Unfortunately, packages are not applicable to many legacy systems—that is, core business functions.

• **Downsize the platform.** If the system needs to be replaced, then it may be wise to consider 'downsizing' it by writing it for a smaller platform such as a mid-range machine or a network server. The advantages of this approach is that, in some systems, operational costs as well as machine costs may be lower. More importantly, the systems may be more flexible if developed with new tools.

Exercising either option (i.e., package substitution or platform downsizing) results in additional application systems which, unfortunately, begin the downward legacy spiral the minute they are placed into production. They are little different than other systems. Indeed, package systems may be legacy on arrival. Management must guard against complacency—*an ounce of prevention is worth a pound of cure!* The next section outlines strategies for the prevention of legacy systems.

PREVENTING LEGACY SYSTEMS

Following an ASAM approach consistently should ensure that systems never become 'legacy' at least in their most pejorative sense. However, the group also addressed ways in which new systems could be built to prevent many of the problems which have occurred with systems built in the past. Many of the strategies are well known but bear repeating here in light of the importance of the legacy situation in most organizations.

The most important feature of creating 'non-legacy' systems is to build them with replacement in mind and, where possible, 'build infrastructure not function.' Application architectures should be developed to promote reusability, shared data, portability, standard interfaces, plug-in components, and easy access to information. This entails getting away from the *concept of system* and moving towards the *concept of componentization* where we 'assemble not build.' This cannot be done immediately but, with an established goal to direct activities, it should be possible to migrate to this architecture over five to ten years using new techniques and technologies.

Group members also suggested that systems be moved to a much greater level of abstraction. Organizations need to design systems like software vendors currently do. Because software vendors have to build for everyone, they must build general capability that can be tailored or customized to apply to specific cases. For example in an insurance company, the starting point would be the statement 'customers buy something from us' leaving aside the identification of a 'customer,' the 'something,' and 'us.' In the past, we have typically decided at the outset who the customer is, what it is that they are buying, and from whom, and with this decision we would proceed to build a system to issue premiums to companies for group coverage. Then we would build a separate system to issue premiums to individuals for life insurance. In contrast, a general system for premium issuance could be built based on a data model that recognized individuals as individual customers and as group customers allowing the company to build accurate customer profile databases while satisfying the need to issue premiums.

CONCLUSION

Organizations today are plagued with legacy systems. This is a problem that can be minimized but will never entirely disappear. Every installed system will someday be classified as legacy unless aggressively managed. Recognizing this, the task that befalls management is twofold: first, build for replacement, and second, attend to your systems regularly so that legacy systems become the valued intellectual property of the organization—a true legacy—rather than its worst nightmare. This chapter has attempted to build a framework to guide IS managers in addressing their legacy systems. Following this framework should guarantee that an organization's legacy systems will continue to provide benefit for many more years.

17

Preparing for the Millennium Change

INTRODUCTION

On Sunday, January 2, 2000, you get a call at home, during the game. The problem reported to you on Saturday turned out to be worse than believed. The events that occurred, as best as can be determined, are described below.

Event #1. *A problem using the high volume manufacturing database trashed the database on Saturday (January 1) at 10 AM. Actually, Japan discovered this problem 12 hours before we did. They called and left a message in voice mail at 11 PM EST December 31 (Friday). Unfortunately, the automated purge routine in voice mail deleted the message before the covering manager received it. The program decided that records with a year's date after '00' (current year) were invalid and flagged them for deletion. Thus the records for '1999' were flagged for deletion. The cleanup step then deleted them and the reorganization step then used that space. The error was discovered when an end-of-year processing found no records for 1999 and issued an error message about a missing database.*

Event #2. *The restore of the database failed. The restore of the database was attempted on Sunday (January 2) at 2 AM. [The programmers on call had problems in getting into the building. It seems that the badge system determined that all badges were expired. Fortunately, that problem belongs to someone else!]. The restore program went into a loop. The routine that determines which tape to restore does a binary search and did not expect '00' entries after '99' entries. The author was located (he retired last year) and we were able to get by that problem. We then found that the automatic backup done Sunday (January 2) at 1 AM had used the tapes created Saturday because it thought they were the oldest ones. The database was finally reconstructed using the tapes made on Friday (December 31) and the transaction log.*

Event #3. *While the database recovery effort was going on, the program that trashed the database was being worked on. The compilation to correct the program failed. An effort to recompile showed that the compiler will not work unless the system is IPLed with a year before 2000. However, the new hardware has the data and time built in and they cannot be modified. We tried to fool it by time zone offsets but the maximum offset allowed was a plus or minus 12 hours. Compiles can only be done at the moment using the old hardware. However, the old hardware does not support the new compiler. An attempt was made to report the problem to the support group but the PBX they are on has been down since early Saturday (January 1). With some code modifications, we compiled the code with an old compiler and shipped the result to the program library.*

Event #4. *The program library manager program kept giving us the wrong version. Finally, it was determined that it thought the '00' version was older than the '99' version. This was resolved by moving the new version to a separate structure and proceeding.*

Event #5. *On Sunday (January 2) morning, an attempt was made to look at the operator logs for the previous day. The Saturday (January 1) logs are missing. The daily process (2 AM) that keeps the latest 15 days of logs thought that the January 1 log was the oldest and erased it. The weekly archival of the operator logs collection is normally done on Sunday mornings at 1 AM. The archival run on early Sunday (January 2) should have contained operator logs for January 1. That archival run did not happen. The routine that figures out the day of the week thought that January 1 was a Monday so no archival was done.*

Event #6. *The job tracking system had problems tracking jobs that started in 1999 and finished in 2000. Still, the data in the tracking system does show several application failures.*

Event #7. *The operator log for Sunday (January 2) shows twelve other programs that are suspect. What the missing Saturday log would contain is worrisome.*

Event #8. *Personnel in manufacturing called indicating that the online reports were useless. An emergency shipment is in jeopardy. The tracking system indicates the application ran fine. The application programmer is looking at this.*

Event #9. *A second group reports that a retrieval system is not working. It turned out that an update program failed. The application program constructed a hash code by dividing a number by several values including the last two digits of the year creating a 'division by zero' error.*

This scenario was created by IBM Canada (1994) to demonstrate the situation that could face organizations when the year 2000 arrives.[1] What happened here is commonly referred to as the millennium problem. Particularly alarming about this scenario is the breadth of the problem and the existence of ripple effects throughout the organization. Organizations that are prepared will glide smoothly into the next century; those unprepared will face disruptions in computer processing. This is a certainty. The only uncertainty is the magnitude of these disruptions. In some cases, the disruptions might be limited to a few hours of relatively inconsequential inconvenience. In others, the interruption could last for a few days with realized losses in activities like billings, orders, or shipments. And in some organizations, it is predicted that the losses will be unrecoverable and the organization's health will be jeopardized. Furthermore, the worst situation arises, not when something fails (as we have outlined here), but when systems proceed incorrectly! It seems that the year 2000 is the bearer of bad tidings. On the positive side, it should be noted that 31 December, 1999 is a Friday; if things go bad, we will have the whole weekend to fix it!

In order to understand the nature of this problem and to develop strategies for IS management to deal with the millennium change in their organizations, Forum members were asked to describe their view of the millennium problem, to address the issues that are involved, and finally to discuss the strategies they have implemented to address the problem. The results of that investigation are presented herewith. This chapter examines the nature of the millennium problem from a number of perspectives. Proven strategies for managing this situation are then presented including a methodology for approaching the problem in a logical fashion.

THE NATURE OF THE MILLENNIUM PROBLEM

The millennium problem has a very humble origin—the date field or, to be more exact, an inadequate date field. Quite

---

[1] Reprinted by permission of International Business Machines Corporation. Another scenario involving a distributed architecture is presented in the Appendix.

simply, if all computer programs had used a date field which identified the day, month, year *and century*, we would not have a problem! The fascinating aspect of this situation is the promulgation of a simple problem into a vast and complex situation—that being faced by almost every organization today. Date fields are ubiquitous in organizations. Virtually every transaction is 'date-stamped' and the comparison of dates is endemic to business functioning. The extent to which this is true will become clear. By way of analogy, if you count the number of places in your home where you must reset the time (e.g., VCRs, microwaves, stoves, radio alarm clocks, TVs, coffee makers, thermostats, etc.) after a power outage, you will become aware of the extent to which date and time keeping devices permeate even your home.

The Date Field

The majority of computerized information systems store dates in Julian (YY/DDD), Gregorian (MM/DD/YY) or standard (YYMMDD) formats. Common to all formats is the use of two digits to describe the year. Unfortunately, two digits are insufficient for an orderly transition into the 21st century. Furthermore, since at the end of this century the millennium changes too, three digits are not enough either. Pleptea (1986) cites the following example to illustrate the point. In medical insurance claims processing, the system checks each claim to see if the policy's effective date precedes the date of medical service for which coverage is claimed. Suppose the policy's effective date is 1 April, 1997 and medical service was rendered after the effective date on 1 April, 2002. The traditional system would compare the dates represented in standard format (i.e., YYMMDD) and the test would incorrectly reject the claim since 970401 is greater than 020401.

The solution to the problem is the adoption of 'century dates'; that is, the use of four digits to represent the year. With the use of century dates in the previous example, the policy's effective date and the medical service date would have been recorded as 19970401 and 20010401 respectively and the mathematical manipulation of these century dates would have correctly identified the policy's effective date as preceding the medical service date. The solution to the problem is as simple as the problem itself. Rectifying the problem, however, may be anything but simple! Had we only had the foresight to code all date fields as century dates, the millennium change would be a far less dramatic event in our lives than it portends to be.

Date Logic versus Date Data

There are really two problems here; one involving the date logic and another involving the date data. *Date data* refers to the methods used to code and store dates while *date logic* refers to the means by which we manipulate date data. The distinction is important for understanding the nature of the millennium change problem facing us. Both date data and date logic will be described.

• **Date Data.** We have already mentioned some common formats such as Gregorian, Julian, and Standard. But even within these formats, there is variation. According to Lips (1993), it is common to find 'standard formats' as YYMMDD or MMDDYY or even DDMMYY—often at the whim of the original programmer. Furthermore, date data can be stored as either numeric (i.e., numbers only) or as alphanumeric (i.e., a combination of numbers and characters). April 4, 1997 could be stored numerically as '970401' or alphanumerically as '97/04/01.' Numeric dates may be DISPLAY, PACKED or BINARY. Numeric and alphanumeric dates' fields may contain special constants such as all zeros or all nines. Alphanumeric dates may contain those same special constants or others such as spaces, low values and high values. In OS/VS, the date is represented by PIC X(8) as MM/DD/YY while in ANSI 1985 and COBOL II, the date is represented by PIC 9(6) as YYMMDD. The difficulty with different date data is not new and, by in large, not a major concern. The reason is that we have had to deal with different date formats for years and, once identified, it is simply a matter of converting one to another. The real difficulty with date data in terms of the millennium change, as will be discussed, is simply *finding* all the locations where date data has been stored.

- **Date Logic.** It is surprising to discover how pervasive date logic is within information systems. The reason for this is because date logic is pervasive throughout the conduct of business. Very few transactions are without dates—dates to indicate the time of transaction, the date of expiry, the duration of special conditions, dates of documents that take precedence over others, future dates that are part of similarly oriented instruments, antecedent dates, etc. You get the picture.

  Not only is date logic endemic, it can be very complex. The development of information systems requires 'calendaring' processing such as identifying today's date and the date 30 days from now. Some calculations need to take holidays into account, some do not. That is, it is not always as simple as subtracting today's date from some future date. Something as straightforward as a leap year can be anything but. The following three rules help make this determination.

  Rule #1. If the year is divisible by 4, then it *is* a leap year.
  Rule #2. But, if the year is divisible by 100, then it *is not* a leap year.
  Rule #3. However, if the year is divisible by 400, then it *is* a leap year.

  As it turns out, the year 2000 is a leap year; the year 1800 was not. Go ahead, try out the rules!

Date Storage

Not only are dates stored in many different formats but they are stored in many different locations. In addition, we need to be concerned with the storage of both date data and date logic (as discussed above). Many applications retrieve dates from the computer's internal clock. For example, in a batch IBM environment, the program may retrieve the date from a special register. According to Lips (1993), 'the new COBOL II compiler does not offer the century date through any of its special registers. However, in IBM COBOL 370, the century date is available through CURRENT-DATE, which has been resurrected as an intrinsic function conforming to the 21-character ANSI 89 standard. Within a CICS on-line environment, a program might retrieve the current date from the EIBDATE field that is in Julian format but has no century date. However, with CICS 1.7 and beyond, dates of various formats with and without century are available through combined use of ABSTIME and FORMATTIME.'

In many applications, however, dates are retrieved instead from an external source. This kind of date is known as the business date, parm date, run date or as-of date. Its value might be found in a file, table, or a database. It could also be a parameter passed through the EXEC statement or ACCEPTED from SYSIN. We can see from this that the location of date data can be highly varied.

When it comes to date logic, the situation worsens. Most IS departments have at least one date routine (i.e., a program to determine the date and time) and many shops have more than one. Some of these routines are written in a very *ad hoc* fashion; some are highly specialized; some are written in Assembler; some may have very unique invocation protocols; and the source code for some may not be available. Some applications programmers invoke the supplied version and some, for reasons known only to themselves, choose to write their own date routine(s). In the worst case, date calculations are 'hard coded' in the application program itself ! Fixing a common date routine is a manageable problem; attempting to find (let alone fix) all applications with embedded date data and/or logic is a different matter entirely!

Age Fallacy

The age fallacy, as the term is coined by Lips (1993), is the belief that newer systems have capabilities to handle the millennium change. He suggests that, at the moment, this does not appear to be true. Vendor supplied software does not always offer century dates. Nor does third-party software. It is not uncommon for newer applications (which may handle century dates) to call older applications (which may not handle century dates). The basic vulnerabilities are the date data and the date logic—the newness of the technology matters little. Lips (1993) states that

> 'it does not matter if dates are stored in flat files, VSAM files, IMS databases or DB2 tables. It does not matter if the logic is written in COBOL, Assembler, C++ or PL/1. It does not matter if CASE tools and/or code generators were used. It does not matter if the software is running on a mainframe, mini or PC. It does not matter whether the operating system is MVS or Windows NT. It does not matter if the application is running on a single platform or on a client/server LAN. What does matter is that the data and the logic be century-sensitive.'

Problem Genesis

The genesis of the problem lies in part with the mindset of programmers with regard to *risk taking* ('the system will be gone before its impact is felt'), *selfishness* ('I'll be gone before there is an impact'), *procrastination* ('lots of costs with no benefits'), and *infallibility* ('science will fix it'). The larger part of the genesis of the problem, however, can be attributed to the fact that no programmer in the 1960s, 1970s, and even in the 1980s would have guessed that the programs that they were writing would still be functioning in 1996—and heading for the year 2000! Because of this belief, they did not think that two-digit dates and non-standard dates would pose any problem. It was not that programmers did not know about century dates, nor was it that they did not understand the potential problem that this would create. They were concerned only with simplifying the coding and, in some cases, saving space by minimizing the length of the date fields. Saving this amount of space today seems somewhat inconsequential; however, in the 1960s, this saving would have been significant across a number of applications in an organization. So the problem was less one of ignorance than poor prediction. It was just that these programs exceeded our wildest estimates of their useful life. Adopting this viewpoint leads us to conclude that the problem facing organizations with the onset of the year 2000 is that our programs were just too good! Their functionality has continued to be valuable and they have not worn out. Unfortunately, putting such a positive spin on the problem does little to solve the dilemma facing IS management.

Fear of the Unknown

There is currently a general feeling of unease surrounding the millennium problem. Much of this unease results from uncertainty—uncertainty regarding the size of the problem and uncertainty regarding the nature of the solution. Without a clear understanding of the problem, IS organizations are unaware of the level of effort that will be necessary to ensure that the problem is solved by the century change. The fact that it is already 1996 means that these IS organizations are gambling that the task can be accomplished within five years. And they are apparently willing to partake of this gamble without knowing the size of the problem! There is little comfort to be taken with this approach.

Additional 'fuel for the fire' takes the form of published warnings and estimates of the effort to correct the problem. Whiteman cites Ken Orr noting that 'Fortune 50 organizations will spend about 35–40 cents per line of code to convert all their existing systems to accept the year 2000. This translates into $50–100 million for each company.' Steven Whiteman, President and CEO of VIASOFT, Inc. informs us that 'a major insurance company who estimated over 40,000 of their programs would be affected . . . began work in 1991 using 35 programmers full-time. They are doubtful they will be able to make their deadline' (1993). Apparently the New York Stock Exchange started in 1987 with 100 programmers with the expectation of finishing in 1994 (Whiteman, 1993). These prognostications add to the unease.

While we have presented possible doomsday scenarios to add realism to the discussion, we have not addressed the ramifications of such scenarios beyond the organization. That is, the discussion has limited itself to how an organization would reload its software, regenerate its systems, recreate its database, etc., but what would be the effects on customers? And how far would the organization's liabilities extend? These problems are monumental and add to the fear of the unknown. Prudence suggests attacking the problem at source to remove these possibilities.

Information systems play a critical role in the majority of organizations. Without the continued and uninterrupted functioning of these systems, many organizations would soon collapse. The realization of this dependence has prompted organizations to implement elaborate and expensive disaster recovery programs to ensure against the possibility of disruption of their information systems. By playing out scenarios of various types of disaster, organizations are able to justify their expenditures on disaster recovery programs by balancing the risk of disaster against the costs of prevention and recovery. The millennium change represents a similar situation with a single exception—the disaster is perfectly predictable! Furthermore, the year 2000 will arrive on time! Information systems departments have faced significant problems before and risen to the occasion. In the next section, a number of management strategies are suggested for organizations to prepare for the millennium change. With careful planning and decisive action, the year 2000 should arrive without notice.

STRATEGIES FOR MANAGING THE MILLENNIUM CHANGE

Forum participants collectively generated the following strategies for organizations to follow in preparation for the millennium change. Adoption of these strategies should proceed without delay.

1. *Start Immediately*

Steps must be taken immediately. As stated earlier, because it is now 1996, organizations have already limited some of their options. One of the possible options would have been to plan to replace all applications and system software by the year 2000 in an orderly fashion. That is, all new systems would be designed with century dates and each time maintenance activities were carried out on a system, those date fields would be updated. This approach addresses the legacy problem discussed in the previous chapter, at the same time as it addresses the millennium problem. Unfortunately, it is the rare organization that is capable of replacing all its systems and applications within the time remaining in this century. Certainly, many of these systems can and will be replaced but doing so does not eliminate the problem—it only reduces it. The fact is that this total replacement strategy, unless already underway, is fast becoming a non-alternative.

Other approaches to the problem involve 'fixing' dates (i.e., both data and logic). Here, there are many options but, as with the total replacement option, many of these will not be possible if further delays occur. The point is that, in order to address the millennium problem with the fullest range of strategies, action must be taken now. There is no advantage to be gained by further postponement. This recommendation is really a call for action. The remaining strategies suggest what specific action or actions should be taken.

2. *Size the Problem*

Sizing the problem is the first order of business; that is, we need to know how much effort is required in order to combat the uncertainty surrounding the year 2000. As described previously, this involves locating every occurrence of date data and date logic within the organizational systems. This is not an easy task. Date data and date logic occur in business application systems (e.g., accounts receivable), in job control language (JCL), in systems software (operating systems, database software), systems management software (e.g., tape library management, job/task schedulers), in internal systems registers, and in vendor supplied software and systems where the source is not available. The people who are in the best position to locate date fields and logic are experienced IS personnel who are familiar with the organization's systems. The expertise of these people must be marshalled to support this activity. It makes sense to assign a senior IS analyst to investigate the systems within the area of the business for which they have responsibility. It is common practice to 'time box' this activity—perhaps using a six-month framework.

Sizing the problem accurately involves two activities. Finding all data fields and logic is the first task and this lets you know how big the problem is. The second part of sizing is deciding on a methodology for solving the problem. Some approaches are likely to be less expensive than others. For instance, an organization might decide to replace all data fields and all data logic. Another organization may simply trap all attempts to perform date calculations and call a routine that adjusts for the century wraparound. The solution chosen will dictate the total effort required. Many of the alternative approaches will be discussed later. Proceeding with this initial analysis will not only produce an estimate of the required effort but, equally important, it will help to reduce the feelings of unease surrounding the year 2000.

3. *Elevate the Issue to Senior Management*

Raising this issue to the level of senior management is imperative. Senior management in many organizations are totally unaware of the issue and its ramifications. There are many reasons for this. In some organizations, the year 2000 is seen as an 'IS issue.' Something as mundane as the length of a date field rarely is elevated to the level of senior management. Furthermore, the problem is of IS' own making. In fact, many IS managers find it difficult to even explain the predicament to their management fearing that they will look foolish. Perhaps more relevant is the fact that significant resources will be required to take corrective action which means that these resources are not available for other more pressing matters.

Locating and rewriting date code ensures safe passage into the next millennium but adds no new functionality. Explanations aside, we are too close to the year 2000 to evade, procrastinate or even apologize.

Forum members felt that it was the task of IS to size the problem before bringing it before senior management. It is important for IS to get ahead of the issue. Once the problem has been sized, a plan of action can be brought before senior management. Perhaps the most important reason for presenting this to senior management is because the problem is not exclusively an IS issue. Certainly, century dates and their attendant difficulties reside within the domain of IS but, as was seen in the fictitious scenarios, the millennium change goes beyond IS due to the pervasiveness of date logic. A date problem could easily de-authorize company personnel from entering a building, a specific area of a building, or a parking area. This range of problems is not under the exclusive purview of IS.

The question then becomes one of who owns the issue. All aspects of the millennium change should be administered by one body; this avoids fragmentation and provides the necessary catalyst. It seems logical to establish a high-level project office under the CIO with membership from the business side so that general management gains recognition of the problem. One group member felt that a recently retired senior member of IS would be an excellent person to chair such a committee. Such a person might be enticed back on a contractual basis. Whatever organizational mechanism is instituted, it should also be remembered that fixing this problem will be viewed as 'repair cost' and repair cost is 'sunk cost.' It will be management's task to determine whether or not this sunk cost can be applied against a replacement business case. In order to address these questions, it is vital to secure management involvement and buy-in.

4. Develop a Methodology

A company-wide approach is necessary; piece-meal solutions will just get us back into trouble. For this reason, a methodology should be developed and implemented across the firm. We see such a methodology consisting of five steps as described below.

- **Discovery.** Find all occurrences of date fields/logic embedded in all systems.

- **Classification.** Classify these occurrences into categories requiring different types of corrective action. A possible classification scheme could be (1) ignore, (2) eliminate, (3) replace, and (4) fix. Applications falling within the first category have date fields whose impact is not relevant. Remember that problems only occur during 'compares.' The second category of application can or will be redundant before the impact is felt due to a business change. The third category includes those applications which will be replaced before the impact is realized due to a business, technology or process change. The final category includes those applications or systems which must be fixed in order to move smoothly into the next century. Corrective action must be applied. See next step.

- **Correction.** Apply the appropriate type of action to correct the date field. The potential solutions which were identified are described below. We refer to them as the 'CURE' approach:

  1. Change year to 'alpha' and translate.

     The alpha date is an alpha representation of the two key parts of a year statement. One alpha character represents the millennium, century, and decade. The second character represents the actual year.[2] Translation inside the application would be required. The sequence is

---

[2] For example, the millennium/century/decade could be represented by the following sequence: A = 190, B = 191, C = 192, D = 193, etc. The year could be represented by the following sequence: A = 0, B = 1, C = 2, etc. Combining this scheme with a Julian format for the day of the year means that January 1, 1900 would be represented as 'AA001' and November 22, 1931 would be represented as 'DB325.'

started from an arbitrary point in time. This scheme allows century dates to be represented within a two-character field but requires extra translation.

2. *U*se absolute elapsed days from an arbitrary start.

    One technique which has been used successfully is to adopt an arbitrary start date and then record all dates as absolute elapsed days from this start date. The start date is usually chosen far enough back so that no living person or contract would precede it. The year 1850 might serve as the start date for an insurance company. This option entails recoding all date fields while much of the date logic remains unchanged. The date logic would have to convert absolute differences into actual dates and would still have to keep track of holidays, end of month, end of cycle, week days versus non-business days, etc.

3. *R*euse existing space (if available).

    Many date fields have embedded characters such as slashes (' / ') and alphanumeric month expressions ('Jan'). These redundant characters can be replaced with a four-digit date field without a loss of space.

4. *E*xpand existing fields to accommodate four-digit year.

    This involves rebuilding all databases and making changes within all programs which reference this data. This would involve changes to the data definition segment as well as the data logic segment of these programs.

- **Test**—perform complete testing to ensure that the changes are guaranteed to perform accurately and predictably. (For a more complete discussion on testing software, see Chapter 13, Improving Testing.) In the next section, testing aids that are specific to the millennium problem are discussed. Using these tools, you can trick the system into thinking that the actual date is beyond the year 2000 to see how well your applications run. This is an advantageous way to simulate the occurrence of the millennium change before the real thing. The role of testing is to guarantee that you are prepared for the year 2000.

- **Document**—modify the existing systems documentation to describe all changes. This should go without saying but we will say it anyway. The time spent in this activity should be built into the estimate of the total effort required to adjust systems and applications for the century change.

5. *Seek Outside Help*

The year 2000 will be faced by every organization. Everyone is in much the same predicament. Differences pertain only to the progress each organization has already achieved. There is some solace to be gained here. As the old adage says, 'misery loves company.' This is not the only solace. Since everyone is facing the same task, there is a huge opportunity to benefit from others. Organizations should not retreat within themselves and concoct a home remedy. Help is available in many forms.

Assistance is available from *consultants*. In fact, whole consulting practices have emerged just to help organizations with this single problem. These consultancies offer a wide range of services from assistance with the identification of the problem in your organization right through to implementing solutions. Many *analysis tools* are available. Some of these run through your source libraries (plus JCL and file definitions segments) looking for date fields. They usually use the data dictionary to trace the date synonyms used in your organization. Some are used to assist with testing. Others involve techniques for artificially advancing your internal system clocks beyond the millennium in order to test the changes you have made to your software. *Outsourcing* offers many options. Once identified, enacting the actual changes to your software is repetitious and requires low skill levels. One group member described it as 'mind-numbing' work. Rather than using higher skilled IS personnel, it should be possible to outsource much of this work. This could include programming, testing, and documentation. Some organizations are planning on going *offshore* to get much of the repair work done. Finally, *all vendors and suppliers* should be considered as a potential source of assistance in this matter. Certainly, it is to be expected that suppliers of operating systems, database software, and other products will have versions of their software that is 'century-ready.' Industry pressures will perhaps entice these players to develop products to assist their clients with the millennium change.

6. *Do Not Forget End-User Computing (EUC)*

Most, if not all, problems mentioned above also apply to the EUC environment. The difference is that most IS departments do not have strict control over the software and application systems being run on the various user platforms. Even where organizations have limited the software to very specific offerings, different versions and releases of common software can be significant. As with senior management, most users are likely unaware of the possible difficulties with the oncoming century change. It is the role of IS to inform them and solicit their help. From the centrally administered project office whose task is to oversee the millennium change (described above) should come information to all user departments. At a minimum, all mission critical applications running on PC or network servers should be identified and tested for possible date field problems. The size and nature of this task will depend directly on each organization's distributed architecture. The scenario in the Appendix depicts an example organization with distributed computing. The reader is advised to consider these potential difficulties.

CONCLUSION

The year 2000 presents a unique set of problems to be solved by organizations. This chapter has attempted to characterize these problems—their nature, their origins, and their ramifications. While not wishing to be alarmist, the message which we hope to create is motivational. Preparing for the century change is not an insignificant task. The sooner started the better. With careful planning, an appropriate level of resourcing, senior management support, and an organization-wide strategy, the transition should be smooth. Will there be 'hiccups' at the stroke of the millennium change? Certainly. The odds of this not happening are remote. Every effort should be made, however, to ensure that it is not your organization suffering from hiccups.

APPENDIX

WOULD IT HAPPEN?— A DISTRIBUTED COMPUTING SCENARIO[3]

The customer called early on Saturday, January 1. The customer had been working on year-end work. The customer had made progress fine on Friday, December 31st; then went home at 6 P.M. on Friday. When the customer arrived on Saturday, January 1, nothing seemed to work. The following problems were subsequently found.

Event #1. Licenced software claims the licence has expired. The software refused to run. The vendor hot line was called. Fortunately, it was staffed. After a significant delay and some hassle, we got a fix air-expressed in (vendor refused to supply a down-loadable fix—we later learned their bulletin board system was down). The air-express shipment took longer than expected because of flight delays—the air traffic control system deleted all aircraft whose departure was in 1999 but arrival was in 2000. The automatic flight tracking system was shut down and the manual tracking system in use is still causing delay.

Event #2. The network path the user was on suffered a severe slowdown because another user's terminal had gone

---

[3] Reprinted by permission of International Business Machines Corporation.

into a tight loop in requesting files from a conference server disk. It thought that the latest file had to be after the year 99 and was rejecting the year 00 dated files that were returned. There were also a couple of workstations that had a "Year 2000 had arrived!!" broadcast task running. Messages were sent to workstations as they logged on the network. As any new workstation logged on the network, they received the broadcast. One message might have been cute; two thousand per workstation was not cute. It is not clear if this was triggered by a virus.

Event #3. *A network server was in a loop checking for data to back up. The customer application was unable to access data on that server.*

Event #4. *Two machines with part of the database were located in a remote area where the power company cut power to numerous customers. Their automated system mistakenly thought customers had failed to pay bills, and in spite of some checks in the system, persons were dispatched to cut power on Friday. Actual power apparently was cut around 7 P.M. December 31. Another small database used by the customer had the records that came in on Saturday (and later for that matter) deleted, because the year code of 00 was used to flag the record for deletion.*

Event #5. *One printer server refused to boot. The server was running old software. New software was installed (remote installation option not possible, it required physically going to the system location).*

Event #6. *The staging DASD for the backup print server filled up. An application on the network, instead of producing a one-week report for Sunday, December 26, 1999, to Saturday, January 1, 2000, produced a report for the entire database due to a year calculation error. This problem actually happened after you were called, but while you were still struggling with other problems.*

Event #7. *The date/time server, running an old version of software, supplied 1900 as the year. Another time server, thought no longer to be used as the production time server, was actually still in use by a few workstations. It had gone into a loop and then crashed. Both problems were fixed, though there were problems with locked rooms and other complicating factors.*

Executive Interview:

John Loewenberg
Senior Vice President
Aetna Insurance

Could you tell us a little about your specific role at Aetna?

Well, my role has changed recently. Formerly, I was the Chief Executive Officer of Aetna Information Technology and was responsible for providing the overall information technology (IT) direction for Aetna as well as leading the delivery of all IT solutions, products and services to Aetna and its business units. This was treated as a separate business within Aetna and has now been disbanded. In my current role, I am responsible for creating a business focused on developing clinical and administrative information and information analysis tools to Aetna Health Plans (AHP) internally as well as to customers, providers and vendors. In addition, I lead the delivery of a managed care operating environment for the future that effectively integrates process, people, information and technology. In addition, the information technology functions for AHP report to me.

It is not clear whether you are the CIO, the business executive, or both.

I am in the health business as both a business and a technology type. Actually, I do not know what the difference is because IT folks are business people. I will go even further to suggest that continuing the distinction between the business and the technology is counterproductive and creates unnatural barriers. I am a part of the health business at Aetna. This is just one of our major business areas which include the property casualty business, the life insurance business, and the investment business. AHP accounts for about 60% of Aetna's business which makes it the largest area. Each of the areas has a technology function reporting to a group executive. Obviously technology has played and will continue to play a significant role in the functioning of our business. For this reason, I feel that technology and the business are intricately interwoven to the point that it makes little sense to attempt to differentiate them. Besides, at Aetna, we may have trouble with the title 'CIO' since it might refer to the Chief Investment Officer or the Chief Information Officer (Public Relations).

It sounds like you have worked hard at integrating IT with the business at Aetna. Can you elaborate on how you have done this?

Well, for one thing, rather than running IT as a separate internal business, we have placed it back into the various business areas at Aetna (as I mentioned). We think that this brings IT into much closer alignment with the business. Let me give you the background on this. Even when IT was run as an internal company, it was aligned by business function and physically located within the four businesses with the head of the application area reporting to the head of the business on a dotted line basis. About a year and a half ago, we decided to decentralize Aetna—to put more accountability into each of the businesses. That was when I went to the Chairman to suggest that we decentralize the application areas and integrate them right into the business. IT needs to be an integral part of the business plans and the implementation of those plans. One of the positive aspects of this is that we do not pursue a technology until it has been identified by the business. That is, we are not interested in chasing technology for technology's sake. There has to be a well-defined business reason and opportunity for the use of a specific technology.

Another example of how we work to integrate IT with the business is in our planning activities. Our IT plan is buried within the business plans of each of the four major business areas of the organization. In fact, I do not have an IT development budget—it is all in the business. I will explain how it works. We have IT people called 'account executives' who work within the various business areas and their main role is to assist these business units in identifying business-driven projects. By projects, I mean business opportunities or problems which involve changes in process and technology. The business units then attach priorities to these projects and integrate them into their business plans. Once these plans are approved, the business establishes delivery agreements. In the end, IT bills back to the business for the development of these systems. It is in this sense that IT really does not have a budget; it is all in the business and I collect it after the fact. This is more than an internal transfer or an accounting shuffle. It signals to the organization that business drives technology investment and spending and, indeed, that technology is an indistinguishable part of the business.

Does this mean you are not interested in being a technology leader?

Not at all. If we feel that there is a business opportunity to use technology for differentiation, we will go after it. As a company, we spend in the range of $810 million on IT every year. IT accounts for about 10% of our total employees at Aetna. So we are a major player when it comes to technology. We have a corporate staff of about eight people whose job is to investigate the technology's applicability, its technological implications, the cost implications and what it would take to use the technology as a business application. These are very senior people with expertise covering a broad range of topics (such as telecommunications or workflow management, etc.). They are charged with setting the overall direction for IT at Aetna. This includes IT architecture (application architecture is done in the business units), standards, and human resources in addition to emerging technologies. This group keeps us on top of the applicable technologies.

I think that we need to clarify this term 'technology leader.' We have no interest in being a technology leader. We are very interested in being a 'leader in the use of technology.' There is a big difference. As a company, it is our job to make sure that we are using IT to produce differentiation. That is, using technology to better serve our customers. In some cases, this is very advanced technology and in some cases, it is not as advanced, as long as it does the job. That is why I like to differentiate the usage you make of the technology from the technology itself. It is usage that makes you a leading edge organization, not whether you run Version 3.1 or 3.2. Focusing solely on technology is a mistake. Technology changes so rapidly and it's getting so complex that, if we are not careful, the economics of IT will kill us. We must carefully manage technology absorption and focus on effective use.

Can you elaborate on what you mean by complexity and economics?

I think that complexity is perhaps the least understood issue in managing information technology today. As we move from the staid, very well developed large-scale systems into the distributed world, there are incredible hidden costs, subtleties, and complexities that arise which are not well understood by the user community (and perhaps not well understood by the IT community as well). If we fail to come to terms with this increasing complexity and if we fail to understand what are the fundamental drivers behind it, we expose our organizations to huge financial risk. That is what I mean by the economics of information technology. For example, the number of applications at the fingertips of our users has increased dramatically. This means that they must become knowledgeable with each of these in terms of both the technology and the business function behind it. It is safe to say that, as a company, we have the potential to have a 10% hit in productivity by requiring these users to master this increase in complexity. In a company like AHP which has roughly a $1 billion payroll, this loss in productivity translates into $100 million! This is why I see complexity as so important to the economic health of our organization. Either you manage it or it will manage you. The upside is a 40% gain in productivity by hiding the complexity and allowing people to productively use the technology.

What do you see as driving this complexity?

I think there are a number of factors. I alluded to the new distributed environment. This plays a significant role in creating complexity. I will give you an example of what I mean. Version management (i.e., upgrading from one version or release of a software package to another) is a real complexity issue. We have about 4500 servers at Aetna and of those about 300 are office servers—that is, they have all the Microsoft software on them to be drawn down to the desktop machines when needed. There would be no way for us to upgrade 50,000 PCs with any assurance that it was done correctly. Even on the servers, we have different versions of software like DOS and Windows.

The second driver is the fact that we have a well informed and demanding user community who are requesting the support of IT to run their business. I would guess that, at the moment, each user deals with about five to nine applications at the desktop. At the present rate of growth, I can see this number becoming 60 applications within three to five years. This will create an enormous amount of complexity for the user community to deal with and it will create a huge task for the IT people to make all this technology manageable. In effect, we would like to make much of the interface to the technology invisible to the user. If we do not, I have a fear that the technical requirements that we would place on the users would be so high that we could end up swamped with users who are technically literate but unable to understand the business functionality.

The third factor is the difficulty we face in managing the desktop workplace. Unlike the mainframe environment where we have many years of experience is managing security, access, restart, backup, etc., we are currently not as good and, more importantly, lack the systems management tools to automate the operation of this new distributed environment. This means that we are having to use too many people in this task. We are running this distributed system about the same way we ran the mainframe data centres 15–20 years ago and the industry is making many of the same mistakes. The difference is that, instead of one or two data centres, we now have 50,000 data centres to manage—every desktop looks like a data centre!

What needs to be done to manage this level of complexity?

Well, at the desktop level, we need to adopt standardized interfaces so that the user community can navigate from application to application without having to face different and unique front-ends. If we had established a common interface a few years ago for all our applications, it would have helped enormously in managing this complexity. In fact, even if this had been the world's worst interface, it still would be to our advantage just because it was consistent from application to application. This benefits developers as well. It would simply eliminate the developer's need to design the interface over and over for each new system. They would not even get a vote—they just implement the interface according to the standard and put their energy into developing the business application.

I think equally important is the consistency of the data. Even if you have consistent front-ends to your applications, each application will manipulate data in different ways and until you get back to a common data file, you will get 'funny things' happening like inconsistent customer identification across applications. Some of these applications were written years ago so it is the old legacy problem. Actually, I prefer to call these systems the 'workhorse' systems since they run our business and they do it as well today as they did ten years ago. But they add to the complexity because you need to rework parts of them to be consistent with your other systems.

One strategy which we have adopted to help manage this complexity is to use standard software. For instance, we have standardized on Microsoft at the desktop; AIX, Microsoft and Novell at the midrange; and basically have an IBM software architecture at the mainframe platform. In order to help implement the adoption of these standards, we negotiated world-wide licensing contracts with our vendors so that Aetna pays for and supplies all desktop software. If a user wants something else, they must justify it to a division executive who will have to pay for it. In addition, we developed the Aetna standard interface which is cloned off the Microsoft interface. I consider the hardware to be generic and therefore less important in this regard. To get at data standards, we are developing software which traps requests for information and funnels these requests off to the appropriate database in the hope of eliminating the need for all the temporary databases which get created over time by different applications. This ensures that the data always appears in a consistent form for each application.

Our philosophy towards managing complexity is really two-fold. As I have mentioned, we adopt standards as much as possible and work to those standards. And I do not just mean industry standards because in a company the size of ours, we really need to create and adhere to our own standards. To put this into perspective, when I arrived at Aetna eight years ago, we had 108 different word processors (or versions of processors) and 19 different E-mail systems! This is probably not uncommon in organizations of this size. The second aspect of our philosophy is to limit our exposure to all this complexity. Let me explain what I mean by this. A common front-end does not eliminate complexity—it hides it. Behind that seamless interface that enables users to ask for information without knowing where it comes from (and better yet, not caring where it comes from), is an incredible amount of complex programming that enables diverse databases to talk to each other and a lot of intricate processing logic. This is the world in which our system people work and it is not easy. However, I would rather expose 1000 systems people to this murky world than 50,000 users! That is what I mean by limiting our exposure to this complexity.

We can even take this one step further. If we have 50,000 users, 1000 developers and 50 systems experts, I would choose to expose only those 50 experts (for example, database administrators) to the real unabridged complexity.

Obviously there are difficulties implementing standards and sometimes there are very good cases to be made for unique systems. How have you handled these situations?

It really comes down to the degree of value added from being different. Technology does not, in and of itself, give you advantage. Advantage arises from the *effective use* of technology. Each time you change, you put yourself on a new learning curve. Therefore, there should be a huge gain to be realized by going with something different just to offset the loss in productivity associated with the learning curve climb. My experience has indicated that many of the wonderful features of a new system are not really justifiable in light of the productivity downside. Besides, we typically only use a small portion of the functionality of most systems, so we would be better off leveraging our knowledge base with the existing system to greater advantage. This is what I mean by effective use.

Economics also dictate this approach. Consider how much time you personally spend coming up to speed with a new system. Now multiply that by 50,000 and you can see the cost to a company like Aetna. On the other hand, a system that makes you productive also results in large benefit numbers when multiplied by 50,000. These decisions cannot be taken lightly simply because of their huge impact on the overall organization. I may be sounding like a bit of a sceptic, but all this technology is incredibly seductive and many IT professionals have a demonstrated affinity for new stuff. Combine these two and you have a dangerous situation. The only way to protect yourself is to enforce standards and focus on effective and economical usage. Technology makes a lot of promises. Many do not pan out. If we had received all the quantum leaps in productivity promised by all the new development tools, we could handle all our development here at Aetna with a single developer! We do go with non-standard technology on occasion, but not without an air-tight business case behind it.

We have talked a lot about the complexity of IT. What is your forecast of the future in this regard?

Well, my crystal ball is not any better than yours, but my personal feelings are that IT will continue to become more and more complex if for no other reason than the incredible need that the business has for new initiatives looking to improve customer service, delivering new products and improving operating costs. All include information technology. There are countless opportunities for the provision of additional products and services to our members. The challenge is to identify the best of these opportunities and, as I previously stated, this can only happen through an effective close collaboration between business and IT specialists. We think we have come a good way along that road and are starting to fully realize the promise and potential of what IT can deliver.

A last word?

Well, as you see from my responses to your questions, I am a pragmatist. I think that it helps to be pragmatic in this field. We have chased a lot of rainbows and this has cost us a lot of time, effort and money. Like all pioneers, I too carry a lot of arrow wounds in my back from getting too far ahead of the pack with unproven technology and new ideas. So I am careful and try not to repeat those mistakes. On the other hand, in this business, IT continues to be extremely important. Our business is manufacturing—information manufacturing—so technology is what runs the factory. Technology and people are our two major resources and both are complex. Therefore, we must manage them carefully in order to be successful in the marketplace. This presents both a challenge and an opportunity depending on your outlook. I am pretty positive about the future of the business I am a part of. It is an exciting place to be right now.

AETNA INSURANCE

Aetna Health Plans provides group health, life, and disability benefits to corporations, government units, and other institutions and associations and is a leading provider of managed health care programmes such as preferred provider organizations (PPOs), health maintenance organizations (HMOs), point-of-service plans (POS), managed mental health and managed dental networks.

With over 19,300 employees nationwide, Aetna Health Plans has the largest network of providers available with 141,615 physicians and 1482 hospitals in 45 states, Puerto Rico and the District of Columbia covering 211 metropolitan statistical areas. In 1993, in excess of 84 million claims were processed with total payments in excess of $14 billion. More than 13.5 million members around the world have mental health and substance abuse coverage through Aetna's managed mental health networks, operating in every state in the US.

Aetna Health Plans is one part of the Aetna organization, the fifteenth largest US corporation with total assets of $100 billion. Aetna is one of the largest financial institutions in the country; one of the nation's largest insurance company providers of group health and life benefits; one of the largest underwriters of commercial property-casualty coverages; the eleventh largest underwriter of personal property-casualty products; among the twenty largest managers of pension assets in the US, with $67.1 billion in assets under management; and a provider of employee benefits since 1913.

18

Information Systems Management and Your Organization

INTRODUCTION

In business, groups are often formed to solicit best practices within an industry to share information about IT—its uses and its problems. What has made The IT Management Forum and this book different from these are the breadth and focus of the topics covered. These include:

· **Industry–Academic Collaboration.** This book has been the result of a collaboration of many individuals—from industry and from academia. Those from industry brought insight and perspective to the managerial issues based on the unique perspective of their organizations. Academics, through their formulation of the issue, their facilitation of the discussion, and their writing of the chapters, supplied the organizing structure for the effective presentation of each issue. These perspectives, when combined, resulted in a composite picture much richer than could have been produced by any of the individuals in isolation—a case of the whole being larger than the parts. It is hoped that other groups of academics and practitioners will be encouraged by this book to pursue similar collaborative efforts.

- **Cross-Industry Representation.** Rather that limiting itself to a single industry with its embedded biases and assumptions, the Forum has endeavoured to include multiple industries amongst its membership. In this way, members have benefitted from seeing how others address similar problems, but from slightly differing perspectives. Frequently, this has resulted in a useful cross-pollination of ideas. For example, one member, representing a financial institution, was amazed to learn that other organizations did not have anywhere near the number of infrastructure groups that he did. In other cases, members have felt a tremendous sense of affirmation that the problems they are experiencing are not unique to their particular organization, but are common to IS in general.

- **Management Focus.** As we have made clear throughout this book, effective information technology management is essential to the effective use of IT in organizations. It is no longer possible (if it ever was!) to simply throw technology at a problem and hope to (a) save money and (b) improve service and quality. Technology can be a boon to a business leading it to offer hitherto unheard of products or turnaround time, or a millstone around its corporate neck, costing money and delivering little value. It is IT management that makes the difference; management of people, practices, and technology and all their interfaces.

- **Best and Worst Practices.** The Forum has been used productively as a focal mechanism for eliciting best-practice information for IT management. (Interestingly, our experience in this area suggests that the elicitation of 'worst' practice is equally important to managers. That is, managers are interested in discovering what different organizations have tried unsuccessfully.) In this way, our members have been able to capitalize on a larger body of collected wisdom regarding the practice of technology management. There is a huge opportunity in the field of IS management to learn from other organizations. There has been an inordinate amount of activity which effectively 'reinvents the wheel' over and over from organization to organization. By building on the combined talents of many individuals and many organ-izations, it is possible to advance the practice of management much more effectively. The production of this book has been rooted in this belief of sharing, collaboration, and mutual benefit.

IS MANAGEMENT:
LOOKING BACK . . . LOOKING AHEAD

The management of information technology (IT) represents a formidable task. IS management must keep abreast of a technology which changes at the speed of light; decide how best to harness this technology to further the organization's business strategy; operate a 'business within a business,' form partnerships and alliances with the business and with other businesses for mutual benefit; organize itself for maximum efficiency and effectiveness; implement a technology infrastructure which is open, flexible, secure, and manageable; and seek out and deliver strategic uses of IT while continuing to run operational systems with the goal of 100% uptime. Few would question the fact that the management of the IS function is a daunting task. Couple this with the fact that CEOs are not prepared to wait for results—the average life of a senior IS manager is less than three years—and IS management's urgent need for information becomes understandable.

Looking back over the last few years, the key IS issues raised by Forum members show several important trends:

* an increase in the importance of information systems in organizations;
* increasing awareness of IT issues among the leadership of companies;
* increasing emphasis on responsiveness to and alignment of IS with the business;
* emphasis on 're'—re-engineering, revitalizing, reducing, rethinking, retrofitting, refocusing, and reinventing.

IS departments have grown, not only in size, but in stature within most organizations. They have matured and become more aware of the business which is their *raison d'etre*.

Yet at the same time, greater and greater demands have been placed on IS: business is more likely to perceive IT as its salvation in tight economic times; technology has grown more complex; users are more knowledgeable and experienced, leading them to challenge technology decisions; greater controls are required on systems; and staff are expected to work both harder and smarter. These pressures are felt most acutely by IS managers who act as the interface between IS and the rest of the organization. Never have we seen IS managers work harder at their job.

As we look ahead, there are no signs that these pressures will disappear. What *is* changing is an ever-increasing emphasis on technology management. Whereas a few years ago, IS managers were focused on the *business* aspects of IS, now they appear to be spending more and more time on its *technical* components. This is because the technology is heralding changes that were unforeseen even four or five years ago. In the future, many issues of IS management as we know them today will disappear. As information technology becomes even more pervasive throughout organizations, many current IS functions will be subsumed within the business itself. Much of what is currently perceived today as IS as separate from business, may no longer be as distinct in the future.

There are signs that the concept of a 'system' is becoming dated. With increasing standardization among software, hardware and telecommunications industries, the delivery of computing function will be much more 'utility like.' Computing platforms and networks will become seamless to the point where users can ask for information without knowing (or caring) where the data is stored and how it is enacted. This means that the IS function will be increasingly concerned with managing an 'information utility.' This utility would be organized around four main activities: data transportation (similar to today's networks), data warehousing, data service (similar to operational systems), and data presentation (similar to today's graphical user interfaces).

However, while we may be able to foresee the future with some clarity, getting there is not at all clear. Organizations are riddled with legacy systems and overwhelmed with contradictory data. They have a heavy investment in existing technology, which they may not be able to afford to replace in the immediate term. Technology is anything but 'seamless'; the interface of multiple vendor equipment and software is likely to cause major headaches over the next few years. At the same time, new and better hardware, software, development tools, and methods are being churned out at an ever-increasing rate. In short, while IS is changing, it is also staying the same.

'Hot topics' for IS managers over the next five years are likely to be technical or to relate to improved productivity as managers keep their heads down and focus on delivering technology to feed a voracious organizational appetite. They should look for:

- software to facilitate prototype development—especially to manage the transition from prototype to an operational system;
- improved productivity measurement techniques and standards;
- the opportunity to benchmark productivity data;
- software to facilitate testing, particularly testing in object-based systems;
- better object library management systems;
- improved methods for evaluating new technologies;
- techniques to encapsulate legacy systems;
- common user interfaces or user workbenches that limit the number of commands or icons a user needs to learn;
- software to control distribution of software to LANs;
- the rebirth of the mainframe—as a giant server;
- increasing sophistication of PCs and servers as they become true multi-purpose computers.

From a non-technical perspective, people management will continue to be a challenge for IS managers, particularly dealing with retraining large numbers of traditional systems analysts and programmers in new techniques and technologies. If retraining fails, IS will lose the wealth of knowledge about the organization and its processes that it has laboriously built up throughout the previous decade and a half. IS may then find itself back where it started—with a lot of technical 'hotshots' who know nothing about business and do not really want to learn.

FINAL THOUGHTS

Managing IS is like riding on a pendulum. Over the past three decades, the job of implementing information technology in the organization has been to balance the competing pressures of business and technology—get too far away from the technology and too close to business and the technology will pull you back; get too focused on technology and lose sight of the business and the business will make sure you know about it. Naturally, we would all like to find the point of equilibrium where business needs and technological imperatives are perfectly and completely balanced. This is a desirable goal, but one that is highly unlikely to be achieved. Like life, managing IS is the business of dealing with all the problems that arise—some of which may be predictable and preventable, and some of which are not.

We hope that this book has not only provided some useful information to IS managers and others who are seeking some practical guidelines about how to deal with particular issues, but also a more general template for how to address any issue of technology management. This template emphasizes working towards *balance*, while recognizing that it will never truly be achieved:

- The goal of this book has been to provide IS managers with *balanced information* to guide them in their struggle with managing the IS function. While the increasing pressures on IS managers may mean that they have less time to reflect on their work, never has it been more important to reflect on the 'bigger picture.' Keeping both in perspective will enable IS managers to avoid rushing down expensive and embarrassing blind alleys. Information must be balanced to ensure that the debate is not biased in terms of pet solutions or preconceived notions, and yet ensure that it entertains novel ideas and approaches. Too many times the field of IS has been led astray by the seductive powers of technology—those 'silver bullets' promising quantum leaps in productivity.

- IS managers must also maintain a *balanced vision* of their internal organization and its relationship with the larger organization. As we have noted, achieving perfect balance may never be possible, but having this as a vision can save an IS manager from the worst excesses of IS management fads in structuring their organization.

- Finally, IS managers must remember to balance the competing demands for their *time*. While technology is an important part of their job, they cannot afford to lose sight of the context in which it is implemented or of the people who use it. It is the rare technology whose real impact does not come about by careful management.

The future of our organizations and our institutions is, in many ways, in the hands of today's IS managers. It is our hope that this book will be helpful to them in making wise and thoughtful choices.

References

Alavi, M. 'An Assessment of the Prototyping Approach to IS Development,' *Communications of the ACM*, Vol. 27, No. 6, June, 1984.

Agrawal, P. IBM Canada Presentation, 4 September, 1991.

Baldridge National Quality Award Criteria, 1993. American Society for Quality Control, Milwaukee, WI.

Barki, H. Presentation to the 1992 HEC-Queen's Research Conference, Queen's University, Kingston.

Bassett, P.G. 'Perspectives on Software Reusability,' *CASE Trends*, July/August, 1990.

Bessen, J. 'Riding the Marketing Information Wave,' *Harvard Business Review*, September–October, 1993, pp. 150–160.

Boehm, B. *Software Engineering Economics*. Englewood Cliffs, NJ: Prentice-Hall, 1981.

Bostrom, R.P. and Heinen, J.S. 'MIS Problems and Failures: A Socio-Technical Perspective,' *MIS Quarterly*, Vol. 9, 1977, pp. 17–32.

Boudette, N. 'Creating the computer-integrated enterprise, Special Report,' *Industry Week*, 1991.

Bozman, J.S. 'OMG Strives to Create On-Line Object Brokerage,' *Computerworld*, 19 July, 1993.

Brooks, F. *The Mythical Manmonth: Essays on Software Engineering*. Reading, MA: Addison-Wesley Publishing, 1975.

Busch, E.A., Jarvenpaa, S.L., Tractinsky, N. and Glick, W.H. 'External Versus Internal Perspective in Determining a Firm's Progressive Use of Information Technology,' *Proceedings of the 12th International Conference on Information Systems*, New York, 1991.

Cappello, D. [Producer]. 'Implementing Distributed Object Computing Solutions' in *Paradigm Shift: A Guide to the Information Revolution*, Vol. 4, No. 5, Rounder Records, 1-800-44DISCS.

Carlyle, R. 'The Tomorrow Organization,' *Datamation*, 1 February, 1990, pp. 22–28.

Cerveny, R.P., Garrity, E.J. and Sanders, L.G. 'The Application of Prototyping to System Development: A Rationale and Model,' *Journal of Management Information Systems*, Fall, 1986.

Couger, J.D. 'Communications of Motivation Norms for Programmer/ Analysts in the Pacific Rim and the U.S.,' *International Information Systems*, 1990, pp. 41–46.

Daft, R., Lengel, R. and Trevino, L. 'Message Equivocality, Media Selection, and Manager Performance: Implication for Information Systems,' *MIS Quarterly*, Vol. 11, No. 3, September, 1987, pp. 355–366.

Davenport, T. *Process Innovation: Re-engineering Work Through Information Technology*, Harvard Business School Press, 1993.

Davenport, T. and Short, J. 'The New Industrial Engineering: Information Technology and Business Process Redesign,' *Sloan Management Review*, Vol. 31, No. 4, Summer, 1990, pp. 11–27.

Davis, G.B. and Olson, M.H. *Management Information Systems: Conceptual Foundations, Structure, and Development.* New York, NY: McGraw-Hill, Inc., 1985.

DeMarco, T. and Lister, T. *Peopleware: Productive Projects and Teams.* New York, NY: Dorset House Publishing, 1987.

Deyo, N. and Gillach, J. 'Object Lessons,' *CIO*, 15 September, 1993.

Dietrich, W., Nackman, L. and Gracer, F. 'Saving a Legacy With Objects,' *Proceedings of the OOPSLA 1989 Conference*, pp. 77–83.

Doll, W.J. and Ahmed, M.U. (1986) 'Diagnosing and Treating the Credibility Syndrome,' *MIS Quarterly*, Vol. 10, pp. 21–32.

Donovan, J. *Business Re-engineering with Technology.* Cambridge, MA: Cambridge Technology Group, 1993.

Drucker, Peter. *Post-Capitalist Society.* New York, NY: Harper Collins, 1993.

Ellul, J. *The Technological Society.* New York, NY: Vintage Books, 1964.

Emery, J. 'Re-engineering the Organization,' *MIS Quarterly* [Editor's Comments] March, 1991, pp. iii–iv.

Fichman, R.G. and Kemerer, C.F. 'Adoption of Software Engineering Process Innovations: The Case of Object Orientation,' *Sloan Management Review*, Winter, 1993, pp. 7–22.

Galbraith, J. *Strategies of Organizational Design.* Reading, MA: Addison-Wesley, 1973.

Giordano, R. 'The Information ' Where? ' House,' *Database Programming and Design*, Vol. 6, No. 9, September, 1993.

Goldratt, E.M. and Cox, J. *The Goal: Excellence in Manufacturing.* New York, NY: North River Press, Croton-on-Hudson, 1984.

Guinan, P.J. 'Achieving Excellence in Application Development,' Interim Report (May 1994), Boston University, School of Management.

Haeckel, S. and Nolan, R. 'Managing by Wire,' *Harvard Business Review*, September–October, 1993, pp. 122–132.

Hammer, M. 'Re-engineering Work: Don't Automate, Obliterate,' *Harvard Business Review*, July–August 1990, pp. 104–112.

Hammer, M. Notes from the *Hammer Forum*, 1991.

Hammonds, K.H. 'Software Made Simple: Will Object-Oriented Programming Transform the Computer Industry?' *Business Week*, 30 September, 1991.

Hartog, C. and Herbert, M. '1985 Opinion Survey of MIS Managers: Key Issues,' *MIS Quarterly*, Vol. 10, No. 4, December, 1986, pp 351-361.

Hetzel, W. *The Complete Guide to Software Testing* [2nd edn], Wellesley, MA: QED Information Sciences, 1988.

Hewlett-Packard. 'Accessing Your Information More Effectively Through Data Warehousing,' Presentation to Insurance Executives, February, 1994.

Holland, R.H. 'Guiding Executive Commitment to R/AD,' Keynote Address to *Annual CIPS Congress*, Victoria, B.C., Canada, 1991.

Huff, S. 'Re-engineering The Business,' *Business Quarterly*, Vol. 56, No. 3, Winter 1992, pp. 38–42.

Information Week. 'Fad or Phenomenon?' 15 July, 1991, pp. 36–37.

Inmon, W.H. 'Building the Data Warehouse: Getting Started,' *Prism Solutions (Tech Topics)*, Vol. 1, No. 21, 1990.

Ives, B. 'The IS Executive: CIO or VP in Charge of Water and Gas,' Invited Guest Speaker, Annual Meetings of the *Administrative Sciences Association of Canada—IS Division*, Niagara Falls, June, 1991.

Jones, C. Presentation overheads from *Software Measurement and Evaluation* course, 1990.

Jones, C. *Applied Software Measurement.* New York, NY: McGraw-Hill, 1991.

Kaiser, K.M. and King, W.R. 'The Manager-Analyst Interface in Systems Development,' *MIS Quarterly,* Vol. 6, No. 1, 1982, pp. 49–55.

Kay, A. 'OOP in a Nutshell: From Clockwork to Biology,' INDEX/vanguard white paper, April, 1993.

Kottler, P., MacDougall, G.H.G., and Armstrong, G. *Marketing (Canadian Edition).* Toronto, ON: Prentice-Hall Canada, 1988.

Krass, P. 'Building a Better Mousetrap,' *Information Week*, 25 March, 1991, pp. 24–30.

Levine, H.G. and Rossmoore, D. 'Understanding Barriers to IT Implementation: A Case Study of ' Rationality, ' Human Error, and Undiscussable Issues,' *Proceedings of the Hawaii International Conference on Computer Systems*, Maui, Hawaii, January, 1993, pp. 850–858.

Lips, M. 'Six Digit Dates and The Century Date: Complex Problem. Simple Solution?,' *Enterprise Systems Journal*, October, 1993, pp. 68–72.

Lukes, S. *Power: A Radical View*. New York, NY: Macmillan, 1974.

Mangurian, G.E. *Alternatives to Replacing Obsolete Systems*, Cambridge, MA: Index Systems Inc., 1985.

Markus, M.L. *Systems in Organizations*. Marshfield, MA: Pitman, 1984.

Markus, M.L. and Bjorn-Andersen, N. 'Power Over Users: Its Exercise by System Professionals,' *Commununications of the ACM*, Vol. 30, June, 1987.

Markus, M.L. and Soh, C. 'Banking on Information Technology: Converting IT Spending into Firm Performance,' in Banker, R., Kauffman, R. and Mahmood, M. eds *Strategic Information Technology Management: Perspectives on Organizational Growth and Competitive Advantage*. Harrisburg, PA: Idea Group Publishing, 1993, pp. 375–403.

McKeen, J.D., Smith, H.A., Agrawal, P.C. and Smyth, D.R. 'The Investment in Information Technology: 1977–1989,' *Proceedings of the Administrative Sciences Association of Canada*, Vol. 11(4), 1990.

McKeen, J.D. and Smith, H.A. 'The Relationship Between Information Technology Use and Organizational Performance.' in Banker, R., Kauffman, R. and Mahmood, M. eds *Strategic Information Technology Management: Perspectives on Organizational Growth and Competitive Advantage*. Harrisburg, PA: Idea Group Publishing, 1993, pp. 405–444.

Mintzberg, H. *The Rise and Fall of Strategic Planning*. Toronto, ON: Maxwell Macmillan Canada, 1994.

Morgan, G. *Images of Organization*. Beverly Hills, CA: Sage Publications Inc., 1986.

Moynihan, T. 'What Chief Executives and Senior Managers Want From Their IT Departments,' *MIS Quarterly*, Vol 14, March, 1990, pp. 15-25.

Oman, R.C. and Ayers, T. 'Productivity and Benefit-Cost Analysis for Information Technology Decisions,' *Information Management Review*, Vol. 3, No. 3, Winter 1988, pp. 31–41.

Ouchi, W. *Theory Z*. Reading, MA: Addison-Wesley, 1981.

Peters, T. 'The Curse of Déjà Vue,' *Report on Business Magazine*, January, 1995.

Pleptea, D.R. 'What Will the Change of the Millennium Do to Our Data Processing Systems? ' *MIS Quarterly*, Vol. 10, No. 2, June, 1986, pp. 103-104.

Postman, N. *Technopoly*. New York, NY: Alfred A. Knopf, 1992.

Richmond, W.B., Seidmann, A. and Whinston, A.B. 'Incomplete Contracting Issues in Information Systems Development Outsourcing,' *Decision Support Systems*, Vol. 8, No. 5, 1992, pp. 459–477.

Ricketts, J. 'How Information Systems Renovation Affects Systems Analysis and Design,' *Informatica*, Vol. 1, No. 1, December, 1992.

Roach, S.S. 'The Case of the Missing Technology Payback,' Presentation at the *Tenth International Conference on Information Systems*, Boston, MA, December, 1989.

Ross-Flanigan, N. 'New Science of Complexity May Simply Solve Everything,' *Toronto Star*, 24 January, 1993.

Senge, P. *The Fifth Discipline*. New York, NY: Doubleday, 1990.

Senn, J. 'Reshaping Business Processes Through Re-engineering,' *Insight*, Society of Information Management Publication, 1991.

Smith, H. 'Get Your Requirements Right—Prototype!' *Canadian Data Systems*, October, 1986.

Southerst, J. 'Customer Crunching,' *Canadian Business*, September 1993.

Sprague, R.H. (Jr) and McNurlin, B.C. *Information Systems Management in Practice* [2nd edn]. Englewood Cliffs, NJ: Prentice-Hall, Inc., 1992.

Sprague, R.H. (Jr) and McNurlin, B.C. *Information Systems Management in Practice* [3rd edn]. Englewood Cliffs, NJ: Prentice-Hall, Inc., 1993.

Stewart, T. 'Managing in the Era of Change,' *Fortune*, 13 December, 1993.

Strassmann, P., Berger, P., Swanson, E.B., Kriebel, C.H. and Kauffman, R.J. *Measuring Business Value of Information Technologies*. Washington, DC: ICIT Press, 1988.

The, L. 'How to Get Started on the OOP Trail,' *Datamation*, 1 November, 1993.

Thierauf, R.J., Klekamp, R.C. and Geeding, D.W. *Management Principles and Practices: A Contingency and Questionnaire Approach*. Santa Barbara: John Wiley & Sons, 1977.

Todd, P.A., McKeen, J.D. and Gallupe, R.B. 'The Evolution of IS Job Skills: A Content Analysis of IS Job Advertisements From 1970 to

1990,' Working Paper No. 93-01, School of Business, Queen''s University, Kingston, Canada, K7L 3N6, 1993.

Wang, S. 'Object-Oriented Methods Shorten the Information Systems Lifecycle,' *Proceedings of the ASAC Conference*, June, 1991.

Wiesendanger, B. 'Benchmarking by Numbers,' *Sales and Marketing*, November, 1992.

Whiteman, S.D. 'MIS Faces Year 2000 Challenge,' *VIA Link*. Phoenix, AR: VIASOFT, Inc., 1993, p. 2.

Wilson, D., 1993. 'Assessing the Impact of Information Technology on Organizational Performance,' in Banker, R., Kauffman, R. and Mahmood, M. eds *Strategic Information Technology Management: Perspectives on Organizational Growth and Competitive Advantage.* Harrisburg, PA: Idea Group Publishing, 1993, pp. 471–514.

Womak, J., Jones, D. and Roos, D. *The Machine that Changed the World.* New York, NY: Harper Collins, 1991.

Yourdon, E. *Decline and Fall of the American Programmer.* Englewood Cliffs, NJ: Yourdon Press, 1993.

Yourdon, E. 'The Coming Object Backlash,' *Computerworld*, 3 January, 1994.

Zuboff, S. 'New Worlds of Computer-Mediated Work,' *Harvard Business Review*, Vol. 60, No. 5, September–October, 1982.

Index